Everym...
a...

C000121624

THE EVERYMAN
LIBRARY

The Everyman Library was founded by J. M. Dent
in 1906. He chose the name Everyman because he wanted
to make available the best books ever written in every
field to the greatest number of people at the cheapest possible
price. He began with Boswell's 'Life of Johnson';
his one-thousandth title was Aristotle's 'Metaphysics',
by which time sales exceeded 40 million.

Today Everyman paperbacks remain true to
J. M. Dent's aims and high standards, with a wide range
of titles at affordable prices in editions which address
the needs of today's readers. Each new text is reset to give
a clear, elegant page and to incorporate the latest thinking
and scholarship. Each book carries the pilgrim logo,
the character in 'Everyman', a medieval mystery play,
a proud link between Everyman
past and present.

THE EVERYMAN BOOK OF VICTORIAN VERSE:
THE PRE-RAPHAELITES TO THE NINETIES

Edited by
DONALD THOMAS
University of Wales, Cardiff

EVERYMAN
J. M. DENT · LONDON
CHARLES E. TUTTLE
VERMONT

Selection, introduction, chronology and bibliography
© Donald Thomas 1993

This edition first published in Everyman in 1993

J. M. Dent
Orion Publishing Group
Orion House, 5 Upper St Martin's Lane,
London WC2H 9EA
and
Charles E. Tuttle Co. Inc.
28 South Main Street,
Rutland, Vermont 05701, USA

Typeset in Sabon by CentraCet, Cambridge
Printed in Great Britain by
The Guernsey Press Co. Ltd, Guernsey, C.I.

British Library Cataloguing-in-Publication Data
is available upon request.

ISBN 0 460 87310 5

for
Linda Shakespeare

CONTENTS

NOTE ON THE EDITOR

DONALD THOMAS is the author of two collections of poetry, including *Points of Contact*, for which he won the Eric Gregory Award, as well as fiction, biography, and the history of literary censorship in *A Long Time Burning*. His recent fiction includes *Dancing in the Dark* (1992) and *The Raising of Lizzie Meek* (1993). His latest biographies are *Henry Fielding* (1990) and *The Marquis de Sade* (1992). He has edited two volumes of *State Trials*, devised two series of Radio 4's 'The Detectives', and his latest documentary volume, *Dead Giveaway* (1993), describes the forensic detection of Cardiff's 'Body in the Carpet' murder in 1991. He is also Professor of English at the University of Wales.

CHRONOLOGY OF THE TIMES

Year	Artistic Events
1844	William Barnes, *Poems of Rural life*
	Benjamin Disraeli, *Coningsby*
1846	Edward Lear, *A Book of Nonsense*
	Daily News appears
1848	Pre-Raphaelite Brotherhood formed
	Charles Dickens, *Dombey and Son*
1849	Dante Gabriel Rossetti, 'Ecce Ancilla Domini'
	Macaulay's *History of England*, Vol. I
1850	*The Germ*
	Elizabeth Barrett Browning, *Sonnets from the Portuguese*
	Tennyson, *In Memoriam*
1851	William Holman Hunt, 'The Hireling Shepherd'
	John Ruskin, *Stones of Venice*
1852	John Everett Millais, 'Ophelia'
	Matthew Arnold, *Empedocles on Etna*
1853	William Holman Hunt, 'Dante Gabriel Rossetti'
	Charlotte Brontë, *Villette*
1854	Coventry Patmore, *The Angel in the House*
	Tennyson illustrated by Millais and Rossetti
1855	Ford Madox Brown, 'The Last of England'
	Anthony Trollope, *The Warden*
1856	John Everett Millais, 'Autumn Leaves'
	Charles Reade, *It is Never too Late to Mend*
1857	Frederick Locker, *London Lyrics*
	Charles Baudelaire, *Les Fleurs du Mal*
1858	William Morris, *The Defence of Guenevere*
	Dean Mansel, *The Limits of Religious Thought*
1859	Charles Darwin, *Origin of Species*
	Edward Fitzgerald, *The Rubáiyát of Omar Khayyám*
	John Stuart Mill, *On Liberty*
1862	Christina Rossetti, *Goblin Market*
	George Meredith, *Modern Love*
	Victor Hugo, *Les Misérables*
1864	Robert Stephen Hawker, *The Quest of the Sangraal*
	Charles Dickens, *Our Mutual Friend*

CHRONOLOGY OF THE TIMES

Year	Historical Events
1844	Royal Commission on the Health of Towns
1846	Irish Potato Famine
1848	Revolutions in France, Germany, Austria, Italy, Poland
1849	Annexation of the Punjab
1850	Submarine telegraph cable between Dover and Calais
1851	Great Exhibition
1852	French Second Empire proclaimed under Napoleon III
1853	Turkish fleet destroyed by Russia
1854	British expeditionary force to the Crimea
1855	Siege and fall of Sebastopol
1856	Peace of Paris ends Crimean War
1857	Indian Mutiny
1858	Brunel's steamship *The Great Eastern* launched
1862	Abraham Lincoln declares freedom of slaves

Year	Artistic Events
1866	Algernon Charles Swinburne, *Poems and Ballads*
	John Henry Newman, *The Dream of Gerontius*
1868	William Morris, *The Earthly Paradise*
	Robert Browning, *The Ring and the Book*
1870	Dante Gabriel Rossetti, *Poems*
1872	Lewis Carroll, *Through the Looking-Glass*
	George Eliot, *Middlemarch*
1874	Dante Gabriel Rossetti, 'Prosperpine'
	Paul Verlaine, *Romances Sans Paroles*
1877	Dante Gabriel Rossetti 'Astarte Syriaca'
	Henry James, *The American*
1880	James Thomson, *The City of Dreadful Night*
	Emile Zola, *Nana*
1881	Dante Gabriel Rossetti, *Ballads and Sonnets*
	Guy de Maupassant, *La Maison Tellier*
1884	Eugene Lee-Hamilton, *Apollo and Marsyas*
	Art Workers' Guild
1885	Robert Louis Stevenson, *A Child's Garden of Verses*
	Richard Burton (tr.) *The Arabian Nights*
1886	Rudyard Kipling, *Departmental Ditties*
	A. V. Dicey, *The Law of the Constitution*
1888	Eugene Lee-Hamilton, *Imaginary Sonnets*
	Matthew Arnold, *Essays in Criticism: Second Series*
1889	Sir Alfred Lyall, *Verses Written in India*
	Sir Arthur Conan Doyle, *The Sign of the Four*
1891	John Davidson, *In a Music-Hall*
	Thomas Hardy, *Tess of the D'Urbervilles*
1892	Rudyard Kipling, *Barrack-Room Ballads*
	W. B. Yeats, *The Countess Cathleen*
1893	Francis Thompson, *Poems*
	Giuseppe Verdi, *Falstaff*
1894	John Davidson, *Ballads and Songs*
	The Yellow Book
1895	Arthur Symons, *London Nights*
	Lionel Johnson, *Poems*
	H. G. Wells, *The Time Machine*
1896	Ernest Dowson, *Verses*
	Giacomo Puccini, *La Bohème*
1897	Vincent O'Sullivan, *The Houses of Sin*
	Joseph Conrad, *The Nigger of the Narcissus*

Year	Historical Events
1866	Benjamin Disraeli, Leader of the Commons
1868	W. E. Gladstone, Prime Minister
1870	Franco-Prussian War Royal Commission on Science (Duke of Devonshire)
1871	Purchase of military commissions abolished
1874	H. Solomon introduces canned foods
1877	Britain annexes the South African Transvaal
1880	First test match between English and Australian cricket teams
1881	British army defeated by South African Boers at Majuba Hill
1884	Grover Cleveland wins United States presidential election
1885	Fall of Khartoum to Mahdi and death of General Gordon
1886	Gladstone's government defeated on Irish Home Rule Bill
1888	George Eastman's 'Kodak' box camera
1889	Henry Vizetelly gaoled for publishing Zola in England
1891	Prince of Wales gives evidence in the 'Baccarat' cheating case
1892	Automatic telephone switchboard
1893	Karl Benz's four-wheeled motor-car
1894	Sino-Japanese War
1895	Oscar Wilde tried and imprisoned
1896	S. P. Langley's flying machine
1897	Celebration of Queen Victoria's Diamond Jubilee

Year	Artistic Events
1898	Oscar Wilde, *The Ballad of Reading Gaol* Henry James, *The Turn of the Screw*
1899	Arthur Symons, *Images of Good and Evil* Rudyard Kipling, *Stalky & Co*
1900	W. E. Henley, *For England's Sake* Anton Chekov, *Uncle Vanya*
1901	Bernard Shaw, *Plays for Puritans*
1902	Thomas Hardy, *Poems of Past and Present*
1918	Gerard Manley Hopkins, *Poems*, ed. Robert Bridges

Year	Historical Events
1898	United States invades Puerto Rico
1899	Outbreak of the Second South African 'Boer' War
1900	Boxer rebellion against Europeans in Peking
1901	Death of Queen Victoria, accession of Edward VII

INTRODUCTION

In May 1836, the future novelist and biographer Arsène Houssaye was sent to London by the *Revue de Paris* to report on a Royal Academy exhibition. A keen observer of the social scene, the twenty-one-year-old Frenchman was struck by the difference between the status of the artist in London and Paris. He was surprised to find 'no artistic friendships, no groups, no schools in England'. He thought it was probably the consequence of the English class-system which appeared to treat artists of all kinds as menials. He was shocked that when a great painter like Sir Edwin Landseer undertook the portrait of a lady, 'she forces him to paint religiously her Amazon's robe, her gloves, her dogs and her riding-crop — and all that with such condescending disdain that one wonders why Landseer does not take that riding-crop to whip her as she whips her dogs.'

There was nothing in England comparable to the bohemian life of Parisian writers and artists which, for example, formed the setting of Henri Murger's fiction of 1848, *Scènes de la vie de Bohème*. The book's popularity was enduring enough for Puccini to base *La Bohème* upon it forty-eight years later. Nor had England ever had a true equivalent to the French *salon*, where wit, ability and sheer cleverness might count for more than the rank or sex of the participants. Nor in England was there evidence of the bohemian comradeship in which poets, artists, novelists might group themselves together, other than in coteries. Perhaps the plainest allegiance in England was to magazines or journals, whereby the Utilitarians of the 1820s attached themselves to the *Westminster Review*, literary Tories to the *Quarterly* and their Whig rivals to the *Edinburgh Review*.

When the Pre-Raphaelite Brotherhood — the 'PRB' — was formed in 1848, it was exclusive both in its ideals and its membership of seven. Influenced by the publication in 1843 and 1846 of the first two volumes of John Ruskin's *Modern Painters*, the object of the PRB was to restore art and poetry to the more vivid simplicity which existed before the florid and overblown influence of the later Renaissance. Clarity of design, brilliance of colour, and a sensuous appeal were to be balanced by dedication and spirituality of subject.

John Ruskin, who was something of a father-figure to the artists of the PRB, described the new movement in *Pre-Raphaelitism* (1851). The earlier 'teaching' which he deplores had urged young painters to 'improve' upon nature, to be 'clever' and to strive for 'bright effects'. The result was, in this view, that painters merely imitated one another or the prevailing styles in art.

> The Pre-Raphaelites imitate no pictures: they paint from nature only. But they have opposed themselves as a body, to that kind of teaching above described, which only began after Raphael's time: and they have opposed themselves as sternly to the entire feeling of the Renaissance schools; a feeling composed of indolence, infidelity, sensuality and shallow pride. Therefore they have called themselves Pre-Raphaelite. If they adhere to their principles, and paint nature as it is around them, with the help of modern science, with the earnestness of the men of the thirteenth and fourteenth centuries, they will, as I said, found a new and noble school in England.

These remarks might apply as directly to the poetry as to the paintings of the 'new and noble school', though that poetry often recalled the thirteenth or fourteenth centuries in its subject-matter as well as in the directness of its vision.

Dante Gabriel Rossetti, twenty years old in 1848, was the most celebrated of the seven original members. His brother William Michael Rossetti and Thomas Woolner were the other poets, Woolner being also a sculptor. The four other painters included two of great future fame, John Everett Millais and William Holman Hunt, as well as Frederick George Stephens and James Collinson. Yet these first Pre-Raphaelites were also a brotherhood in a vocational, if not a religious, sense. The soul, as well as the pen or the brush, was to be purged of the meretricious and debased qualities which recent art too often exhibited. Nor was the new movement to be an easy excursion into fake medievalism. John Ruskin in 1846 had laid down that natural phenomena 'can only be seen with their properly belonging joy and interpreted up to the measure of proper human intelligence, when they are accepted as the work and the gift of a Living Spirit greater than our own.'

To be an artist or a poet was to have a divine calling. Yet it was also to have a lively interest in earthly pleasures. In the history of Pre-Raphaelitism, high ideals and a more fleshly appreciation of 'stunners' like Lizzie Siddal and Jane Morris went together. The Victorian 'artist', whether Dante Gabriel Rossetti or Oscar Wilde, was increasingly seen as one whose dedication to art entitled him to a less strict moral code in matters of women, drink, or regular hours than the factory manager or his clerk.

In 1850 there appeared four issues of the PRB's magazine, *The Germ: Thoughts towards Nature in Poetry, Literature and Art.* Dante Gabriel Rossetti published his early poetry in it, including the jewelled and enamelled paradise of 'The Blessed Damozel' and 'My Sister's Sleep'. His sister, Christina Rossetti, and Coventry Patmore were among its other poets. 1850 was also the year in which Rossetti met a tall, beautiful, red-haired shopgirl, Elizabeth Siddal, first his mistress, then his wife.

As the poetry of the Pre-Raphaelites appeared in print, and as their paintings drew attention and excitement to the Royal Academy or the so-called Free Exhibition at Hyde Park Corner, the PRB lost something of its exclusivity. Holman Hunt moved towards the mainstream of Victorian religious and didactic painting, John Everett Millais towards that commercialism which the Pre-Raphaelites had first deplored. During the 1860s, the composition of the group changed. It was hard to say whether some of the new figures, particularly in poetry, were strictly Pre-Raphaelite or not. Christina Rossetti had been closely associated with the group. A younger man like William Morris had most of the credentials. Swinburne showed an affinity in some of his poetry. Among painters, Edward Burne-Jones was an enthusiastic adherent, though he rather modified the idealism of the PRB to a gospel of beauty.

> I mean by a picture a beautiful romantic dream of something that never was, never will be — in a light better than any light that ever shone — in a land no one can ever remember, only desire — and from the forms divinely beautiful.

While this might seem like a contradiction of Ruskin's view of Pre-Raphaelitism as representing nature with scientific clarity, it illustrated how easily the movement and its followers might slip into the 'Aesthetic' fashions of the 1880s or the creed of 'Art for Art's sake' in the 1890s.

Though Pre-Raphaelitism, as Ruskin preached it and Dante Gabriel Rossetti practised it, was a novelty of the 1840s, its literary impact was delayed until that more general movement of younger Victorians in the 1860s. Swinburne and William Morris were poets of the later decade, while Dante Gabriel Rossetti's general fame came with the publication of his verse in 1870. The significant delay in publication of *Poems by D. G. Rossetti* had little to do with literary fashion. When Lizzie Rossetti, formerly Lizzie Siddal, took an overdose of chloral in 1862, Rossetti in his grief buried his poems in her coffin, many of them unpublished. As time passed, he regretted this quixotic sacrifice. An exhumation order was obtained. In best Gothic style, Lizzie was unearthed from Highgate cemetery at night by candlelight, under the supervision of the swindler and blackmailer Charles Augustus Howell. Rossetti's poems were retrieved for publication.

By this time, Pre-Raphaelitism as a literary movement also owed much to a mid-century rebellion among the middle-class young. The great names of the early Victorian period, those who had published their first books or achieved their first fame when the Queen came to the throne in 1837, had had their day in the view of such rebels. Tennyson and Dickens seemed of that old order. Now there were young men ready to excite or shock the drawing-rooms and deaneries of England with the poetry of a new age. Even older Pre-Raphaelites, including Dante Gabriel Rossetti, regarded this with unease. Pre-Raphaelite idealism might slide into bohemian self-indulgence.

In this new mood, Pre-Raphaelitism was no longer as neatly defined as in its first phase. Was a young man like Swinburne at any point or in any aspect Pre-Raphaelite? There were certainly lines, for example in his early verse play *Rosamund* at the end of 1860, which sounded like Pre-Raphaelite word-painting. The description of the medieval heroine and the women who dress her might be a Rossetti painting.

> Maids will keep round me, girls with smooth worn hair,
> When mine is hard, no silk in it to feel,
> Tall girls to dress me, laughing underbreath,
> Too low for gold to tighten at the waist

The literary barrister Arthur Munby described Swinburne in the 1860s as Rossetti's 'young disciple'. Though Swinburne later disavowed Pre-Raphaelitism, he did so only in respect of his work after 1865. For the moment he was, as Munby saw him, a 'strange incarnation' of the movement. To yet another observer of the 1860s, Edmund Gosse, Swinburne was more radical, 'not merely a poet, but a flag, and not merely a flag but the Red Flag incarnate'. Young men at Cambridge linked arms and swept their elders from the pavements as they advanced, chanting the lines of Swinburne's scandalous ode to 'Dolores'.

Nothing better illustrated the convergence of earnest Pre-Raphaelite ideals and bohemian manners than the way in which many of the leading figures lived communally at 16 Cheyne Walk, Chelsea, the house taken by Rossetti after Lizzie's death. Eccentricity, exhibitionism, and disorder prevailed. The house, overlooking the Thames, had a garden large enough for Rossetti to keep a menagerie. It included a wombat, a kangaroo and an armadillo. Dante Gabriel and William Michael Rossetti, Swinburne, George Meredith, Fanny Cornforth the new model and mistress of Dante Gabriel, and William Morris were among the residents.

Bohemia did not thrive. The wombat ate the cigars. Meredith proved wittier than Dante Gabriel Rossetti and made fun of him in front of his guests. Rossetti threw a cup of tea in his face. Swinburne's energy, 'dancing all over the studio like a wild cat', irritated Rossetti. Meredith was revolted by Rossetti's gargantuan breakfasts, a mound of bacon surrounded by a circle of eggs. Swinburne knocked Morris into the china cabinet and smashed some of Rossetti's finest pieces. With the painter Simeon Solomon, Swinburne romped naked about the house, sliding down the banisters and shrilly waking the echoes. Rossetti introduced Fanny Cornforth, whom Swinburne always referred to as 'The Bitch' out of loyalty to Lizzie's memory. It was one of the more interesting households in the history of English literature but it soon broke up. Meredith was first to leave, unable to endure the noise, swearing that he would have kicked Swinburne down the stairs, 'had he not foreseen what a clatter his horrid little bottom would have made as it bounced from step to step'.

Yet the household was a literary example. It contained Dante Gabriel and William Michael Rossetti, original members of the PRB, William Morris who followed their example and Swinburne who was seen as Pre-Raphaelite at times. It included George Meredith, who was not evidently Pre-Raphaelite but who certainly matched many of Ruskin's ideals of contemporary realism in his poetic sequence, *Modern Love*.

To put a limit to the PRB in anything but pedantic terms is difficult. Christina Rossetti was not a founder member but she was a blood-relation, who wrote about the movement and shared a good deal of its moral earnestness. William Morris was not associated with the PRB until two decades after its beginning, yet he was the most famous name associated with it apart from Dante Gabriel Rossetti. He also shared its earnestness and a yearning for the simple communal life of the fourteenth century. Indeed, in the 1880s he was to become a communist, though his art still owed far more to Chaucer than to Karl Marx.

The men and women of the Victorian bourgeoisie had not suffered such a performance in silence. For some readers, Rossetti and Swinburne had flouted all standards of decency in their writing by 1870. In October 1871, in the *Contemporary Review*, there appeared 'The Fleshly School of Modern Poetry'. This was by 'Thomas Maitland', who proved to be the critic Robert Buchanan, and it was reprinted in a longer version in 1872. He accused Swinburne of having imported the 'dunghill' of Baudelaire's *Fleurs du Mal* (1857) into his own poetry, notably in 'Anactoria' which shares with 'Femmes Damnées' the subject of lesbianism, 'the vilest act conceivable in human debauchery', as Buchanan described it. In Rossetti's poetry, 'I see no gleam of nature, nor a sign of humanity; I hear only the heated ravings of an affected lover, indecent for the most part, and often blasphemous. I attempt to describe Mr Swinburne; and lo! the Bacchanal screams, the sterile Dolores sweats, serpents dance, men and women wrench, wriggle and foam in an endless alliteration of heated and meaningless words . . .' The product of such writing, wrote Buchanan tersely, was 'the veriest garbage of Baudelaire'.

Even Pre-Raphaelitism, according to Buchanan, was submerged in the 'evil dream' of a new hedonism. In a passage that might have inspired an anti-pornography vigilante a century later, Buchanan assures us that 'photographs of nude, indecent, and hideous harlots, in every possible attitude that vice can devise, flaunt from the shop windows'. The high ideals of the PRB in 1848 had been corrupted beyond redemption, in Buchanan's view. English art and literature had come to this.

Like most vigilantes, however, Buchanan saw what he wanted to see or perhaps directed his attention to shop windows of a rather specialist kind. He also made himself a little ridiculous by being a moralist under a pseudonym. His view was not generally shared. Others, like the young novelist George Gissing, found only a prudish self-righteousness in what might be called the political correctness of late Victorian England.

For practical purposes, the PRB as a group lost its impetus after 1870. Swinburne and Morris went their separate ways. Rossetti's best work was finished. Christina Rossetti's poetry reflected her patient invalidism. On the horizon were other new developments which were to turn what remained of the beauty of religion into a religion of beauty.

Yet the experience of the PRB had brought about some sense of community in art and poetry, which Arsène Houssaye had missed thirty years before. The 1880s, by contrast, was to be a decade of cheap editions and a proliferation of literature. Yet the literary world remained small enough for there to be shared anticipation over the appearance of a new book by a favourite author. It was the first age in which mass-produced editions enabled a poet to be truly popular and to have a general following. Arthur Machen, coming to London from Wales as a young man in the 1880s, recalled something of this in his autobiography *Far Off Things*, published in 1922. As so often, it was Swinburne who was the cause of excitement, while the act of purchasing a book of poetry was in itself an intellectual adventure.

> I was possessed by an eager curiosity concerning this Swinburne, convinced in advance — I cannot remember how — that here I should surely find an unexpected, unsurmised treasure. And so, one hot, shiny afternoon, I came up from the old Georgian suburb by the black stream, crossed Hungerford Bridge and made my way into the Strand; into that Strand which is as lost as Atlantis. And going eastward past many vanished things, past the rich odours of Messrs. Rimell's soap-boiling, I came to St Mary-le-Strand, and the entrance of Holywell Street. At the southern corner of this street, facing the east end of the church, there stood Denny's bookshop, and, gold in my pocket, I went in with a bold appearance, and said, "Have you got Swinburne's 'Songs Before Sunrise?'" The shopman did not seem in the least astonished at my question. He said he had got the book, and produced it, and showed it me, and the very cover was such as I had never seen before, provocative, therefore, in a high degree. And so I bought the book and carried it out of Denny's into the sunlight in a great amazement.

On enthusiasm of this kind, the still greater success of the 1890s was to be founded. The cult of personality, so evident in Swinburne's life, was commemorated in Oscar Wilde's wistful observation that he had put his genius into his life and only his talent into his art.

For most readers, the prevailing impression of English culture between the first Pre-Raphaelitism of the later 1840s and the less strictly defined aestheticism of 'Art for Art's Sake' in the 1890s is one of diversity and even confusion. A period which included such names as Gerard Manley Hopkins, Thomas Hardy, and Rudyard Kipling, as well as the continued writing of Elizabeth Barrett Browning, George Meredith, Swinburne and the Rossettis was hardly insignificant. To many observers, however, it lacked the sense of direction which came before and after. F. T. Palgrave, famous as the compiler of *The Golden Treasury* (1861), complained of this state of affairs when writing in the *Nineteenth Century* for

January 1888. He lamented the way in which so many demands of modern culture 'saturate our attention'.

As Palgrave saw it, modern life and society rather than modern art lay at the root of this fragmentation, the sense that culture had lost direction in its development. 'The fret and hurry of the age diverting us from all calm, enduring sources of pleasure, are fatal at once to the growth of genius in art, and to our enjoyment of its creations . . . Art has enlarged its boundaries; but it is extensive now, not intensive.'

Though one may modify Palgrave's view, there is no doubt that throughout the Victorian period the mere subject-matter of poetry appeared to expand. The experience of military and imperial life was a new development. The religious debate in the nineteenth century was reflected in some of the greatest poetry of the age. The analysis of the relationship between men and women, whether in the writing of Elizabeth Barrett Browning or George Meredith, showed a new subtlety and immediacy which the Victorian novel seldom matched. There were also innovations in children's verse, on a scale and of a type which had not been evident before. Despite the Pre-Raphaelites, England was still not a country of literary movements but of individuals, writing for themselves and going in their separate directions. For a variety of reasons, social rather than literary, that was to change by the 1890s.

In the earlier Victorian period, certain major figures who were the direct heirs of the Romantics — Tennyson, Browning, Arnold, for example — stand apart. So do the literary movements of the PRB and the Nineties. In an anthology of Victorian verse, however, there is something to be said for meeting the difficulty which Palgrave states by grouping other poems under headings. To some extent this must be an arbitrary division. Yet the themes which most fairly reflect the preoccupations of the age may be described as: 'Men and Women', 'England, my England', 'The Way of the Cross', 'Army and Empire', 'The Child's World', and 'Dreams of Elsewhere'. The arrangement of the poems in the present selection is not strictly chronological in each category but rather a development of the particular theme. A few of the poems in these intervening groups are contemporary with the early years of the PRB and some with the beginnings of 'Art for Art's Sake'.

The mid-nineteenth century is rich in a poetic analysis of the relationships between men and women. Elizabeth Barrett Browning's *Sonnets from the Portuguese* celebrates one of the most dramatic love-matches in English letters, made yet more famous by Rudolf Besier's play *The Barretts of Wimpole Street* in 1930 and its screen adaptations. The sonnet form gives a concision and power to the sequence which also shows Elizabeth Barrett Browning's writing at its best. Its subject, her redemption from sickness and death by the younger poet Robert Browning, is a compelling personal drama, the more so when described from her point of view.

Because *Sonnets from the Portuguese* is so personal a testament, it is to be taken on its own valuation or not at all. Coventry Patmore and George Meredith stand more clearly in opposition. Patmore's very title, *The Angel in the House*, was to be seen in a later and more sceptical age as an undesirable idealisation of womanhood in marriage. There were to be no more goddesses. Yet because Patmore's poem is set among everyday objects and experiences, its sentiment carries conviction in such passages as the couple on their seaside honeymoon. In contrast to this, George Meredith, brooding on his desertation by his wife and her subsequent death, makes a meticulous analysis of betrayal and violent feeling in *Modern Love*.

These three mid-century poems are irreconcilable as statements of human love. Yet they share the intensity and skill with which eternal sentiments are expressed through the almost mythological imagery of *Sonnets from the Portuguese* or by Coventry Patmore through scenes as trivial as trying on a pair of shoes. Whatever the framework, they have an instinctive modernity.

Some of the most popular Victorian poetry presented relationships between men and women, even the most tragic, as comic or farcical. Edmund Gosse in *Father and Son* (1907) recalled that Dickens was allowed him as childhood reading by his evangelical father because the great novelist 'exposes the passion of love in a ridiculous light'. It was a light in which a good many Victorians, for a variety of reasons, felt more comfortable than in the presence of Elizabeth Barrett Browning or George Meredith. The *vers de société* of Frederick Locker or Charles Stuart Calverley, Thackeray's parody and the music-hall ballads of 'Vilikins and his Dinah' or 'Polly Perkins' all came within this dispensation.

Yet the lives of men and women, as poetry reflected them, were frequently exercises in individual analysis rather than contemplations of love and marriage. Nowhere is this better illustrated than in one of the most gifted poets of the century, John Clare, writing within the confines of Northampton Asylum, or in the sonnets of the bedridden Eugene Lee-Hamilton. At another level, both Lee-Hamilton in a sonnet like 'The Eagles of Tiberius' and the botanist Lord De Tabley's poem 'The Study of a Spider' remind the reader that one of the richest gifts bequeathed by the Romantics to their successors was a sense of the grotesque.

> What have I done for you,
> England, my England?

The answer to W. E. Henley's question in *Invictus* was, so far as the poets of the age were concerned, that they had created an enduring image of the land and its landscape. They did so with varying degrees of truth to life. John Keble celebrates its purity and innocence, John Clare its homely beauty. Elizabeth Barrett Browning's England is a modified vision of a country created by nature, courtesy of William Wordsworth.

Sometimes the poetry of English life and landscape is less contemplative, describing the vigour of the industrial age in William Cosmo Monkhouse's poem 'The Night Express' or the ravens who feed on the flesh of drowned mariners in Robert Stephen Hawker's macabre piece 'A Croon on Hennacliff'. The rural or fashionable society of mid-Victorian England fills the landscape of Charles Tennyson Turner's sonnet 'After the School Feast' or Henry Sambrooke Leigh's laconic picture of the riders in Hyde Park's 'Rotten Row'.

Of the three major figures in this section, Gerard Manley Hopkins was a poet of nature even before his first devotional poetry. Frequently, of course, as in a poem like 'The Windhover', the two elements were to combine. His natural world is limpid and lightly coloured, a contrast to the drama of faith and despair that was to follow. Thomas Hardy shows a spare modernity which characterises his earlier writing. The style is easy and conversational, even in his elegy for William Barnes, a balance to the compressed energy of Hopkins. Few poets of the age gained the popular success of A. E. Housman in *A Shropshire Lad*. Perhaps more than his great contemporaries he tapped an English instinct of loyalty to place and people. Yet even in that he seems to draw on powers which both Hardy and Kipling had shown, one in a sense of locality and the other in an easy delineation of character or type.

The success of such poetry is not to be wondered at. It frequently described an England which readers feared either existed no longer or was disappearing. Leslie Stephen writing of George Eliot in *Hours in a Library* (1892) praised her depiction of 'quiet English country life'. But he adds, 'Its last traces are vanishing so rapidly amidst the changes of modern revolution that its picture could hardly be drawn again, even if there were an artist of equal skill and penetration.' The appeal of the poets who attempted to draw a similar picture was in their imaginative preservation of something which their contemporaries believed was, in reality, lost for ever.

'The Way of the Cross' is a long one in Victorian verse, stretching from the popular thumping rhythms of salvationist hymns to the verbal and metrical intricacies of 'The Wreck of the Deutschland.' In perspective, it appears that Hopkins gave an intensity and personal drama to English devotional poetry, which had not been matched since Donne or Milton in the seventeenth century. As in Donne, the personal and sometimes egotistical element is central. Victorian hymns are communal but such poetry is individual. And just as Victorian marriage was no longer always a matter of wedding bells and happy-ever-after in the poetry of the age, so religious conversion is not for Hopkins an end to spiritual agony. His poems of praise are finely written but his so-called 'Sonnets of Desolation' are an eloquent expression of a mind at the end of its tether.

By no means is all Victorian poetry in this genre an expression of grateful acceptance. The spiritual vacuum of James Thomson's *City of Dreadful Night* seems to have more in common with Hopkins' sonnets than those sonnets have with the steady faith expressed by Newman in 'The Pillar of the Cloud' or *The Dream of Gerontius*. Newman had been born almost in the age of reason, Hopkins and Thomson suggest the subconscious visions which were to fuel Breuer, Freud and psychoanalysis. Hopkins was more than forty years younger than Newman but only twelve years older than Freud. At the time of the poet's early death, the first work on which Freud and Breuer's *Studies in Hysteria* (1895) was based had been completed.

Most Victorian devotional poetry was more traditional, a tradition which incorporated the revival of medievalism. Arthurian legends offered material to Tennyson, Rossetti, and Morris alike. The quest for the Holy Grail, as the cup used by Christ at the Last Supper and by Joseph of Arimathea to catch the precious blood at the foot of the Cross, was a potent symbol in poetry and myth. Like the Flowering Thorn of Glastonbury, the Holy Grail had been Joseph of Arimathea's gift to Britain on his visit in the years after the Crucifixion. Victorian rationalism would have none of this. One of Max Beerbohm's unkindest cartoons shows the sceptical figure of Benjamin Jowett, Modern Churchman and future Master of Balliol, confronting Rossetti severely in 1857 at the Oxford Union, where the Pre-Raphaelites were decorating the walls with frescoes of such subjects. 'And what were they going to *do* with the Grail when they found it, Mr Rossetti?'

None the less, visionary poems on such themes had a wide audience in the Victorian period. Robert Stephen Hawker's 'Quest of the Sangraal' is one of the best examples of the genre, set within the landscape of a wild Cornish coast where he had spent his life. Its narrative is filled with local detail and yet portrays the scene of great events in the story of King Arthur. For those drawn to such myths, the Victorian literary ethic encouraged an attitude toward Arthur which anticipated Winston Churchill's comment that if there was not such a man, there should have been.

Army and empire were difficult subjects for readers and critics in the post-Victorian period. There was a sense of guilt at having had an empire. Indeed, there was a sense of double-guilt among those like the Bloomsbury Group who both abhorred the fact that England had colonised much of the world, while living rather well themselves on the proceeds. Lytton Strachey was able to debunk the Victorians in comfort, supported by the wealth which his family had acquired in India.

At a greater distance, it is possible to view such controversies in perspective. No one need be a militarist in order to be moved by the courage and sacrifice of the Light Cavalry Brigade at Balaclava. Later still, Rudyard Kipling is no mere jingoist but characteristically the voice of the underdog or the other ranks. Henry Newbolt is an imperialist, though interesting as a reflection of that imperial turn of the century in which he wrote, and a skilful portrayer of type and class in a poem like 'He Fell Among Thieves'.

There are two principal themes in such poetry. First there is the affection and nostalgia that soldiers or civil servants felt for the empire over which they presided. Second is the hardship of ordinary soldiers and junior officers or administrators. Far from having an urge to go out and colonise India or Africa, most men would avoid it if they could. As Walter Yeldham describes it, a regiment posted to India might expect to see half its men die of disease or in action within a few years. There was little prestige either. In the mess rooms of the British army before the Indian Mutiny of 1857, the term 'Indian Officer' was used as a form of disparagement for a British officer who had served in India, rather than in a more fashionable posting at home.

The most important military and imperial verse comes after 1857 and it is instructive to see how much of it speaks for those who have not done well out of either army or empire. By contrast, there was an intellectual snobbery in the Victorian novel. In Victorian India, novelists had a subject of Tolstoyan potential. It seldom appears, except in chapters like the opening of *The Moonstone* or such characters as Major Bagstock in *Dombey and Son*. It was left to Kipling and his kind to remedy this in poetry.

Victorian imperial greed is so readily accepted as a cliché that it is perhaps as well to recall, in the culture of the day, the scheme to break up the Empire in 1863. This impulse came not from the ranks of revolution but from Queen Victoria herself who put the plan to Charles Wood, Secretary of State for India. An empire, in 1863, seemed not to be worthwhile and in the end not sustainable. The cost had been lately represented by the Crimean War and the Indian Mutiny. Such doubts were to be overruled by thoughts of duty and destiny but they had existed in the minds of the nation's leaders. In poetry, they continued as a wistful and ironic undertone, heard frequently in Kipling.

Among the other themes of Victorian verse, 'The Child's World' and 'Dreams of Elsewhere' are more briefly represented. Edward Lear and Lewis Carroll dominate Victorian poetry for children. Their originality scarcely needs emphasising, yet they owed more to the past than might sometimes be thought. Even before Lear's first 'Nonsense' was published, nonsense of a rather macabre kind had been served up to children by such publications as *Hood's Annual* in the 1830s with its comic sketches and verses. Crime, punishment and judgment were as much a part of Hood's world as of Carroll's.

> Then turning round his head again,
>   He saw before his eyes
> A great judge, and a little judge,
>   The judges of a-size . . .

There is also the graveyard humour of 'Mary's Ghost', the girl whose body has been dug up and anatomised, so that its parts are in jars of preservative all over London. Where is her lover to find her?

> I can't tell where my head is gone,
> But Doctor Carpue can:
> As for my trunk, it's all pack'd up
> To go by Pickford's van . . .

Much early nonsense might cause unease or protest in the present day, if aimed at young children, reflecting the difference between Victorian and modern prudery. Death and cruelty were more often witnessed in Victorian experience and so more easily objects of humour. Indeed, until the abolition of public executions in 1868, there was nothing whatever to prevent children watching a man or woman struggling for life in the hangman's noose.

The nonsense of the age was robust. Both Lear and Carroll infused it with a further sense of mental oddity or unbalance. Lear's Uncle Arly and Carroll's Father William would do for the Victorian nursery but perhaps not for an ethically earnest playgroup.

'Dreams of Elsewhere' presents those visions of other places, remote and idealised, which appeal to all periods of culture. The eighteenth century exploited them as well as the nineteenth. The characteristic of late-Victorian excursions into such fantasies is perhaps the extent to which they offered a flight from reality rather than a neo-classical energy of satire or the sculpted lines of eulogy. If one quality colours Victorian daydream, it is perhaps 'charm', suggesting both its appeal and its limitations. Edward Fitzgerald's translation of Omar Khayyam is in some ways an exception to this. Yet is also appeals as an easy and undemanding refuge from the oppression of modern life.

Like the Pre-Raphaelite period, the 1890s had a unity which was more suggested than real. There were, of course, several names and titles around which poets or artists might be grouped. If the Pre-Raphaelites had a house magazine in *The Germ*, so did their descendants in *The Yellow Book*, an illustrated quarterly which ran from 1894 to 1897, and *The Savoy*, edited by Aubrey Beardsley and Arthur Symons in 1896. There was also The Rhymers' Club, whose poets included Ernest Dowson, Lionel Johnson and the young W. B. Yeats. Arsène Houssaye's complaint about the absence of literary groupings in English society seemed even more fully answered than by the PRB.

The last decade of the century moved under the impulse of Walter Pater, best known for his *Studies in the History of the Renaissance* (1873) and his novel *Marius the Epicurean* (1885). In the conclusion to the first of these, Pater had quoted Victor Hugo's comment that all men are condemned to death but with an unknown period of reprieve. Pater argued that the reprieve was best spent in an intense dedication to immediate artistic experience, 'To burn always with this hard gem-like flame, to maintain this ecstasy, is success in life.' The qualities of the aesthetic soul were, 'the poetic passion, the desire of beauty, the love of art for art's sake . . .'

In the 1880s, the aesthetic movement attracted a good deal of public attention. Beauty was the key to art and life. This was not in

itself hedonistic or immoral. As Pater had said, good actions are to
be commended because they are also beautiful. Yet such aestheti-
cism was soon mocked by George Du Maurier in *Punch* and by the
portrayal of Oscar Wilde as Bunthorne in Gilbert and Sullivan's
opera *Patience* (1881).

> Though the Philistines may jostle,
> You will rank as an apostle,
> In the high aesthetic band,
> If you walk down Piccadilly
> With a poppy or a lily
> In your medieval hand . . .

What seemed like intensity to Pater appeared as pose and affectation
to others. The smell of certain wild flowers was too much for Pater
to bear. So Oscar Wilde insisted to Margot Asquith that the call of
the cuckoo made him feel ill. He must go indoors for protection.
There scarcely seemed scope for mockery of a movement which
parodied itself, though there was parody and satire, of course.
Wilde, shortly before his downfall, was depicted as Mr Amarinth in
Robert Hichens' *The Green Carnation* (1894). Yet aestheticism in
England was sustained principally by the wit and genius of Wilde,
who seldom appeared to take anything — including himself —
seriously. One of the major literary testaments of the 1890s and of
the aesthetic movement was Wilde's preface to his novel *The Picture
of Dorian Gray* (1891) with its mixture of epigram and paradox,
calculated to shock the Philistines even where it did not offend
them. 'There is no such thing as a moral or an immoral book.
Books are well written or badly written that is all . . . No artist has
ethical sympathies. An ethical sympathy in an artist is an unpardon-
able mannerism of style.'

In the face of such dexterity, Wilde's enemies saw in his writing
the reduction of aestheticism to the flippant, the amoral, and the
corrupting. It would surely have offended the earnestness of the
Pre-Raphaelites as gravely as it did the Philistines thirty years later.
It was the mere cleverness which Ruskin had abhorred. Four years
after his novel was published, Wilde was under cross-examination
at the Central Criminal Court, where *The Picture of Dorian Gray*
was used against him. When asked if some of his more outrageous
paradoxes were true, he replied unwisely, 'I rarely think that
anything I write is true.'

Perhaps the most influential literary seminar of the decade was
that cross-examination by Edward Carson of Oscar Wilde, and
subsequent proceedings at the Central Criminal Court in 1895.

Wilde had brought a prosecution for criminal libel against the Marquess of Queensberry, father of Lord Alfred Douglas, after receiving his card, 'For Oscar Wilde posing as a Somdomite'. (Queensberry was better at boxing than spelling.) A good deal of Carson's cross-examination dealt with the literature of the day and its values. Indeed, the most widely read literary criticism in the 1890s came from the editorial columns of papers like the *Daily Telegraph* and the *Evening News* in the aftermath of Wilde's conviction in his subsequent trial.

Both in Wilde's novel and in the cross-examination, reference was made to another book, a second source for the aestheticism of the 1890s. It was Joris-Karl Huysmans' *A Rebours* (1884), whose title may be translated as 'Against Nature'. This novel was the textbook of the decadents and of neurotic sensibility. The pleasures of its wealthy hero, Des Esseintes, are exotic, hedonistic, perverse. The temporary failure of his virility, for example, is the occasion for a grand funeral banquet at which everything, including the food and wine, is black or as dark as possible.

> The dining room was draped in black for the occasion and the garden outside it had been transformed. The paths were strewn with charcoal, the ornamental pond was edged with black basalt and had been filled with ink. The shrubberies had been replanted with cypress and pines. Dinner was served on a black cloth with baskets of scabious and violets. The candelabra cast a green unnatural light over the table and tapers glimmered in the chandeliers. A hidden orchestra played funeral marches and the guests were waited upon by naked negresses wearing only slippers and stockings in cloth of silver embroidered with tears . . .

The humour seems far more modern than the date of publication, suggesting a surrealist joke or a sequence in a Luis Buñuel film half a century later. But as the novel develops, decadent pleasure requires a stronger stimulus. The hero picks up a boy from the streets and takes him to a well-appointed brothel. Des Esseintes pays the madame well, instructing her to provide whatever pleasures the boy may seek. When the money is spent, in a few weeks time, the pleasures will cease. By then the boy will be prepared to rob and murder for the money he needs to continue his enjoyment. 'On that day my object will have been achieved.' The hero settles back hopefully, scanning the newspaper columns for reports of the boy's criminal career and probably his execution. To those brought up on *Great Expectations* and *Adam Bede*, such fiction was not merely outrageous, it was morally incomprehensible.

Artifice, morbidity, decadence seemed to be the tributaries which fed this stream of cultural life in the century's final decade. It was not hard to find examples in such verse as Lionel Johnson's poem 'The Dark Angel' or Ernest Dowson's 'Amor Profanus'. A similar morbidity affected poetic drama. In 1892 Oscar Wilde wrote his only play that was to be banned in England, *Salomé*. With its cadences of blasphemous passion, its dance of the seven veils, its biblical resonance, its obscene demand by Salomé for the head of Jokanaan, John the Baptist, as her amorous plaything, it could belong to no other decade of the Victorian age. Salomé salutes the severed and bleeding head at the play's end, shortly before being put to death herself. 'Ah! thou would'st not suffer me to kiss thy mouth, Jokanaan. Well! I will kiss it now. I will bite it with my teeth as one bites a ripe fruit ...' Whatever horrors Robert Buchanan may have thought he saw in Rossetti or Swinburne, there had been nothing like this. Seduction, sexuality and a thirst for blood were combined in a manner that was not relieved by self-conscious wit of the kind found in Huysmans.

Survivors from the mid-century of Dickens and Tennyson might stand aghast and wonder how private aspiration and public taste could have changed so greatly. It was easy, of course, to see that London was a more cosmopolitan city than it had been, more open to the influences of France and Germany. Maud Allen, who had played Salomé, sued Noel Pemberton Billing for libel in 1918. Lord Alfred Douglas gave evidence at the trial that Oscar Wilde was already reading Krafft-Ebing's *Psychopathia Sexualis* (1886) while he was writing the play in 1892. Forms of behaviour little understood by most men and women in England before this time had now acquired such names as lesbianism, paedophilia, sadism, masochism and so forth. Perhaps it was a short step from defining such behaviour to reflecting it in art. Baudelaire was now translated into English verse. After Wilde's trial and imprisonment, *The Picture of Dorian Gray* passed to the Paris publisher Charles Carrington. But Carrington's main activity was in producing pornography for the English market. *The Picture of Dorian Gray* now stood with novels like *Flossie: A Venus of Fifteen* and *The Yellow Room: or, Alice Darvell's Subjection* on Carrington's shelves. Literature and its underworld had seldom been so close.

Among contemporaries, Max Nordau saw the decadence at the century's end and noted, 'The prevalent feeling is that of imminent perdition and extinction'. The poet Arthur Symons thought that the attraction of decadence to its artists was that of a 'new and beautiful and interesting disease'. As Oscar Wilde went to prison for two years on 25 May 1895, the *Daily Telegraph* editorial warned the artistic community that the nation would tolerate no more.

> Young men at universities, silly women who lend an ear to any chatter which is petulant and vivacious, novelists who have sought to imitate the style of paradox and unreality, poets who have lisped the language of nerveless and effeminate libertinage — these are the persons who should ponder with themselves the doctrines and the career of the man who has now to undergo the righteous sentence of the law.

Within hours of his conviction, the *Evening Standard* also voiced its distaste for all that Oscar Wilde represented.

> He was one of the high priests of a school which attacks all the wholesome, manly, simple ideals of English life, and sets up false gods of decadent culture and intellectual debauchery. The man himself was a perfect type of his class, a gross sensualist veneered with the affectation of artistic feeling too delicate for the appreciation of common clay . . . It has been the fashion to concede a certain amount of immoral licence to men of genius, and it is time that public opinion should correct it . . . all the more when we find a counsel so distinguished as Sir Edward Clarke gravely submitting to a jury that his client should not be judged as an ordinary man in the matter of decent language and manly feeling because forsooth he had intellectual powers above the average.

Decadence had received its due. Yet true to its name, it was already in decay. A stronger and more resilient writing in the final years of the century expressed a form of social commitment. If it was the decade of *Dorian Gray*, it was also the decade of *Tess of the D'Urbervilles* and *Jude the Obscure*. Far more people read Arthur Morrison's *Tales of Mean Streets* than ever set eyes on Huysmans' *A Rebours*. The most outrageously decadent poet must have looked with envy on the sales of Rudyard Kipling's *Barrack-Room Ballads*, published in 1892, or those of Sir Henry Newbolt's *The Island Race* (1898). Even Oscar Wilde's comedies had an appeal for most audiences which was not dissimilar to that of a new young writer of the decade, P. G. Wodehouse.

In poetry, there are few voices of the age more distinctive than the mysticism or symbolism of W. B. Yeats or the social resonance of John Davidson. Aubrey Beardsley shows a fine sardonic humour in his 'Ballad of a Barber'. W. E. Henley describes with unflinching veracity the experience of undergoing surgery and amputation. Decadence was more prone to advertise itself but it was scarcely the sole voice of English culture. It remains a concluding irony of the age that Oscar Wilde should have regained celebrity after his sentence had been served, not through his former writing but by the harrowing and compelling stanzas of *The Ballad of Reading Gaol* and letters to the *Daily Chronicle* arguing for the improvement of conditions in English prisons.

A good deal in both the decadent and social realist writing of the 1890s looked to the past. Yet in a longer view, there seems much that is in advance of its time. Wilde's comedies played as easily and successfully fifty years after as they did at their first productions. In 1905 *Salomé* was the libretto for the operatic modernism of Richard Strauss. Poems like Richard Le Galienne's 'Ballad of London' or Vincent O'Sullivan's 'The Lady' wake anticipations of the early T. S. Eliot. Yeats had begun that span which was to carry him into the 1930s. The first of Ezra Pound's *Personae* was only seven years away from the Victorian period. The Diamond Jubilee in 1897 and the death of the Queen in 1901 set such a seal of finality upon the division that the age and the century seemed to end together. Yet it might be thought that even in the posturing and the surreal qualities of the decadence, no less than in the reflection of social drama, the styles of a new century had crept upon English culture unawares, even before the old century had run its course.

DONALD THOMAS

THE PRE-RAPHAELITES

Dante Gabriel Rossetti
THE BLESSED DAMOZEL

Rossetti's most quoted poem is also one of his earliest. Written in 1847, it appeared in *The Germ* in 1850. Though he revised it in subsequent editions, it is best known in this first version. The combination of Pre-Raphaelite vision and symbolism made it a pattern for such writing. For almost thirty years after the poem's publication, Rossetti tried to match it with a painting of the same title. When he completed the picture in 1878, he called it 'one of my very best'. Theodore Watts-Dunton, however, preferred 'the perfection of the literary rendering' and thought that the picture showed 'the difficulty of rendering by painting subjects that are specially adapted to be rendered by poetry'.

The blessed damozel leaned out
From the gold bar of Heaven;
Her eyes were deeper than the depth
Of waters stilled at even;
She had three lilies in her hand,
And the stars in her hair were seven.

Her robe, ungirt from clasp to hem,
No wrought flowers did adorn,
But a white rose of Mary's gift,
For service meetly worn;
Her hair that lay along her back
Was yellow like ripe corn.

Her seemed she scarce had been a day
One of God's choristers;
The wonder was not yet quite gone
From that still look of hers;
Albeit, to them she left, her day
Had counted as ten years.

(To one, it is ten years of years.
. . . Yet now, and in this place,
Surely she leaned o'er me — her hair
Fell all about my face . . .
Nothing: the autumn fall of leaves.
The whole year sets apace.)

It was the rampart of God's house
　　That she was standing on;
By God built over the sheer depth
　　The which is Space begun;
So high, that looking downward thence
　　She scarce could see the sun.

It lies in Heaven, across the flood
　　Of ether, as a bridge.
Beneath, the tides of day and night
　　With flame and darkness ridge
The void, as low as where this earth
　　Spins like a fretful midge.

Heard hardly, some of her new friends
　　Amid their loving games
Spake evermore among themselves
　　Their virginal chaste names;
And the souls mounting up to God
　　Went by her like thin flames.

And still she bowed herself and stooped
　　Out of the circling charm;
Until her bosom must have made
　　The bar she leaned on warm,
And the lilies lay as if asleep
　　Along her bended arm.

From the fixed place of Heaven she saw
　　Time like a pulse shake fierce
Through all the worlds. Her gaze still strove
　　Within the gulf to pierce
Its path: and now she spoke as when
　　The stars sang in their spheres.

The sun was gone now; the curled moon
　　Was like a little feather
Fluttering far down the gulf; and now
　　She spoke through the still weather.
Her voice was like the voice the stars
　　Had when they sang together.

(Ah sweet! Even now, in that bird's song,
    Strove not her accents there,
Fain to be hearkened? When those bells
    Possessed the mid-day air,
Strove not her steps to reach my side
    Down all the echoing stair?)

'I wish that he were come to me,
    For he will come,' she said.
'Have I not prayed in Heaven? — on earth,
    Lord, Lord, has he not pray'd?
Are not two prayers a perfect strength?
    And shall I feel afraid?

'When round his head the aureole clings,
    And he is clothed in white,
I'll take his hand and go with him
    To the deep wells of light;
We will step down as to a stream,
    And bathe there in God's sight.

'We two will stand beside that shrine,
    Occult, withheld, untrod,
Whose lamps are stirred continually
    With prayer sent up to God;
And see our old prayers, granted, melt
    Each like a little cloud.

'We two will lie i' the shadow of
    That living mystic tree
Within whose secret growth the Dove
    Is sometimes felt to be,
While every leaf that His plumes touch
    Saith His Name audibly.

'And I myself will teach to him,
    I myself, lying so,
The songs I sing here; which his voice
    Shall pause in, hushed and slow,
And find some knowledge at each pause,
    Or some new thing to know.'

(Alas! We two, we two, thou say'st!
    Yea, one wast thou with me
That once of old. But shall God lift
    To endless unity
The soul whose likeness with thy soul
    Was but its love for thee?)

'We two,' she said, 'will seek the groves
    Where the lady Mary is,
With her five handmaidens, whose names
    Are five sweet symphonies,
Cecily, Gertrude, Magdalen,
    Margaret and Rosalys.

'Circlewise sit they, with bound locks
    And foreheads garlanded;
Into the fine cloth white like flame
    Weaving the golden thread,
To fashion the birth-robes for them
    Who are just born, being dead.

'He shall fear, haply, and be dumb:
    Then will I lay my cheek
To his, and tell about our love,
    Not once abashed or weak:
And the dear Mother will approve
    My pride, and let me speak.

'Herself shall bring us, hand in hand,
    To Him round whom all souls
Kneel, the clear-ranged unnumbered heads
    Bowed with their aureoles:
And angels meeting us shall sing
    To their citherns and citoles.

'There will I ask of Christ the Lord
    Thus much for him and me: —
Only to live as once on earth
    With Love, — only to be,
As then awhile, for ever now
    Together, I and he.'

She gazed and listened and then said,
  Less sad of speech than mild, —
'All this is when he comes.' She ceased.
  The light thrilled towards her, fill'd
With angels in strong level flight.
  Her eyes prayed, and she smil'd.

(I saw her smile.) But soon their path
  Was vague in distant spheres:
And then she cast her arms along
  The golden barriers,
And laid her face between her hands,
  And wept. (I heard her tears.)

MY SISTER'S SLEEP

Another early poem of Rossetti's, written in 1847, this was also published in *The Germ*. Its subject is dramatic rather than biographical and its tone illustrates the fusion of religious faith and artistic novelty that was a feature of Pre-Raphaelite work. Its visual qualities, particularly in the vivid winter night of the fourth stanza, recalled the poetry of Keats. Rossetti's use of a metre from old English writers was soon eclipsed when Tennyson's *In Memoriam* appeared in the same form a few months later.

She fell asleep on Christmas Eve:
  At length the long-ungranted shade
  Of weary eyelids overweigh'd
The pain nought else might yet relieve.

Our mother, who had leaned all day
  Over the bed from chime to chime,
  Then raised herself for the first time,
And as she sat her down, did pray.

Her little work-table was spread
  With work to finish. For the glare
  Made by her candle, she had care
To work some distance from the bed.

Without, there was a cold moon up,
  Of winter radiance sheer and thin;
  The hollow halo it was in
Was like an icy crystal cup.

Through the small room, with subtle sound
  Of flame, by vents the fireshine drove
  And reddened. In its dim alcove
The mirror shed a clearness round.

I had been sitting up some nights,
  And my tired mind felt weak and blank;
  Like a sharp strengthening wine it drank
The stillness and the broken lights.

Twelve struck. That sound, by dwindling years
  Heard in each hour, crept off; and then
  The ruffled silence spread again,
Like water that a pebble stirs.

Our mother rose from where she sat:
  Her needles, as she laid them down,
  Met lightly, and her silken gown
Settled: no other noise than that.

'Glory unto the Newly Born!'
  So, as said angels, she did say;
  Because we were in Christmas Day,
Though it would still be long till morn.

Just then in the room over us
  There was a pushing back of chairs,
  As some who had sat unawares
So late, now heard the hour, and rose.

With anxious softly-stepping haste
  Our mother went where Margaret lay,
  Fearing the sounds o'erhead — should they
Have broken her long watched-for rest!

She stooped an instant, calm, and turned;
  But suddenly turned back again;
  And all her features seemed in pain
With woe, and her eyes gazed and yearned.

For my part, I but hid my face,
  And held my breath, and spoke no word:
  There was none spoken; but I heard
The silence for a little space.

Our mother bowed herself and wept:
   And both my arms fell, and I said,
   'God knows I knew that she was dead.'
And there, all white, my sister slept.

Then kneeling, upon Christmas morn
   A little after twelve o'clock
   We said, ere the first quarter struck,
'Christ's blessing on the newly born!'

TROY TOWN

Like 'The Blessed Damozel', Rossetti's portrayal of Trojan legend
in this poem of 1869 is a painting in words and its refrain suggests
a medieval ballad on the subject. It illustrates the sensuous quality
which mingled with spiritual vision in the best Pre-Raphaelite art.
Rossetti had already painted William Morris's model, Annie Miller,
as Helen of Troy.

Heavenborn Helen, Sparta's queen,
      (*O Troy Town!*)
Had two breasts of heavenly sheen,
The sun and moon of the heart's desire:
All Love's lordship lay between.
      (*O Troy's down,*
       Tall Troy's on fire!)

Helen knelt at Venus' shrine,
      (*O Troy Town!*)
Saying, 'A little gift is mine,
A little gift for a heart's desire.
Hear me speak and make me a sign!
      (*O Troy's down,*
       Tall Troy's on fire!)

'Look, I bring thee a carven cup;
      (*O Troy Town!*)
See it here as I hold it up, —
Shaped it is to the heart's desire,
Fit to fill when the gods would sup.
      (*O Troy's down,*
       Tall Troy's on fire!)

'It was moulded like my breast
          (*O Troy Town!*)
He that sees it may not rest,
Rest at all for his heart's desire.
O give ear to my heart's behest!
          (*O Troy's down,*
            Tall Troy's on fire!)

'See my breast, how like it is;
          (*O Troy Town!*)
See it bare for the air to kiss!
Is the cup to thy heart's desire?
O for the breast, O make it his!
          (*O Troy's down,*
            Tall Troy's on fire!)

'Yea, for my bosom here I sue;
          (*O Troy Town!*)
Thou must give it where 'tis due,
Give it there to the heart's desire.
Whom do I give my bosom to?
          (*O Troy's down,*
            Tall Troy's on fire!)

'Each twin breast is an apple sweet
          (*O Troy Town!*)
Once an apple stirred the beat
Of thy heart with the heart's desire: —
Say, who brought it then to thy feet?
          (*O Troy's down,*
            Tall Troy's on fire!)

'They that claimed it then were three:
          (*O Troy Town!*)
For thy sake two hearts did he
Make forlorn of the heart's desire,
Do for him as he did for thee!
          (*O Troy's down,*
            Tall Troy's on fire!)

'Mine are apples grown to the south,
          (*O Troy Town!*)
Grown to taste in the days of drouth,
Taste and waste to the heart's desire:

Mine are apples meet for his mouth.'
    (*O Troy's down,*
     Tall Troy's on fire!)

Venus looked on Helen's gift,
    (*O Troy Town!*)
Looked and smiled with subtle drift,
Saw the work of her heart's desire: —
'There thou kneel'st for Love to lift!'
    (*O Troy's down,*
     Tall Troy's on fire!)

Venus looked in Helen's face,
     (*O Troy Town!*)
Knew far off an hour and place,
And fire lit from the heart's desire;
Laughed and said, 'Thy gift hath grace!'
    (*O Troy's down,*
     Tall Troy's on fire!)

Cupid looked on Helen's breast,
    (*O Troy Town!*)
Saw the heart within its nest,
Saw the flame of the heart's desire, —
Marked his arrow's burning crest.
    (*O Troy's down,*
     Tall Troy's on fire!)

Cupid took another dart,
    (*O Troy Town!*)
Fledged it for another heart,
Winged the shaft with the heart's desire,
Drew the string and said, 'Depart!'
    (*O Troy's down,*
     Tall Troy's on fire!)

Paris turned upon his bed,
    (*O Troy Town!*)
Turned upon his bed and said,
Dead at heart with the heart's desire, —
'O to clasp her golden head!'
    (*O Troy's down,*
     Tall Troy's on fire!)

THE CARD DEALER

Rossetti's parable of love and death is rich in the symbolism of the
coloured rings, the cards and the erotic beauty of the woman. In its
observation of the modern world it gives a new power to the
Romantic mingling of sexuality and death.

Could you not drink her gaze like wine!
　　Yet though its splendour swoon
Into the silence languidly
　　As a tune into a tune,
Those eyes unravel the coiled night
　　And know the stars at noon.

The gold that's heaped beside her hand,
　　In truth rich prize it were;
And rich the dreams that wreathe her brows
　　With magic stillness there;
And he were rich who should unwind
　　That woven golden hair.

Around her, where she sits, the dance
　　Now breathes its eager heat;
And not more lightly or more true
　　Fall there the dancers' feet
Than fall her cards on the bright board
　　As 'twere an heart that beat.

Her fingers let them softly through,
　　Smooth polished silent things;
And each one as it falls reflects
　　In swift light-shadowings,
Blood-red and purple, green and blue,
　　The great eyes of her rings.

Whom plays she with? With thee, who lov'st
　　Those gems upon her hand;
With me, who search her secret brows;
　　With all men, bless'd or bann'd.
We play together, she and we,
　　Within a vain strange land:

A land without any order, —
  Day even as night, (one saith,) —
Where who lieth down ariseth not
  Nor the sleeper awakeneth;
A land of darkness as darkness itself
  And of the shadow of death.

What be her cards, you ask? Even these: —
  The heart, that doth but crave
More, having fed; the diamond,
  Skilled to make base seem brave;
The club, for smiting in the dark;
  The spade, to dig a grave.

And do you ask what game she plays?
  With me 'tis lost or won;
With thee it is playing still; with him
  It is not well begun;
But 'tis a game she plays with all
  Beneath the sway o' the sun.

Thou seest the card that falls, — she knows
  The card that followeth:
Her game in thy tongue is called Life,
  As ebbs thy daily breath;
When she shall speak, thou'lt learn her tongue
  And knows she calls it Death.

WINTER and SPRING

The same Keatsean vividness of description and compression of
phrase appear in Rossetti's sonnets, particularly in the sestet of
'Winter'. These belong to a later and more disciplined period of his
work, published a year before his death in *Ballads and Sonnets*
(1881).

WINTER
How large that thrush looks on the bare thorn-tree!
  A swarm of such, three little months ago,
  Had hidden in the leaves and let none know
Save by the outburst of their minstrelsy.

A white flake here and there — a snow-lily
  Of last night's frost — our naked flower-beds hold;
  And for a rose-flower on the darkling mould
The hungry redbreast gleams. No bloom, no bee.

The current shudders to its ice-bound sedge:
  Nipped in their bath, the stark reeds one by one
  Flash each its clinging diamond in the sun:
'Neath winds which for this Winter's sovereign pledge
Shall curb great king-masts to the ocean's edge
  And leave memorial forest-kings o'erthrown.

SPRING

Soft-littered is the new-year's lambing-fold,
  And in the hollowed haystack at its side
  The shepherd lies o' nights now, wakeful-eyed
At the ewes' travailing call through the dark cold.
The young rooks cheep 'mid the thick caw o' the old:
  And near unpeopled stream-sides, on the ground,
  By her spring-cry the moorhen's nest is found,
Where the drained flood-lands flaunt their marigold.

Chill are the gusts to which the pastures cower,
  And chill the current where the young reeds stand
  As green and close as the young wheat on land:
Yet here the cuckoo and the cuckoo-flower
Plight to the heart Spring's perfect imminent hour
  Whose breath shall soothe you like your dear one's hand.

from THE HOUSE OF LIFE
(Sonnets xxxiii & xxxvi)

Rossetti's long sonnet-sequence occupied him almost until the end
of his life, though it was published in part in 1870. 'Venus Victrix'
commemorates Rossetti's love for Jane Morris who stares with a
rather moody voluptuousness from such paintings of his as 'Proser-
pine' and 'The Day Dream'. The same feeling for sensuous beauty,
shadowed by time and change, informs the second sonnet.

Sonnet xxxiii
VENUS VICTRIX

Could Juno's self more sovereign presence wear
  Than thou, 'mid other ladies throned in grace? —
  Or Pallas, when thou bend'st with soul-stilled face
O'er poet's page gold-shadowed in thy hair?
Does thou than Venus seem less heavenly fair
  When o'er the sea of love's tumultuous trance
  Hovers thy smile, and mingles with thy glance
That sweet voice like the last wave murmuring there?

Before such triune loveliness divine
  Awestruck I ask, which goddess here most claims
The prize that, howsoe'er adjudged, is thine?
  Then Love breathes low the sweetest of thy names;
And Venus Victrix to my heart doth bring
Herself, the Helen of her guerdoning.

Sonnett xxxvi
LIFE-IN-LOVE

Not in thy body is thy life at all
  But in this lady's lips and hands and eyes;
  Through these she yields thee life that vivifies
What else were sorrow's servant and death's thrall.
Look on thyself without her, and recall
  The waste remembrance and forlorn surmise
  That lived but in a dead-drawn breath of sighs
O'er vanished hours and hours eventual.

Even so much life hath the poor tress of hair
  Which, stored apart, is all love hath to show
  For heart-beats and for fire-heats long ago;
Even so much life endures unknown, even where,
  'Mid change the changeless night environeth,
  Lies all that golden hair undimmed in death.

THE WINE OF CIRCE

One of Rossetti's 'Sonnets for Pictures', this was written as a tribute to 'The Wine of Circe' by Edward Burne-Jones. In Rossetti's version, the enchantress of Homer's *Odyssey* becomes the flesh-and-blood beauty of a mid-Victorian daydream.

> Dusk-haired and gold-robed o'er the golden wine
>   She stoops, wherein, distilled of death and shame,
>   Sink the black drops; while, lit with fragrant flame,
> Round her spread board the golden sunflowers shine.
> Doth Helios here with Hecatè combine
>   (O Circe, thou their votaress!) to proclaim
>   For these thy guests all rapture in Love's name,
> Till pitiless Night gave Day the countersign?
>
> Lords of their hour, they come. And by her knee
>   Those cowering beasts, their equals heretofore,
> Wait; who with them in new equality
>   To-night shall echo back the unchanging roar
>   Which sounds for ever from the tide-strown shore
> Where the dishevelled seaweed hates the sea.

LILITH

Rossetti's sonnet of 1868 was written for his own painting 'The Lady Lilith', completed four years earlier. In Talmudic legend, Lilith was Adam's first wife who rebelled against him and lived as a demon. The painting, for which Fanny Cornforth was the model, shows Lilith lounging in an ornate dressing-room, drawing the length of her shining hair through her fingers. It has the familiar Pre-Raphaelite air of mythology transformed into a sensuous Victorian cameo.

> Of Adam's first wife, Lilith, it is told
>   (The witch he loved before the gift of Eve,)
>   That, ere the snake's, her sweet tongue could deceive,
> And her enchanted hair was the first gold.
> And still she sits, young while the earth is old,
>   And, subtly of herself contemplative,
>   Draws men to watch the bright net she can weave,
> Till heart and body and life are in its hold.

The rose and poppy are her flowers; for where
  Is he not found, O Lilith, whom shed scent
And soft-shed kisses and soft sleep shall snare?
  Lo! as that youth's eyes burned at thine, so went
  Thy spell through him, and left his straight neck bent,
And round his heart one strangling golden hair.

Christina Rossetti
IN AN ARTIST'S STUDIO

This is an early poem of Christina Rossetti's, a sonnet of 1856, suggesting her close association with the Pre-Raphaelite Brotherhood, if not her membership of it. There is little doubt, at that period, that the 'nameless girl' of her brother's paintings was Lizzie Siddal.

One face looks out from all his canvases.
One selfsame figure sits or walks or leans:
We found her hidden just behind those screens,
That mirror gave back all her loveliness.
A queen in opal or in ruby dress,
A nameless girl in freshest summer-greens,
A saint, an angel — every canvas means
The same one meaning, neither more or less.
He feeds upon her face by day and night,
And she with true kind eyes looks back on him.
Fair as the moon and joyful as the light:
Not wan with waiting, nor with sorrow dim;
Not as she is, but was when hope shone bright;
Not as she is, but as she fills his dream.

P.R.B.

By 1854, Holman Hunt was in Palestine and Thomas Woolner on his way to Australia. Millais had turned to commercially successful art. Dante Gabriel Rossetti wrote to his sister that the Pre-Raphaelite Brotherhood had run its course and that now 'the whole Round Table is dissolved'. Christina, taking a less solemn view of the development than her brother, replied in the form of a sonnet.

The P.R.B. is in its decadence:
For Woolner in Australia cooks his chops,
And Hunt is yearning for the land of Cheops:
D. G. Rossetti shuns the vulgar optic;
While William M. Rossetti merely lops
His B's in English disesteemed as Coptic;
Calm Stephens in the twilight smokes his pipe
But long the dawning of his public day;
And he at last the champion great Millais,
Attaining Academic opulence
Winds up his signature with A.R.A.
So rivers merge in the perpetual sea;
So luscious fruit must fall when over-ripe;
And so the consummated P.R.B.

THE QUEEN OF HEARTS

Among the poems that reflect the society of the 1860s in which the
Rossettis and their friends moved, the spontaneity and affection of
this exchange is one of the most chrming examples.

How comes it, Flora, that, whenever we
Play cards together, you invariably,
        However pack the parts,
        Still hold the Queen of Hearts?

I've scanned you with a scrutinizing gaze,
Resolved to fathom these your secret ways:
        But, sift them as I will,
        Your ways are secret still.

I cut and shuffle; shuffle, cut again;
But all my cutting, shuffling, proves in vain:
        Vain hope, vain forethought too;
        That Queen still falls to you.

I dropped her once, prepense; but, ere the deal
Was dealt, your instinct seemed her loss to feel:
        'There should be one card more,'
        You said, and searched the floor.

I cheated once; I made a private notch
In Heart-Queen's back, and kept a lynx-eyed watch;
    Yet such another back
    Deceived me in the pack:

The Queen of Clubs assumed by arts unknown
An imitative dint that seemed my own;
    This notch, not of my doing,
    Misled me to my ruin.

It baffles me to puzzle out the clue,
Which must be skill, or craft, or luck in you:
    Unless, indeed, it be
    Natural affinity.

THE THREE ENEMIES

Long illness and religious awakening left their impression on
Christina Rossetti's later poems. Her style was generally lyrical and
reflective but, as here, she also produced religious poems of drama
and vivacity.

THE FLESH
'Sweet, thou art pale.'
    'More pale to see,
Christ hung upon the cruel tree
And bore His Father's wrath for me.'

'Sweet, thou art sad.'
    'Beneath a rod
More heavy, Christ for my sake trod
The winepress of the wrath of God.'

'Sweet, thou art weary.'
    'Not so Christ
Whose mighty love of me sufficed
For Strength, Salvation, Eucharist.'

'Sweet, thou art footsore.'
    'If I bleed,
His feet have bled; yea in my need.
His Heart once bled for mine indeed.'

THE WORLD

'Sweet, thou art young.'
      'So He was young
Who for my sake in silence hung
Upon the Cross with Passion wrung.'

'Look, thou art fair.'
      'He was more fair
Than men, Who deigned for me to wear
A visage marred beyond compare.'

'And thou hast riches.'
      'Daily bread:
All else is His: Who, living, dead,
For me lacked where to lay His Head.'

'And life is sweet.'
      'It was not so
To Him, Whose Cup did overflow
With mine unutterable woe.'

THE DEVIL

'Thou drinkest deep.'
      'When Christ would sup
He drained the dregs from out my cup:
So how should I be lifted up?'

'Thou shalt win Glory.'
      'In the skies,
Lord Jesus, cover up mine eyes
Lest they should look on vanities.'

'Thou shalt have knowledge.'
      'Helpless dust!
In Thee, O Lord, I put my trust:
Answer Thou for me, Wise and Just.'

'And Might.' —
      'Get thee behind me. Lord,
Who hast redeemed and not abhorred
My soul, oh keep it by Thy Word.'

REMEMBER

There is an echo in this poem of Shakespeare's Sonnet LXXI 'No longer mourn for me when I am dead...' Yet Shakespeare's argument is stronger-minded, Christina Rossetti's more wistful and self-effacing.

Remember me when I am gone away,
   Gone far away into the silent land;
   When you can no more hold me by the hand,
Nor I half turn to go, yet turning stay.
Remember me when no more day by day
   You tell me of our future that you plann'd:
   Only remember me; you understand
It will be late to counsel then or pray.
Yet if you should forget me for a while
   And afterwards remember, do not grieve:
   For if the darkness and corruption leave
A vestige of the thoughts that once I had,
Better by far you should forget and smile
   Than that you should remember and be sad.

LAST PRAYER

By contrast with the rather easy-going hymnology of the Victorian period, its best poets produced work of a dramatic and disturbing intensity on religious themes. Christina Rossetti's powerful invocation seems calculated to leave the sceptic unnerved and the critic silent.

Before the beginning Thou hast foreknown the end,
   Before the birthday the death-bed was seen of Thee:
Cleanse what I cannot cleanse, mend what I cannot mend,
   O Lord All-Merciful, be merciful to me.

While the end is drawing near I know not mine end;
   Birth I recall not, my death I cannot foresee:
O God, arise to defend, arise to befriend,
   O Lord All-Merciful, be merciful to me.

Thomas Woolner
MY BEAUTIFUL LADY

Thomas Woolner (1825–92), the sculptor who was one of the
seven members of the PRB in 1848, was known for only a few
poems of which this was the most popular. Its praise of female
beauty is more diffident and formal than Rossetti's but none the
less sustained.

I love my Lady; she is very fair;
Her brow is wan and bound by simple hair;
   Her spirit sits aloft and high,
   But glances from her tender eye
      In sweetness droopingly.

As a young forest while the wind drives thro',
My life is stirr'd when she breaks on my view;
   Her beauty grants my will no choice
   But silent awe, till she rejoice
      My longing with her voice.

Her warbling voice, tho' ever low and mild,
Oft makes me feel as strong wine would a child;
   And tho' her hand be airy light
   Of touch, it moves me with its might
      As would a sudden fright.

A hawk high poised in air, whose nerved wing-tips
Tremble with might suppress'd before he dips,
   In vigilance, scarce more intense
   Than I, when her voice holds my sense
      Contented in suspense.

Her mention of a thing, august or poor,
Makes it far nobler than it was before:
   As, where the sun strikes, life will gush
   And what is pale receive a flush,
      Rich hues, a richer blush.

My Lady's name when I hear strangers use,
Not meaning her, to me seems lax misuse;
   I love none but my Lady's name;
   Maud, Grace, Rose, Marian, all the same
      Are harsh, or blank and tame.

My lady walks as I have watch'd a swan
Swim where a glory on the water shone:
   There ends of willow-branches ride
   Quivering in the flowing tide,
     By the deep river's side.

Fresh beauties, howsoe'er she moves, are stirr'd;
As the sunn'd bosom of a humming-bird
   At each pant lifts some fiery hue,
   Fierce gold, bewildering green or blue —
     The same, yet ever new.

William Morris

from THE DEFENCE OF GUENEVERE

On 19 February 1857, Swinburne read 'The Defence of Guenevere'
to the Old Mortality, an undergraduate society at Oxford, and
announced that its young author was superior to Tennyson. The
theme of the poem, in which the queen who has committed adultery
with Lancelot defends herself, was also one that the mid-Victorians
were prepared to read sympathetically. Morris paid for his headlong
enthusiasm by some technical awkwardness but the poem, dedi-
cated to Dante Gabriel Rossetti, was an impressive debut.

But, knowing now that they would have her speak,
She threw her wet hair backward from her brow,
Her hand close to her mouth touching her cheek,

As though she had had there a shameful blow,
And feeling it shameful to feel aught but shame
All through her heart, yet felt her cheek burned so,

She must a little touch it; like one lame
She walked away from Gauwaine, with her head
Still lifted up; and on her cheek of flame

The tears dried quick; she stopped at last and said:
'O knights and lords, it seems but little skill
To talk of well-known things past now and dead.

'God wot I ought to say, I have done ill,
And pray you all forgiveness heartily!
Because you must be right, such great lords — still

'Listen, suppose your time were come to die,
And you were quite alone and very weak;
Yea, laid a dying while very mightily

'The wind was ruffling up the narrow streak
Of river through your broad lands running well:
Suppose a hush should come, then some one speak:

"One of these cloths is heaven, and one is hell,
Now choose one cloth for ever; which they be,
I will not tell you, you must somehow tell

'"Of your own strength and mightiness; here see!"
Yea, yea, my lord, and you to ope your eyes,
At foot of your familiar bed to see

'A great God's angel standing, with such dyes,
Not known on earth, on his great wings, and hands,
Held out two ways, light from the inner skies

'Showing him well, and making his commands
Seem to be God's commands, moreover, too,
Holding within his hands the cloths on wands;

'And one of these strange choosing cloths was blue,
Wavy and long, and one cut short and red;
No man could tell the better of the two.

'After a shivering half-hour you said,
"God help! heaven's colour, the blue"; and he said, "hell."
Perhaps you then would roll upon your bed,

'And cry to all good men that loved you well,
"Ah Christ! if only I had known, known, known."
Launcelot went away, then I could tell.

'Like wisest man how all things would be, moan,
And roll and hurt myself, and long to die,
And yet fear much to die for what was sown.

'Nevertheless you, O Sir Gauwaine, lie,
Whatever may have happened through these years,
God knows I speak truth, saying that you lie.'

Her voice was low at first, being full of tears,
But as it cleared, it grew full loud and shrill,
Growing a windy shriek in all men's ears,

A ringing in their startled brains, until
She said that Gauwaine lied, then her voice sunk,
And her great eyes began again to fill,

Though still she stood right up, and never shrunk,
But spoke on bravely, glorious lady fair!
Whatever tears her full lips may have drunk,

She stood, and seemed to think, and wrung her hair,
Spoke out at last with no more trace of shame,
With passionate twisting of her body there:

'It chanced upon a day that Launcelot came
To dwell at Arthur's court: at Christmas-time
This happened; when the heralds sung his name,

'"Son of King Ban of Benwick," seemed to chime
Along with all the bells that rang that day,
O'er the white roofs, with little change of rhyme.

'Christmas and whitened winter passed away,
And over me the April sunshine came,
Made very awful with black hail-clouds, yea

'And in the Summer I grew white with flame,
And bowed my head down — Autumn, and the sick
Sure knowledge things would never be the same,

'However often Spring might be most thick
Of blossoms and buds, smote on me, and I grew
Careless of most things, let the clock tick, tick,

'To my unhappy pulse, that beat right through
My eager body; while I laughed out loud,
And let my lips curl up at false or true,

'Seemed cold and shallow without any cloud.
Behold my judges, then the cloths were brought:
While I was dizzied thus, old thoughts would crowd,

'Belonging to the time ere I was bought
By Arthur's great name and his little love,
Must I give up for ever then, I thought,

'That which I deemed would ever round me move
Glorifying all things, for a little word,
Scarce ever meant at all, must I now prove

'Stone-cold for ever? Pray you, does the Lord
Will that all folks should be quite happy and good?
I love God now a little, if this cord

'Were broken, once for all what striving could
Make me love anything in earth or heaven?
So day by day it grew, as if one should

'Slip slowly down some path worn smooth and even,
Down to a cool sea on a summer day;
Yet still in slipping was there some small leaven

'Of stretched hands catching small stones by the way,
Until one surely reached the sea at last,
And felt strange new joy as the worn head lay

'Back, with the hair like sea-weed; yea all past
Sweat of the forehead, dryness of the lips,
Washed utterly out by the dear waves o'ercast

'In the lone sea, far off from any ships!
Do I not know now of a day in Spring?
No minute of that wild day ever slips

'From out my memory; I hear thrushes sing,
And wheresoever I may be, straightway
Thoughts of it all come up with most fresh sting;

'I was half mad with beauty on that day,
And went without my ladies all alone,
In a quiet garden walled round every way;

'I was right joyful of that wall of stone,
That shut the flowers and trees up with the sky,
And trebled all the beauty: to the bone,

'Yea right through to my heart, grown very shy
With weary thoughts, it pierced, and made me glad;
Exceedingly glad, and I knew verily,

'A little thing just then had made me mad;
I dared not think, as I was wont to do,
Sometimes, upon my beauty; if I had

'Held out my long hand up against the blue,
And, looking on the tenderly darken'd fingers,
Thought that by rights one ought to see quite through,

'There, see you, where the soft light yet lingers,
Round by the edges; what should I have done
If this had joined with yellow spotted singers,

'And startling green drawn upward by the sun?
But shouting, loosed out, see now! all my hair,
And trancedly stood watching the west wind run

'With faintest half-heard breathing sound — why there
I lose my head e'en now in doing this;
But shortly listen — In that garden fair

'Came Launcelot walking; this is true, the kiss
Wherewith we kissed in meeting that spring day,
I scarce dare talk of the remember'd bliss,

'When both our mouths went wandering in one way,
And aching sorely, met among the leaves;
Our hands being left behind strained far away.

'Never within a yard of my bright sleeves
Had Launcelot come before — and now, so nigh!
After that day why is it Guenevere grieves?

'Nevertheless you, O Sir Gauwaine, lie,
Whatever happened on through all those years,
God knows I speak truth, saying that you lie . . .

*

'All I have said is truth, by Christ's dear tears.'
She would not speak another word, but stood
Turn'd sideways; listening, like a man who hears

His brother's trumpet sounding through the wood
Of his foes' lances. She lean'd eagerly,
And gave a slight spring sometimes, as she could

At last hear something really; joyfully
Her cheek grew crimson, as the headlong speed
Of the roan charger drew all men to see,
The Knight who came was Launcelot at good need.

from THE HOLLOW LAND

By contrast with his longer poems, some of Morris's shorter pieces
attained a limpid simplicity which other Pre-Raphaelites sought in
vain. The following two short poems are insertions in his early
prose romance *The Hollow Land* (1856).

Christ keep the Hollow Land
All the summer-tide;
Still we cannot understand
Where the waters glide;

Only dimly seeing them
Coldly slipping through
Many green-lipped cavern mouths,
Where the hills are blue.

*

Queen Mary's crown was gold,
King Joseph's crown was red,
But Jesus' crown was diamond
That lit up all the bed
    Mariæ Virginis.

Ships sail through the Heaven
With red banners dress'd,
Carrying the planets seven
To see the white breast
    Mariæ Virginis.

THE HAYSTACK IN THE FLOODS

Morris's vision of the Middle Ages was not so much of purity and innocence as of death and violence. 'The Haystack in the Floods' is a casual and brutal incident in which the historical details are merely hinted at but the sexual blackmail, assassination and mental torment of the woman are described precisely and with care.

Had she come all the way for this,
To part at last without a kiss?
Yea, had she borne the dirt and rain
That her own eyes might see him slain
Beside the haystack in the floods?

Along the dripping leafless woods,
The stirrup touching either shoe,
She rode astride as troopers do;
With kirtle kilted to her knee,
To which the mud splashed wretchedly;
And the wet dripped from every tree
Upon her head and heavy hair,
And on her eyelids broad and fair;

The tears and rain ran down her face.
By fits and starts they rode apace,
And very often was his place
Far off from her; he had to ride
Ahead, to see what might betide
When the roads cross'd; and sometime, when
There rose a murmuring from his men,
Had to turn back with promises;
Ah me! she had but little ease;
And often for pure doubt and dread
She sobb'd, made giddy in the head
By the swift riding; while, for cold,
Her slender fingers scarce could hold
The wet reins; yea, and scarcely, too,
She felt the foot within her shoe
Against the stirrup: all for this,
To part at last without a kiss
Beside the haystack in the floods.
For when they near'd that old soaked hay,
They saw across the only way
That Judas, Godmar, and the three
Red running lions dismally
Grinn'd from his pennon, under which,
In one straight line along the ditch,
They counted thirty heads.
                                So then,
While Robert turn'd round to his men,
She saw at once the wretched end,
And, stooping down, tried hard to rend
Her coif the wrong way from her head,
And hid her eyes; while Robert said:
'Nay, love, 'tis scarcely two to one,
At Poictiers where we made them run
So fast — why, sweet my love, good cheer,
The Gascon frontier is so near,
Nought after this.'
                                But, 'O', she said,
'My God! my God! I have to tread
The long way back without you; then
The court at Paris; those six men;
The gratings of the Chatelet;
The swift Seine on some rainy day
Like this, and people standing by,

And laughing, while my weak hands try
To recollect how strong men swim.
All this, or else a life with him,
For which I should be damned at last,
Would God that this next hour were past!'
He answer'd not, but cried his cry,
'St George for Marny!' cheerily;
And laid his hand upon her rein.
Alas! no man of all his train
Gave back that cheery cry again;
And while for rage his thumb beat fast
Upon his sword-hilt, some one cast
About his neck a kerchief long,
And bound him.

       Then they went along
To Godmar; who said: 'Now, Jehane,
Your lover's life is on the wane
So fast, that, if this very hour
You yield not as my paramour,
He will not see the rain leave off —
Nay, keep your tongue from gibe and scoff,
Sir Robert, or I slay you now.'

She laid her hand upon her brow,
Then gazed upon the palm, as though
She thought her forehead bled, and — 'No.'
She said, and turn'd her head away,
As there were nothing else to say,
And everything were settled: red
Grew Godmar's face from chin to head:
'Jehane, on yonder hill there stands
My castle, guarding well my lands:
What hinders me from taking you,
And doing what I list to do
To your fair wilful body, while
Your knight lies dead?'

       A wicked smile
Wrinkled her face, her lips grew thin,
A long way out she thrust her chin:
'You know that I should strangle you
While you were sleeping; or bite through
Your throat, by God's help — ah!' she said,
'Lord Jesus, pity your poor maid!

For in such wise they hem me in,
I cannot choose but sin and sin,
Whatever happens; yet I think
They could not make me eat or drink,
And so should I just reach my rest.'
'Nay, if you do not my behest,
O Jehane! though I love you well,'
Said Godmar, 'would I fail to tell
All that I know?' 'Foul lies,' she said.
'Eh? lies my Jehane? by God's head,
At Paris folks would deem them true!
Do you know, Jehane, they cry for you,
"Jehane the brown! Jehane the brown!
Give us Jehane to burn or drown!" —
Eh — gag me, Robert — sweet my friend,
This were indeed a piteous end
For those long fingers, and long feet,
And long neck, and smooth shoulders sweet;
An end that few men would forget
That saw it — So, an hour yet:
Consider, Jehane, which to take
Or life or death!'

        So, scarce awake,
Dismounting, did she leave that place,
And totter some yards; with her face
Turn'd upward to the sky she lay,
Her head on a wet heap of hay,
And fell asleep: and while she slept,
And did not dream, the minutes crept
Round to the twelve again; but she,
Being waked at last, sigh'd quietly,
And strangely childlike came, and said:
'I will not.' Straightway Godmar's head,
As though it hung on strong wires, turn'd
Most sharply round, and his face burn'd.
For Robert — both his eyes were dry,
He could not weep, but gloomily
He seem'd to watch the rain; yea, too,
His lips were firm; he tried once more
To touch her lips; she reach'd out, sore
And vain desire so tortured them,
The poor grey lips, and now the hem
Of his sleeve brush'd them.

                                          With a start
Up Godmar rose, thrust them apart;
From Robert's throat he loosed the bands
Of silk and mail: with empty hands
Held out, she stood and gazed, and saw,
The long bright blade without a flaw
Glide out from Godmar's sheath, his hand
In Robert's hair; she saw him bend
Back Robert's head; she saw him send
The thin steel down; the blow told well,
Right backward the knight Robert fell,
And moan'd as dogs do, being half dead,
Unwitting, as I deem: so then
Godmar turn'd grinning to his men,
Who ran, some five or six, and beat
His head to pieces at their feet.

Then Godmar turn'd again and said:
'So, Jehane, the first fitte is read!
Take note, my lady, that your way
Lies backward to the Chatelet!'
She shook her head and gazed awhile
At her cold hands with rueful smile,
As though this thing had made her mad.
This was the parting that they had
Beside the haystack in the floods.

SUMMER DAWN and POMONA

The sonnet presents a succinct genre painting in words, rather like
Tennyson's 'Mariana', in which scene, voice and suggestion are
more important than any explanation as to why the prayer is asked.
The lone house in the cornfield evokes a Victorian rural image
rather than a medieval vision.

'Pomona' is Morris's tribute to the myth and custom which give life
to the country scene of an industrial age.

SUMMER DAWN

Pray but one prayer for me 'twixt thy closed lips,
Think but one thought of me up in the stars.
The summer night waneth, the morning light slips,
Faint and grey 'twixt the leaves of the aspen, betwixt the
    cloud-bars,
That are patiently waiting there for the dawn:
Patient and colourless, though Heaven's gold
Waits to float through them along with the sun.
Far out in the meadows, above the young corn,
The heavy elms wait, and restless and cold
The uneasy wind rises; the roses are dun;
Through the long twilight they pray for the dawn,
Round the lone house in the midst of the corn.
    Speak but one word to me over the corn,
    Over the tender, bow'd locks of the corn.

POMONA

I am the ancient Apple-Queen,
As once I was so am I now.
But evermore a hope unseen,
Betwixt the blossom and the bough.

Ah, where's the river's hidden Gold?
And where the windy grave of Troy?
Yet come I as I came of old,
From out the heart of Summer's joy.

AUGUST

In 1868, ten years after the appearance of *The Defence of Guenev-
ere*, Morris published *The Earthly Paradise*. Appropriately, that
paradise was set in the English countryside with its changing
seasons, which Morris described in a poetic calendar. 'August' is
one of the shorter poems in the sequence.

Across the gap made by our English hinds,
Amidst the Roman's handiwork, behold
Far off the long-roofed church; the shepherd binds
The withy round the hurdles of his fold,
Down in the fosse the river fed of old,
That through long lapse of time has grown to be
The little grassy valley that you see.

Rest here awhile, not yet the eve is still,
The bees are wandering yet, and you may hear
The barley mowers on the trenchèd hill,
The sheep-bells, and the restless changing weir,
All little sounds made musical and clear
Beneath the sky that burning August gives,
While yet the thought of glorious Summer lives.

Ah, love! such happy days, such days as these,
Must we still waste them, craving for the best,
Like lovers o'er the painted images
Of those who once their yearning hearts have blessed?
Have we been happy on our day of rest?
Thine eyes say 'yes', — but if it came again,
Perchance its ending would not seem so vain.

Now came fulfilment of the year's desire,
The tall wheat, coloured by the August fire
Grew heavy-headed, dreading its decay,
And blacker grew the elm-trees day by day.
About the edges of the yellow corn,
And o'er the gardens grown somewhat outworn
The bees went hurrying to fill up their store;
The apple-boughs bent over more and more;
With peach and apricot the garden wall
Was odorous, and the pears began to fall
From off the high tree with each freshening breeze.

So in a house bordered about with trees,
A little raised above the waving gold
The Wanderers heard this marvellous story told,
While 'twixt the gleaming flasks of ancient wine,
They watched the reapers' slow advancing line.

from SENDING TO THE WAR

Morris left the Liberal party in 1880 and founded the Socialist
League five years later. In 1886 he published *The Pilgrims of Hope*,
from which these lines are taken. The contrast between the march-
ing regiment, 'the wrath of England', and 'the want and the woe of
the town', is an inspiration to the poet's vision of a future in which
the revolution is accomplished.

Sick unto death was my hope,
    and I turned and looked on my dear,
And beheld her frightened wonder,
    and her grief without a tear,
And knew how her thought was mine —
    When, hark! o'er the hubbub and noise,
Faint and a long way off,
    the music's measured voice,
And the crowd was swaying and swaying,
    and somehow, I knew not why,
A dream came into my heart
    of deliverance drawing anigh.
Then with roll and thunder of drums
    grew the music louder and loud,
And the whole street tumbled and surged,
    and cleft was the holiday crowd,
Till two walls of faces and rags
    lined either side of the way.
Then clamour of shouts rose upward,
    as bright and glittering gay
Came the voiceful brass of the band,
    and my heart beat fast and fast,
For the river of steel came on,
    and the wrath of England passed
Through the want and the woe of the town,
    and strange and wild was my thought,
And my clenched hands wandered about
    as though a weapon they sought.
Hubbub and din was behind them,
    and the shuffling haggard throng,
Wandering aimless about,
    tangled the street for long;
But the shouts and the rhythmic noise
    we still heard far away,
And my dream was become a picture
    of the deeds of another day.
Far and far was I borne,
    away o'er the years to come,
And again was the ordered march,
    and the thunder of the drum,

And the bickering points of steel,
    and the horses shifting about
'Neath the flashing swords of the captains —
    then the silence after the shout —

Sun and wind in the street,
    familiar things made clear,
Made strange by the breathless waiting
    for the deeds that are drawing anear.
For woe had grown into will,
    and wrath was bared of its sheath,
And stark in the streets of London
    stood the crop of the dragon's teeth.
Where then in my dream were the poor
    and the wall of the faces wan?
Here and here by my side,
    shoulder to shoulder of man,
Hope in the simple folk,
    hope in the hearts of the wise,
For the happy life to follow,
    or death and the ending of lies,
Hope is awake in the faces
    angerless now no more,
Till the new peace dawn on the world,
    the fruit of the people's war.

War in the world abroad
    a thousand leagues away,
While custom's wheel goes round
    and day devoureth day.
Peace at home! — what peace,
    While the rich man's mill is strife,
And the poor is the grist that he grindeth,
    and life devoureth life?

from NEW BIRTH

In a further section from *The Pilgrims of Hope*, Morris describes
the appeal of a Communist street-speaker to his audience. Apart
from its political interest, the poem illustrates the effect of Victorian
oratory upon its hearers. The conversion in this case is political but
the man who is 'born again to-night' might equally well have been
the subject of a religious awakening.

He ceased, and I thought the hearers
    would rise up with one cry,
And bid him straight enrol them;
    but they, they applauded indeed,
For the man was grown full eager,
    and had made them hearken and heed:
But they sat and made no sign,
    and two of the glibber kind
Stood up to jeer and to carp,
    his fiery words to blind.
I did not listen to them,
    but failed not his voice to hear
When he rose to answer the carpers,
    striving to make more clear
That which was clear already;
    not overwell, I knew,
He answered the sneers and the silence,
    so hot and eager he grew;
But my hope full well he answered,
    and when he called again
On men to band together
    lest they live and die in vain,
In fear lest he should escape me,
    I rose ere the meeting was done,
And gave him my name and my faith —
    and I was the only one.
He smiled as he heard the jeers,
    and there was a shake of the hand,
He spoke like a friend long known;
    and lo! I was one of the band.

And now the streets seem gay
    and the high stars glittering bright;
And for me, I sing amongst them,
    for my heart is full and light.
I see the deeds to be done
    and the day to come on the earth,
And riches vanished away
    and sorrow turned to mirth;
I see the city squalor
    and the country stupor gone.
And we a part of it all —
    we twain no longer alone

In the days to come of the pleasure,
    in the days that are of the fight —
I was born once long ago:
    I am born again to-night.

Algernon Charles Swinburne

DOLORES
(Notre-Dame des Sept Douleurs)

In *Poems and Ballads* (1866), Swinburne outraged some readers
and critics by his poeticising of sexual aberrations. To a modern
reader, 'Dolores' may appear as an ode to the goddess of sado-
masochism. Yet such a term was unknown in 1866 and, set in the
context of the time, the figure of Dolores is not so far removed from
the Pre-Raphaelite image of Lilith and her sisters.

Cold eyelids that hide like a jewel
    Hard eyes that grow soft for an hour;
The heavy white limbs, and the cruel
    Red mouth like a venomous flower;
When these are gone by with their glories,
    What shall rest of thee then, what remain,
O mystic and sombre Dolores,
    Our Lady of Pain?

Seven sorrows the priests give their Virgin;
    But thy sins, which are seventy times seven,
Seven ages would fail thee to purge in,
    And then they would haunt thee in heaven:
Fierce midnights and famishing morrows,
    And the loves that complete and control
All the joys of the flesh, all the sorrows
    That wear out the soul.

O garment not golden but gilded,
    O garden where all men may dwell,
O tower not of ivory, but builded
    By hands that reach heaven from hell;

O mystical rose of the mire,
  O house not of gold but of gain,
O house of unquenchable fire,
  Our Lady of Pain!

O lips full of lust and of laughter,
  Curled snakes that are fed from my breast,
Bite hard, lest remembrance come after
  And press with new lips where you pressed.
For my heart too springs up at the pressure,
  Mine eyelids too moisten and burn;
Ah, feed me and fill me with pleasure,
  Ere pain come in turn.

In yesterday's reach and to-morrow's,
  Out of sight though they lie of to-day,
There have been and there yet shall be sorrows
  That smite not and bite not in play.
The life and the love thou despisest,
  These hurt us indeed, and in vain,
O wise among women, and wisest,
  Our Lady of Pain.

Who gave thee thy wisdom? what stories
  That stung thee, what visions that smote?
Wert thou pure and a maiden, Dolores,
  When desire took thee first by the throat?
What bud was the shell of a blossom
  That all men may smell to and pluck?
What milk fed thee first at what bosom?
  What sins gave thee suck?

We shift and bedeck and bedrape us,
  Thou art noble and nude and antique;
Libitina thy mother, Priapus
  Thy father, a Tuscan and Greek.
We play with light loves in the portal,
  And wince and relent and refrain;
Loves die, and we know thee immortal,
  Our Lady of Pain.

Fruits fail and love dies and time ranges;
  Thou art fed with perpetual breath,
And alive after infinite changes,
  And fresh from the kisses of death;

Of languors rekindled and rallied,
  Of barren delights and unclean,
Things monstrous and fruitless, a pallid
  And poisonous queen.

Could you hurt me, sweet lips, though I hurt you?
  Men touch them, and change in a trice
The lilies and languors of virtue
  For the raptures and roses of vice;
Those lie where thy foot on the floor is,
  These crown and caress thee and chain,
O splendid and sterile Dolores,
  Our Lady of Pain.

There are sins it may be to discover,
  There are deeds it may be to delight.
What new work wilt thou find for thy lover,
  What new passions for daytime or night?
What spells that they know not a word of
  Whose lives are as leaves overblown?
What tortures undreamt of, unheard of,
  Unwritten, unknown?

Ah beautiful passionate body
  That never has ached with a heart!
On thy mouth though the kisses are bloody,
  Though they sting till it shudder and smart,
More kind than the love we adore is,
  They hurt not the heart or the brain,
O bitter and tender Dolores,
  Our Lady of Pain.

As our kisses relax and redouble,
  From the lips and the foam and the fangs
Shall no new sin be born for men's trouble,
  No dream of impossible pangs?
With the sweet of the sins of old ages
  Wilt thou satiate thy soul as of yore?
Too sweet is the rind, say the sages,
  Too bitter the core.

Hast thou told all thy secrets the last time,
  And bared all thy beauties to one?
Ah, where shall we go then for pastime,
  If the worst that can be has been done?

But sweet as the rind was the core is;
   We are fain of thee still, we are fain,
O sanguine and subtle Dolores,
   Our Lady of Pain.

By the hunger of change and emotion
   By the thirst of unbearable things,
By despair, the twin-born of devotion,
   By the pleasure that winces and stings,
The delight that consumes the desire,
   The desire that outruns the delight,
By the cruelty deaf as a fire
   And blind as the night,

By the ravenous teeth that have smitten
   Through the kisses that blossom and bud,
By the lips intertwisted and bitten
   Till the foam has a savour of blood,
By the pulse as it rises and falters,
   By the hands as they slacken and strain,
I adjure thee, respond from thine altars,
   Our Lady of Pain.

Wilt thou smile as a woman disdaining
   The light fire in the veins of a boy?
But he comes to thee sad, without feigning,
   Who has wearied of sorrow and joy;
Less careful of labour and glory
   Than the elders whose hair has uncurled;
And young, but with fancies as hoary
   And grey as the world.

I have passed from the outermost portal
   To the shrine where a sin is a prayer;
What care though the service be mortal?
   O our Lady of Torture, what care?
All thine the last wine that I pour is,
   The last in the chalice we drain,
O fierce and luxurious Dolores,
   Our Lady of Pain.

All thine the new wine of desire,
   The fruit of four lips as they clung
Till the hair and the eyelids took fire,
   The foam of a serpentine tongue,

The froth of the serpents of pleasure,
   More salt than the foam of the sea,
Now felt as a flame, now at leisure
   As wine shed for me.

Ah thy people, thy children, thy chosen,
   Marked cross from the womb and perverse!
They have found out the secret to cozen
   The gods that constrain us and curse;
They alone, they are wise, and none other;
   Give me place, even me, in their train,
O my sister, my spouse, and my mother,
   Our Lady of Pain.

For the crown of our life as it closes
   Is darkness, the fruit thereof dust;
No thorns go as deep as a rose's,
   And love is more cruel than lust.
Time turns the old days to derision,
   Our loves into corpses or wives;
And marriage and death and division
   Make barren our lives.

And pale from the past we draw nigh thee,
   And satiate with comfortless hours;
And we know thee, how all men belie thee,
   And we gather the fruit of thy flowers;
The passion that slays and recovers,
   The pangs and the kisses that rain
On the lips and the limbs of thy lovers,
   Our Lady of Pain.

The desire of thy furious embraces
   Is more than the wisdom of years,
On the blossom though blood lie in traces,
   Though the foliage be sodden with tears.
For the lords in whose keeping the door is
   That opens on all who draw breath
Gave the cypress to love, my Dolores,
   The myrtle to death.

And they laughed, changing hands in the measure,
   And they mixed and made peace after strife;
Pain melted in tears, and was pleasure;
   Death tingled with blood, and was life.

Like lovers they melted and tingled,
    In the dusk of thine innermost fane;
In the darkness they murmured and mingled,
    Our Lady of Pain.

In a twilight where virtues are vices,
    In thy chapels, unknown of the sun,
To a tune that enthralls and entices,
    They were wed, and the twain were as one.
For the tune from thine altar hath sounded
    Since God bade the world's work begin,
And the fume of thine incense abounded,
    To sweeten the sin.

Love listens, and paler than ashes,
    Through his curls as the crown on them slips,
Lifts languid wet eyelids and lashes,
    And laughs with insatiable lips.
Thou shalt hush him with heavy caresses,
    With music that scares the profane;
Thou shalt darken his eyes with thy tresses,
    Our Lady of Pain.

Thou shalt blind his bright eyes though he wrestle,
    Thou shalt chain his light limbs though he strive;
In his lips all thy serpents shall nestle,
    In his hands all thy cruelties thrive.
In the daytime thy voice shall go through him,
    In his dreams he shall feel thee and ache;
Thou shalt kindle by night and subdue him
    Asleep and awake.

Thou shalt touch and make redder his roses
    With juice not of fruit nor of bud;
When the sense in the spirit reposes,
    Thou shalt quicken the soul through the blood.
Thine, thine the one grace we implore is,
    Who would live and not languish or feign,
O sleepless and deadly Dolores,
    Our Lady of Pain.

Dost thou dream, in a respite of slumber,
    In a lull of the fires of thy life,
Of the days without name, without number,
    When thy will stung the world into strife;

When, a goddess, the pulse of thy passion
  Smote kings as they revelled in Rome;
And they hailed thee re-risen, O Thalassian,
  Foam-white, from the foam?

When thy lips had such lovers to flatter;
  When the city lay red from thy rods,
And thine hands were as arrows to scatter
  The children of change and their gods;
When the blood of thy foemen made fervent
  A sand never moist from the main,
As one smote them, their lord and thy servant,
  Our Lady of Pain.

On sands by the storm never shaken,
  Nor wet from the washing of tides;
Nor by foam of the waves overtaken,
  Nor winds that the thunder bestrides;
But red from the print of thy paces,
  Made smooth for the world and its lords,
Ringed round with a flame of fair faces,
  And splendid with swords.

There the gladiator, pale for thy pleasure,
  Drew bitter and perilous breath;
There torments laid hold on the treasure
  Of limbs too delicious for death;
When thy gardens were lit with live torches;
  When the world was a steed for thy rein;
When the nations lay prone in thy porches,
  Our Lady of Pain.

When, with flame all around him aspirant,
  Stood flushed, as a harp-player stands,
The implacable beautiful tryant,
  Rose-crowned, having death in his hands;
And a sound as the sound of loud water
  Smote far through the flight of the fires,
And mixed with the lightning of slaughter
  A thunder of lyres.

Dost thou dream of what was and no more is,
  The old kingdoms of earth and the kings?
Dost thou hunger for these things, Dolores,
  For these, in a world of new things?

But thy bosom no fasts could emaciate,
   No hunger compel to complain
Those lips that no bloodshed could satiate,
   Our Lady of Pain.

As of old when the world's heart was lighter,
   Through thy garments the grace of thee glows,
The white wealth of thy body made whiter
   By the blushes of amorous blows,
And seamed with sharp lips and fierce fingers,
   And branded by kisses that bruise;
When all shall be gone that now lingers,
   Ah, what shall we lose?

Thou wert fair in the fearless old fashion,
   And thy limbs are as melodies yet,
And move to the music of passion,
   With lithe and lascivious regret.
What ailed us, O gods, to desert you
   For creeds that refuse and restrain?
Come down and redeem us from virtue,
   Our Lady of Pain.

All shrines that were Vestal are flameless,
   But the flame has not fallen from this;
Though obscure be the god, and though nameless
   The eyes and the hair that we kiss;
Low fires that love sits by and forges
   Fresh heads for his arrows and thine;
Hair loosened and soiled in mid orgies
   With kisses and wine.

Thy skin changes country and colour,
   And shrivels or swells to a snake's.
Let it brighten and bloat and grow duller,
   We know it, the flames and the flakes,
Red brands on it smitten and bitten,
   Round skies where a star is a stain,
And the leaves with thy litanies written,
   Our Lady of Pain.

On thy bosom though many a kiss be,
   There are none such as knew it of old.
Was it Alciphron once or Arisbe,
   Male ringlets or feminine gold,

That thy lips met with under the statue,
　　Whence a look shot out sharp after thieves
From the eyes of the garden-god at you
　　Across the fig-leaves?

Then still, through dry seasons and moister,
　　One god had a wreath to his shrine;
Then love was the pearl of his oyster,
　　And Venus rose red out of wine,
We have all done amiss, choosing rather
　　Such loves as the wise gods disdain;
Intercede for us thou with thy father,
　　Our Lady of Pain.

In spring he had crowns of his garden,
　　Red corn in the heat of the year,
Then hoary green olives that harden
　　When the grape-blossom freezes with fear;
And milk-budded myrtles with Venus
　　And vine-leaves with Bacchus he trod;
And ye said, 'We have seen, he hath seen us,
　　A visible God.'

What broke off the garlands that girt you?
　　What sundered you spirit and clay?
Weak sins yet alive are as virtue
　　To the strength of the sins of that day.
For dried is the blood of thy lover,
　　Ipsithilla, contracted the vein;
Cry aloud, 'Will he rise and recover,
　　Our Lady of Pain?'

Cry aloud; for the old world is broken;
　　Cry out; for the Phrygian is priest,
And rears not the bountiful token
　　And spreads not the fatherly feast.
From the midmost of Ida, from shady
　　Recesses that murmur at morn,
They have brought and baptized her, Our Lady,
　　A goddess new-born.

And the chaplets of old are above us,
　　And the oyster-bed teems out of reach;
Old poets outsing and outlove us,
　　And Catullus makes mouths at our speech.

Who shall kiss, in thy father's own city,
  With such lips as he sang with, again?
Intercede for us all of thy pity,
  Our Lady of Pain.

Out of Dindymus heavily laden
  Her lions draw bound and unfed
A mother, a mortal, a maiden,
  A queen over death and the dead.
She is cold, and her habit is lowly,
  Her temple of branches and sods;
Most fruitful and virginal, holy,
  A mother of gods.

She hath wasted with fire thine high places,
  She hath hidden and marred and made sad
The fair limbs of the Loves, the fair faces
  Of gods that were goodly and glad.
She slays, and her hands are not bloody;
  She moves as a moon in the wane,
White-robed, and thy raiment is ruddy,
  Our Lady of Pain.

They shall pass and their places be taken,
  The gods and the priests that are pure,
They shall pass, and shalt thou not be shaken?
  They shall perish, and shalt thou endure?
Death laughs, breathing close and relentless
  In the nostrils and eyelids of lust,
With a pinch in his fingers of scentless
  And delicate dust.

But the worm shall revive thee with kisses;
  Thou shalt change and transmute as a god,
As the rod to a serpent that hisses,
  As the serpent again to a rod.
Thy life shall not cease though thou doff it;
  Thou shalt live until evil be slain,
And good shall die first, said thy prophet,
  Our Lady of Pain.

Did he lie? did he laugh? does he know it,
  Now he lies out of reach, out of breath,
Thy prophet, thy preacher, thy poet,
  Sin's child by incestuous Death?

Did he find out in fire at his waking,
  Or discern as his eyelids lost light,
When the bands of the body were breaking
  And all came in sight?

Who has known all the evil before us,
  Or the tyrannous secrets of time?
Though we match not the dead men that bore us
  At a song, at a kiss, at a crime —
Though the heathen outface and outlive us,
  And our lives and our longings are twain —
Ah, forgive us our virtues, forgive us,
  Our Lady of Pain.

Who are we that embalm and embrace thee
  With spices and savours of song?
What is time, that his children should face thee?
  What am I, that my lips do thee wrong?
I could hurt thee — but pain would delight thee;
  Or caress thee — but love would repel;
And the lovers whose lips would excite thee
  Are serpents in hell.

Who now shall content thee as they did,
  Thy lovers, when temples were built
And the hair of the sacrifice braided
  And the blood of the sacrifice spilt,
In Lampsacus fervent with faces,
  In Aphaca red from thy reign,
Who embraced thee with awful embraces,
  Our Lady of Pain?

Where are they, Cotytto or Venus,
  Astarte or Ashtaroth, where?
Do their hands as we touch come between us?
  Is the breath of them hot in thy hair?
From their lips have thy lips taken fever,
  With the blood of their bodies grown red?
Hast thou left upon earth a believer
  If these men are dead?

They were purple of raiment and golden,
  Filled full of thee, fiery with wine,
Thy lovers, in haunts unbeholden,
  In marvellous chambers of thine.

They are fled, and their footprints escape us,
    Who appraise thee, adore, and abstain,
O daughter of Death and Priapus,
    Our Lady of Pain.

What ails us to fear overmeasure,
    To praise thee with timorous breath,
O mistress and mother of pleasure,
    The one thing as certain as death?
We shall change as the things that we cherish,
    Shall fade as they faded before,
As foam upon water shall perish,
    As sand upon shore.

We shall know what the darkness discovers,
    If the grave-pit be shallow or deep;
And our fathers of old, and our lovers,
    We shall know if they sleep not or sleep.
We shall see whether hell be not heaven,
    Find out whether tares be not grain,
And the joys of thee seventy times seven,
    Our Lady of Pain.

RONDEL and LOVE AND SLEEP

In two short pieces from his early work, Swinburne lays claim to a
sensuous and even a sensual appreciation of female beauty that is a
reflection of the Pre-Raphaelite vision, not least in a preoccupation
with tresses of hair and the lily-imagery of beauty. The explicitness
of Swinburne's sexual suggestiveness is the principal distinction
between the two styles.

RONDEL
Kissing her hair I sat against her feet,
Wove and unwove it, wound and found it sweet;
Made fast therewith her hands, drew down her eyes,
Deep as deep flowers and dreamy like dim skies;
With her own tresses bound and found her fair,
    Kissing her hair.

Sleep were no sweeter than her face to me,
Sleep of cold sea-bloom under the cold sea;
What pain could get between my face and hers?
What new sweet thing would love not relish worse?
Unless, perhaps, white death had kissed me there,
    Kissing her hair?

LOVE AND SLEEP

Lying asleep between the strokes of night
  I saw my love lean over my sad bed,
  Pale as the duskiest lily's leaf or head,
Smooth-skinned and dark, with bare throat made to bite,
Too wan for blushing and too warm for white,
  But perfect-coloured without white or red.
  And her lips opened amorously, and said —
I wist not what, saving one word — Delight.
  And all her face was honey to my mouth,
And all her body pasture to mine eyes;
    The long lithe arms and hotter hands than fire,
The quivering flanks, hair smelling of the south,
  The bright light feet, the splendid supple thighs
    And glittering eyelids of my soul's desire.

MEN AND WOMEN

Elizabeth Barrett Browning
from SONNETS FROM THE PORTUGUESE

The story of Robert Browning's rescue of Elizabeth Barrett from death and domestic tyranny in 1846 is so well-known as to be something of a cliché. The dying patient escaped with her lover to a new life of married happiness in Florence. She lived for another fifteen years and, though her health was not always good, she was to write her best poetry and give birth to her son. On 22 June 1846, she had written to Robert Browning from her sick room in Wimpole Street, 'You shall see some day at Pisa what I will not show you now. Does not Solomon say that "there is a time to read what is written"? If he doesn't, he *ought*.'

Browning first saw the sonnets in 1849 at Bagna di Lucca, where he and Elizabeth had gone to escape the summer heat of Florence. One morning, after they had been discussing the propriety of expressing personal love in poetry that might be publicly read, Elizabeth said, 'Do you know I once wrote some poems about *you*?... There they are, if you care to see them.' Writing of the incident fifteen years later, after Elizabeth's death in 1861, Browning found it so clear in his mind that he could recall her precise tone and gesture, even the mimosa beyond the window at which he was standing.

The sequence of forty-four sonnets had been written during their courtship, the last dated two days before their marriage. In poetic terms they give the lie to that other cliché of the Victorian age as one of sexual and marital oppression and misery. Publication of the sonnets presented a difficulty, however. To read them a century later is still to feel something of an intruder. Yet it was unthinkable that the noblest sonnets since Shakespeare in their expression of physical and spiritual love between man and woman should remain unpublished. It was decided to publish them as though they had been written in the sixteenth century to the Portuguese poet Luis de Camoens by his mistress Catarina. They appeared as 'Sonnets from the Portuguese' in Elizabeth's *Poems* of 1850.

i

I thought once how Theocritus had sung
Of the sweet years, the dear and wished-for years,
Who each one in a gracious hand appears
To bear a gift for mortals, old or young:
And, as I mused it in his antique tongue,
I saw, in gradual vision through my tears,
The sweet, sad years, the melancholy years,
Those of my own life, who by turns had flung
A shadow across me. Straightway I was 'ware,
So weeping, how a mystic Shape did move
Behind me, and drew me backward by the hair,
And a voice said in mastery while I strove, . . .
'Guess now who holds thee?' — 'Death', I said. But, there,
The silver answer rang . . . 'Not Death, but Love'.

ii

But only three in all God's universe
Have heard this word thou hast said, Himself, beside
Thee speaking, and me listening! and replied
One of us . . . *that* was God, . . . and laid the curse
So darkly on my eyelids, as to amerce
My sight from seeing thee, — that if I had died,
The deathweights, placed there, would have signified
Less absolute exclusion. 'Nay' is worse
From God than from all others, O my friend!
Men could not part us with their worldly jars,
Nor the seas change us, nor the tempests bend;
Our hands would touch for all the mountain-bars, —
And, heaven being rolled between us at the end,
We should but vow the faster for the stars.

iii

Unlike are we, unlike, O princely Heart!
Unlike our uses and our destinies.
Our ministering two angels look surprise
On one another, as they strike athwart
Their wings in passing. Thou, bethink thee, art
A guest for queens to social pageantries,
With gages from a hundred brighter eyes
Than tears even can make mine, to ply thy part

Of chief musician. What has *thou* to do
With looking from the lattice-lights at me,
A poor, tired, wandering singer, . . . singing through
The dark, and leaning up a cypress-tree?
The chrism is on thine head, — on mine, the dew, —
And Death must dig the level where these agree.

iv
Thou hast thy calling to some palace-floor,
Most gracious singer of high poems! where
The dancers will break footing, from the care
Of watching up thy pregnant lips for more.
And dost thou lift this house's latch too poor
For hand of thine? and canst thou think and bear
To let thy music drop here unaware
In folds of golden fulness at my door?
Look up and see the casement broken in,
The bats and owlets builders in the roof!
My cricket chirps against thy mandolin.
Hush, call no echo up in further proof
Of desolation! there's a voice within
That weeps . . . as thou must sing . . . alone, aloof.

v
I lift my heavy heart up solemnly,
As once Electra her sepulchral urn,
And, looking in thine eyes, I overturn
The ashes at thy feet. Behold and see
What a great heap of grief lay hid in me,
And how the red wild sparkles dimly burn
Through the ashen greyness. If thy foot in scorn
Could tread them out to darkness utterly,
It might be well perhaps. But if instead
Thou wait beside me for the wind to blow
The grey dust up, . . . those laurels on thine head,
O my Belovèd, will not shield thee so,
That none of all the fires shall scorch and shred
The hair beneath. Stand farther off then! go.

vi

Go from me. Yet I feel that I shall stand
Henceforward in thy shadow. Nevermore
Alone upon the threshold of my door
Of individual life, I shall command
The uses of my soul, nor lift my hand
Serenely in the sunshine as before,
Without the sense of that which I forbore, . . .
Thy touch upon the palm. The widest land
Doom takes to part us, leaves thy heart in mine
With pulses that beat double. What I do
And what I dream include thee, as the wine
Must taste of its own grapes. And when I sue
God for myself, He hears that name of thine,
And sees within my eyes, the tears of two.

vii

The face of all the world is changed, I think,
Since first I heard the footsteps of thy soul
Move still, oh, still, beside me, as they stole
Betwixt me and the dreadful outer brink
Of obvious death, where I, who thought to sink,
Was caught up into love, and taught the whole
Of life in a new rhythm. The cup of dole
God gave for baptism, I am fain to drink,
And praise its sweetness, Sweet, with thee anear.
The names of country, heaven, are changed away
For where thou art or shalt be, there or here;
And this . . . this lute and song . . . loved yesterday,
(The singing angels know) are only dear,
Because thy name moves right in what they say.

viii

What can I give thee back, O liberal
And princely giver, who hast brought the gold
And purple of thine heart, unstained, untold,
And laid them on the outside of the wall
For such as I to take or leave withal,
In unexpected largesse? am I cold,
Ungrateful, that for these most manifold
High gifts, I render nothing back at all?

Not so; not cold, — but very poor instead.
Ask God who knows. For frequent tears have run
The colours from my life, and left so dead
And pale a stuff, it were not fitly done
To give the same as pillow to thy head.
Go farther! let it serve to trample on.

xxii
When our two souls stand up erect and strong,
Face to face, silent, drawing nigh and nigher,
Until the lengthening wings break into fire
At either curvèd point, — what bitter wrong
Can the earth do to us, that we should not long
Be here contented? Think. In mounting higher,
The angels would press on us, and aspire
To drop some golden orb of perfect song
Into our deep, dear silence. Let us stay
Rather on earth, Belovèd, — where the unfit
Contrarious moods of men recoil away
And isolate pure spirits, and permit
A place to stand and love in for a day,
With darkness and the death-hour rounding it.

xxvi
I lived with visions for my company,
Instead of men and women, years ago,
And found them gentle mates, nor thought to know
A sweeter music than they played to me.
But soon their trailing purple was not free
Of this world's dust, — their lutes did silent grow,
And I myself grew faint and blind below
Their vanishing eyes. Then THOU didst come . . . to be,
Belovèd, what they seemed. Their shining fronts,
Their songs, their splendours, (better, yet the same,
As river-water hallowed into fonts)
Met in thee, and from out thee overcame
My soul with satisfaction of all wants —
Because God's gifts put man's best dreams to shame.

xxvii

My own Belovèd, who has lifted me
From this drear flat of earth where I was thrown,
And, in betwixt the languid ringlets, blown
A life-breath, till the forehead hopefully
Shines out again, as all the angels see,
Before thy saving kiss! My own, my own,
Who camest to me when the world was gone,
And I who looked for only God, found *thee*!
I find thee; I am safe, and strong, and glad.
As one who stands in dewless asphodel,
Looks backward on the tedious time he had
In the upper life, — so I, with bosom-swell,
Make witness, here, between the good and bad,
That Love, as strong as Death, retrieves as well.

xxviii

My letters! all dead paper, . . . mute and white! —
And yet they seem alive and quivering
Against my tremulous hands which loose the string
And let them drop down on my knee tonight.
This said, . . . he wished to have me in his sight
Once, as a friend: this fixed a day in spring
To come and touch my hand . . . a simple thing,
Yet I wept for it! — this, . . . the paper's light . . .
Said, *Dear, I love thee*; and I sank and quailed
As if God's future thundered on my past.
This said, *I am thine* — and so its ink has paled
With lying at my heart that beat too fast.
And this . . . O Love, thy words have ill availed,
If, what this said, I dared repeat at last!

xxx

I see thine image through my tears tonight,
And yet to-day I saw thee smiling. How
Refer the cause? — Belovèd, is it thou
Or I? who makes me sad? The acolyte
Amid the chanted joy and thankful rite,
May so fall flat, with pale insensate brow,
On the altar-stair. I hear thy voice and vow
Perplexed, uncertain, since thou art out of sight,

As he, in his swooning ears, the choir's Amen.
Belovèd, dost thou love? or did I see all
The glory as I dreamed, and fainted when
Too vehement light dilated my ideal,
For my soul's eyes? Will that light come again,
As now these tears come . . . falling hot and real?

XXXV

If I leave all for thee, wilt thou exchange
And be all to me? Shall I never miss
Home-talk and blessing and the common kiss
That comes to each in turn, nor count it strange,
When I look up, to drop on a new range
Of walls and floors . . . another home than this?
Nay, wilt thou fill that place by me which is
Filled by dead eyes too tender to know change?
That's hardest. If to conquer love, has tried,
To conquer grief, tries more . . . as all things prove;
For grief indeed is love and grief beside.
Alas, I have grieved so I am hard to love.
Yet love me — wilt thou? Open thine heart wide,
And fold within, the wet wings of thy dove.

XXXVI

When we met first and loved, I did not build
Upon the event with marble. Could it mean
To last, a love set pendulous between
Sorrow and sorrow? Nay, I rather thrilled,
Distrusting every light that seemed to gild
The onward path, and feared to overlean
A finger even. And, though I have grown serene
And strong since then, I think that God has willed
A still renewable fear . . . O love, O troth . . .
Lest these enclaspèd hands should never hold,
This mutual kiss drop down between us both
As an unowned thing, once the lips being cold.
And Love, be false! if *he*, to keep one oath,
Must lose one joy, by his life's star foretold.

xxxvii

Pardon, oh, pardon, that my soul should make
Of all that strong divineness which I know
For thine and thee, an image only so
Formed of the sand, and fit to shift and break.
It is that distant years which did not take
Thy sovranty, recoiling with a blow,
Have forced my swimming brain to undergo
Their doubt and dread, and blindly to forsake
Thy purity of likeness, and distort
Thy worthiest love to a worthless counterfeit.
As if a shipwrecked Pagan, safe in port,
His guardian sea-god to commemorate,
Should set a sculptured porpoise, gills a-snort,
And vibrant tail, within the temple-gate.

xxxviii

First time he kissed me, he but only kissed
The fingers of this hand wherewith I write;
And, ever since, it grew more clean and white, . . .
Slow to world-greetings . . . quick with its 'Oh, list',
When the angels speak. A ring of amethyst
I could not wear here, plainer to my sight,
Than that first kiss. The second passed in height
The first, and sought the forehead, and half missed,
Half falling on the hair. O beyond meed!
That was the chrism of love, which love's own crown,
With sanctifying sweetness, did precede.
The third upon my lips was folded down
In perfect, purple state; since when, indeed,
I have been proud and said, 'My love, my own'.

xxxix

Because thou hast the power and own'st the grace
To look through and behind this mask of me,
(Against which years have beat thus blanchingly
With their rains,) and behold my soul's true face,
The dim and weary witness of life's race! —
Because thou hast the faith and love to see,
Through that same soul's distracting lethargy,
The patient angel waiting for a place

In the new Heavens! — because nor sin nor woe,
Nor God's infliction, nor death's neighbourhood,
Nor all which others viewing, turn to go, . . .
Nor all which makes me tired of all, self-viewed, . . .
Nothing repels thee, . . . Dearest, teach me so
To pour out gratitude, as thou dost, good.

xl
Oh, yes! they love through all this world of ours!
I will not gainsay love, called love forsooth.
I have heard love talked in my early youth,
And since, not so long back but that the flowers
Then gathered, smell still. Mussulmans and Giaours
Throw kerchiefs at a smile, and have no ruth
For any weeping. Polypheme's white tooth
Slips on the nut, if, after frequent showers,
The shell is over-smooth, — and not so much
Will turn the thing called love, aside to hate,
Or else to oblivion. But thou art not such
A lover, my Belovèd! thou canst wait
Through sorrow and sickness, to bring souls to touch,
And think it soon when others cry 'Too late'.

xli
I thank all who have loved me in their hearts,
With thanks and love from mine. Deep thanks to all
Who paused a little near the prison-wall,
To hear my music in its louder parts,
Ere they went onward, each one to the mart's
Or temple's occupation, beyond call.
But thou, who, in my voice's sink and fall,
When the sob took it, thy divinest Art's
Own instrument didst drop down at thy foot,
To harken what I said between my tears, . . .
Instruct me how to thank thee! — Oh, to shoot
My soul's full meaning into future years,
That *they* should lend it utterance, and salute
Love that endures, from Life that disappears!

xlii

'*My future will not copy fair my past*' —
I wrote that once; and thinking at my side
My ministering life-angel justified
The word by his appealing look upcast
To the white throne of God, I turned at last,
And there, instead, saw thee, not unallied
To angels in thy soul! Then I, long tried
By natural ills, received the comfort fast,
While budding, at thy sight, my pilgrim's staff
Gave out green leaves with morning dews impearled.
I seek no copy now of life's first half:
Leave here the pages with long musing curled,
And write me new my future's epigraph,
New angel mine, unhoped for in the world!

xliii

How do I love thee? Let me count the ways.
I love thee to the depth and breadth and height
My soul can reach, when feeling out of sight
For the ends of Being and ideal Grace.
I love thee to the level of everyday's
Most quiet need, by sun and candle-light.
I love thee freely, as men strive for Right;
I love thee purely, as they turn from Praise.
I love thee with the passion put to use
In my old griefs, and with my childhood's faith.
I love thee with a love I seemed to lose
With my lost saints, — I love thee with the breath,
Smiles, tears, of all my life! — and, if God choose,
I shall but love thee better after death.

xliv

Belovèd, thou hast brought me many flowers
Plucked in the garden, all the summer through
And winter, and it seemed as if they grew
In this close room, nor missed the sun and showers.
So, in the like name of that love of ours,
Take back these thoughts which here unfolded too,
And which on warm and cold days I withdrew
From my heart's ground. Indeed, those beds and bowers

Be overgrown with bitter weeds and rue,
And wait thy weeding; yet here's eglantine,
Here's ivy! — take them, as I used to do
Thy flowers, and keep them where they shall not pine.
Instruct thine eyes to keep their colours true,
And tell thy soul, their roots are left in mine.

Coventry Patmore
HUSBAND AND WIFE

Coventry Patmore (1823–96) was a friend of the Pre-Raphaelites and a contributor to *The Germ* in 1850. He remains best known for his sequence *The Angel in the House* (1854–62), a celebration of courtship and marriage as Patmore had experienced them. More conventional than Elizabeth Barrett Browning, Patmore surveys marriage with something of the eye of a Metaphysical poet for objects and everyday paradoxes. 'Husband and Wife' describes the newly-weds on their seaside honeymoon, meeting a cousin whose Royal Navy ship is anchored off-shore.

Patmore has a quick eye for social observation and the nuances of behaviour. Sometimes attacked for his portrayal of conventional relationships as bringing happiness, he was nonetheless praised in 1886 by a fellow Catholic poet, Gerard Manley Hopkins. 'Your poems are a good deed done for the Catholic Church and another for England, the British Empire, which now trembles in the balance held in the hand of unwisdom.' Patmore was converted to Catholicism in 1864.

I

I, while the shop-girl fitted on
  The sand-shoes, look'd where, down the bay,
The sea glow'd with a shrouded sun.
  'I'm ready, Felix; will you pay?'
That was my first expense for this
  Sweet Stranger, now my three days' Wife.
How light the touches are that kiss
  The music from the chords of life!

2

Her feet, by half-a-mile of sea,
  In spotless sand left shapely prints;
With agates, then, she loaded me;
  (The lapidary call'd them flints);
Then, at her wish, I hail'd a boat,
  To take her to the ships-of-war,
At anchor, each a lazy mote
  Black in the brilliance, miles from shore.

3

The morning breeze the canvas fill'd,
  Lifting us o'er the bright-ridged gulf,
And every lurch my darling thrill'd
  With light fear smiling at itself;
And, dashing past the Arrogant,
  Asleep upon the restless wave,
After its cruise in the Levant,
  We reach'd the Wolf, and signal gave
For help to board: with caution meet,
  My bride was placed within the chair,
The red flag wrapp'd about her feet,
  And so swung laughing through the air.

4

'Look, Love,' she said, 'there's Frederick Graham,
  'My cousin, whom you met, you know.'
And seeing us, the brave man came,
  And made his frank and courteous bow,
And gave my hand a sailor's shake,
  And said, 'You ask'd me to the Hurst:
'I never thought my luck would make
  'Your wife and you my guests the first.'
And Honor, cruel, 'Nor did we:
  'Have you not lately changed your ship?'
'Yes: I'm Commander, now,' said he,
  With a slight quiver of the lip.
We saw the vessel, shown with pride;
  Took luncheon; I must eat his salt!
Parting he said, (I fear my bride
  Found him unselfish to a fault),
His wish, he saw, had come to pass,
  (And so, indeed, her face express'd),
That that should be, whatever 'twas,

Which made his Cousin happiest.
We left him looking from above;
  Rich bankrupt! for he could afford
To say most proudly that his love
  Was virtue and its own reward.
But others loved as well as he,
  (Thought I, half-anger'd), and if fate,
Unfair, had only fashion'd me
  As hapless, I had been as great.

5

As souls, ambitious, but low-born,
  If raised past hope by luck or wit,
All pride of place will proudly scorn,
  And live as they'd been used to it,
So we two wore our strange estate:
  Familiar, unaffected, free,
We talk'd, until the dusk grew late,
  Of this and that; but, after tea,
As doubtful if a lot so sweet
  As ours was ours in very sooth,
Like children, to promote conceit,
  We feign'd that it was not the truth;
And she assumed the maiden coy,
  And I adored remorseless charms,
And then we clapp'd our hands for joy,
  And ran into each other's arms.

George Meredith
from MODERN LOVE

George Meredith (1828–1909) was a friend and companion of the Pre-Raphaelites, sharing Tudor House, Cheyne Walk with the Rossettis, Swinburne and Morris. He had married the widowed daughter of Thomas Love Peacock. She deserted Meredith and their son in 1858. Meredith's caustic response may be seen in the studied misogyny of his semi-autobiographical novel *The Ordeal of Richard Feverel* (1859) — 'Kissing don't last: cookery do!' or 'I expect that Woman will be the last thing civilized by Man'. However, Mary Ellen Meredith died in 1861 and the high spirits of fiction became a sombre study of love's decay in his long poem *Modern Love*, a linked sequence of fifty poems of sixteen lines each, describing the disintegration of love between husband and wife, followed by the woman's death from poison. Though it lacks the self-conscious plot of a contemporary novel and is more advanced in its analysis of mood and character than most Victorian fiction, it shares with poems like Tennyson's *Maud* qualities of a mid-century novel-in-verse. This selection is taken from the opening of the sequence.

i

By this he knew she wept with waking eyes:
That, at his hand's light quiver by her head,
The strange low sobs that shook their common bed,
Were called into her with a sharp surprise,
And strangled mute, like little gaping snakes,
Dreadfully venomous to him. She lay
Stone-still, and the long darkness flowed away
With muffled pulses. Then, as midnight makes
Her giant heart of Memory and Tears
Drink the pale drug of silence, and so beat
Sleep's heavy measure, they from head to feet
Were moveless, looking through their dead black years,
By vain regret scrawled over the blank wall.
Like sculptured effigies they might be seen
Upon their marriage-tomb, the sword between;
Each wishing for the sword that severs all.

ii

It ended, and the morrow brought the task.
Her eyes were guilty gates, that let him in
By shutting all too zealous for their sin:
Each sucked a secret, and each wore a mask.
But, oh, the bitter taste her beauty had!
He sickened as at breath of poison-flowers:
A languid humour stole among the hours,
And if their smiles encountered, he went mad,
And raged deep inward, till the light was brown
Before his vision, and the world forgot,
Looked wicked as some old dull murder-spot.
A star with lurid beams, she seemed to crown
The pit of infamy: and then again
He fainted on his vengefulness, and strove
To ape the magnanimity of love,
And smote himself, a shuddering heap of pain.

iii

This was the woman; what now of the man?
But pass him. If he comes beneath a heel,
He shall be crushed until he cannot feel,
Or, being callous, haply till he can.
But he is nothing: — nothing? Only mark
The rich light striking out from her on him!
Ha! what a sense it is when her eyes swim
Across the man she singles, leaving dark
All else! Lord God, who mad'st the thing so fair,
See that I am drawn to her even now!
It cannot be such harm on her cool brow
To put a kiss? Yet if I meet him there!
But she is mine! Ah, no! I know too well
I claim a star whose light is overcast:
I claim a phantom-woman in the Past.
The hour has struck, though I heard not the bell!

iv

All other joy of life he strove to warm,
And magnify, and catch them to his lip:
But they had suffered shipwreck with the ship,
And gazed upon him sallow from the storm.
Or if Delusion came, 't was but to show
The coming minute mock the one that went.
Cold as a mountain in its star-pitched tent,
Stood high Philosophy, less friend than foe:
Whom self-caged Passion, from its prison-bars,
Is always watching with a wondering hate.
Not till the fire is dying in the grate,
Look we for any kinship with the stars.
Oh, wisdom never comes when it is gold,
And the great price we pay for it full worth:
We have it only when we are half earth.
Little avails that coinage to the old!

v

A message from her set his brain aflame.
A world of household matters filled her mind,
Wherein he saw hypocrisy designed:
She treated him as something that is tame,
And but at other provocation bites.

Familiar was her shoulder in the glass,
Through that dark rain: yet it may come to pass
That a changed eye finds such familiar sights
More keenly tempting than new loveliness.
The 'What has been' a moment seemed his own:
The splendours, mysteries, dearer because known,
Nor less divine: Love's inmost sacredness,
Called to him, 'Come!' — In his restraining start,
Eyes nurtured to be looked at, scarce could see
A wave of the great waves of Destiny
Convulsed at a checked impulse of the heart.

vi

It chanced his lips did meet her forehead cool.
She had no blush, but slanted down her eye.
Shamed nature, then, confesses love can die:
And most she punishes the tender fool
Who will believe what honours her the most!
Dead! is it dead? She has a pulse, and flow
Of tears, the price of blood-drops, as I know,
For whom the midnight sobs around Love's ghost,
Since then I heard her, and so will sob on.
The love is here; it has but changed its aim.
O bitter barren woman! what's the name?
The name, the name, the new name thou hast won?
Behold me striking the world's coward stroke!
That will I not do, though the sting is dire.
— Beneath the surface this, while by the fire
They sat, she laughing at a quiet joke.

vii

She issues radiant from her dressing-room,
Like one prepared to scale an upper sphere:
— By stirring up a lower, much I fear!
How deftly that oiled barber lays his bloom!
That long-shanked dapper Cupid with frisked curls,
Can make known women torturingly fair;
The gold-eyed serpent dwelling in rich hair,
Awakes beneath his magic whisks and twirls.
His art can take the eyes from out my head,
Until I see with eyes of other men;
While deeper knowledge crouches in its den,

And sends a spark up: — is it true we are wed?
Yea! filthiness of body is most vile,
But faithlessness of heart I do hold worse.
The former, it were not so great a curse
To read on the steel-mirror of her smile.

viii

Yet it was plain she struggled, and that salt
Of righteous feeling made her pitiful.
Poor twisting worm, so queenly beautiful!
Where came the cleft between us? whose the fault?
My tears are on thee, that have rarely dropped
As balm for any bitter wound of mine:
My breast will open for thee at a sign!
But, no: we are two reed-pipes, coarsely stopped:
The God once filled them with his mellow breath;
And they were music till he flung them down,
Used! used! Hear now the discord-loving clown
Puff his gross spirit in them, worse than death!
I do not know myself without thee more:
In this unholy battle I grow base:
If the same soul be under the same face,
Speak, and a taste of that old time restore!

ix

He felt the wild beast in him betweenwhiles
So masterfully rude, that he would grieve
To see the helpless delicate thing receive
His guardianship through certain dark defiles.
Had he not teeth to rend, and hunger too?
But still he spared her. Once: 'Have you no fear?'
He said: 't was dusk; she in his grasp; none near.
She laughed: 'No, surely; am I not with you?'
And uttering that soft starry 'you,' she leaned
Her gentle body near him, looking up;
And from her eyes, as from a poison-cup,
He drank until the flittering eyelids screened.
Devilish malignant witch! and oh, young beam
Of heaven's circle-glory! Here thy shape
To squeeze like an intoxicating grape —
I might, and yet thou goest safe, supreme.

William Barnes
THE BWOAT

Far removed from the sustained intellectualism of *Modern Love*,
the bulk of Victorian poetry on human themes dealt with the life of
the age more simply and briefly. William Barnes (1801–86) was a
Dorset dialect poet and in some respects Thomas Hardy's prede-
cessor. The son of a farmer in the Blackmoor Vale, he became an
undergraduate at St John's College, Cambrdge, in middle age and
took Holy Orders. He published three series of *Poems of Rural Life*
between 1844 and 1863.

Where cows did slowly seek the brink
O' *Stour*, drough sunburnt grass, to drink;
Wi' vishèn float, that there did sink
    An' rise, I zot as in a dream.
The dazzlèn zun did cast his light
On hedge-row blossom, snowy white,
Though nothèn yet did come in zight,
    A-stirrèn on the straÿèn stream;

Till, out by sheädy rocks there show'd,
A bwoat along his foamy road,
Wi' thik feäïr maid at mill, a row'd
    Wi' Jeäne behind her brother's oars.
An' steätely as a queen o' vo'k,
She zot wi' floàten scarlet cloak,
An' comen on, at ev'ry stroke,
    Between my withy-sheäded shores.

The broken stream did idly try
To show her sheäpe a-ridèn by,
The rushes brown-bloom'd stems did ply,
    As if they bow'd to her by will.
The rings o' water, wi' a sock,
Did break upon the mossy rock,
An' gi'e my beätèn heart a shock,
    Above my float's up-leapèn quill.

Then, lik' a cloud below the skies,
A-drifted off, wi' less'nèn size,
An' lost, she floated vrom my eyes,
    Where down below the stream did wind;

An' left the quiet weäves oonce mwore
To zink to rest, a sky-blue' vloor,
Wi' all so still's the clote they bore,
    Aye, all but my own ruffled mind.

Lord Lytton
THE CHESS BOARD

Edward Robert Bulwer-Lytton, 1st Earl of Lytton (1831–91), was
the son of the famous historical novelist, Edward Bulwer-Lytton,
author of *The Last Days of Pompeii* (1834) and of the successful
play *Money* (1840). The Earl of Lytton began his career as a poet
under the pseudonym 'Owen Meredith'. After serving in the diplo-
matic service, he became Viceroy of India in 1876. 'The Chess
Board' is an exercise in wistful intimacy.

Irene, do you yet remember
Ere we were grown so sadly wise,
Those evenings in the bleak December,
Curtain'd warm from the snowy weather,
When you and I play'd chess together,
    Checkmated by each other's eyes?
    Ah, still I see your soft white hand
Hovering warm o'er Queen and Knight,
    Brave Pawns in valiant battle stand:
The double Castles guard the wings:
The Bishop, bent on distant things,
Moves, sidling, through the fight,
    Our fingers touch; our glances meet,
    And falter; falls your golden hair
    Against my cheek; your bosom sweet
Is heaving. Down the field, your Queen
Rides slow her soldiery all between,
    And checks me unaware.
    Ah me! the little battle's done,
Disperst is all its chivalry;
Full many a move, since then, have we
'Mid Life's perplexing chequers made,
And many a game with Fortune play'd, —
    What is it we have won?
    This, this at least — if this alone; —
That never, never, never more,

As in those old still nights of yore,
  (Ere we were grown so sadly wise)
  Can you and I shut out the skies,
Shut out the world, and wintry weather,
And, eyes exchanging warmth with eyes,
  Play chess, as then we play'd together!

William Makepeace Thackeray
WERTHER

Despite the intensity and solemnity of much Victorian poetry on the theme of sexual love, there was a good deal which treated such matters flippantly or, at least, with a veneer of social comedy. The great romantic statements of love at the turn of the century fell victim to parody or mockery. William Makepeace Thackeray (1811–63) here administers the *coup de grâce* to Goethe's *Sorrows of Young Werther* (1774), in which the lovesick hero kills himself after his sweetheart Charlotte marries Albert. In Thackeray's version, the beautiful heroine of romance becomes, with ludicrous bourgeois propriety, the 'well-conducted person' of mid-Victorian domestic morals.

Werther had a love for Charlotte
  Such as words could never utter;
Would you know how first he met her?
  She was cutting bread and butter.

Charlotte was a married lady,
  And a moral man was Werther,
And, for all the wealth of Indies,
  Would do nothing for to hurt her.

So he sighed and pined and ogled,
  And his passion boiled and bubbled,
Till he blew his silly brains out,
  And no more was by it troubled.

Charlotte, having seen his body
  Borne before her on a shutter,
Like a well-conducted person,
  Went on cutting bread and butter.

Frederick Locker
OUR PHOTOGRAPHS

Victorian *vers de société* derived much of its style and tone from poets of the Romantic Revival such as Winthrop Mackworth Praed and, indeed, from Byron. The relationships of men and women in society, as opposed to private life, offered a good deal of material to poets like Frederick Locker (1821–95), who became Frederick Locker-Lampson in 1885. He remains best known for his volume *London Lyrics* (1857) and for his anthology of light verse *Lyra Elegantarium* (1867). Metropolitan sophistication and the tone of smart society anticipate something of the 1890s and Oscar Wilde's comedy. 'Our Photographs' is an up-to-date lament by a jilted lover whose Di has chosen a staff officer instead of him.

She play'd me false, but that's not why
I haven't quite forgiven Di,
    Although I've tried:
This curl was hers, so brown, so bright,
She gave it me one blissful night,
    And — more beside!

In *photo* we were group'd together;
She wore the darling hat and feather
    That I adore;
In profile by her side I sat
Reading my poetry — but that
    She'd heard before.

Why, after all, Di threw me over
I never knew, and can't discover,
    Or even guess;
May be Smith's lyrics she decided
Were sweeter than the sweetest I did —
    I acquiesce.

A week before their wedding day,
When Smith was call'd in haste away
    To join *the Staff*,
Di gave to him, with tearful mien,
Our *only photograph*. I've seen
    That photograph,

I've seen it in Smith's album-book!
Just think! her hat — her tender look,
   Are now that brute's!
Before she gave it, off she cut
My body, head, and lyrics, but
She was obliged, the little slut,
   To leave my Boots.

AT HURLINGHAM

In Frederick Locker's second poem the right degree of devotion
rather than jilting is the theme. After a curious epigraph, the setting
is the exclusive Hurlingham Club near London, where Willy's team
is competing with the House of Commons in a pigeon-shoot. The
tone of the girl as narrator has more in common with Lorelei from
Little Rock in Anita Loos' *Gentlemen Prefer Blondes* than with
Sonnets from the Portuguese. However, it reminds us that a
successful career as a social butterfly requires intelligence, hard
work, constant dedication, and an undeviating eye for the main
chance.

I recollect a nurse call'd Ann,
   Who carried me about the grass,
And one fine day a fine young man
   Came up, and kiss'd the pretty Lass:
She did not make the least objection!
      Thinks I, 'Aha!
When I can talk I'll tell Mamma.'
— And that's my earliest recollection.
A TERRIBLE INFANT

This was dear Willy's brief despatch,
   A curt and yet a cordial summons; —
'Do come! I'm in to-morrow's match,
   And see us whip the *Faithful Commons*.'
We trundled out behind the bays,
   Through miles and miles of brick and garden;
Mamma was drest in mauve and maize, —
   She let me wear my *Dolly Varden*.

A charming scene, and lively too;
   The paddock's full, the band is playing

Boulotte's song in *Barbe bleue*;
  And what are all these people saying?
They flirt! they bet! There's Linda Reeves
  Too lovely! I'd give worlds to borrow
Her yellow rose with russet leaves! —
  I'll wear a yellow rose to-morrow!

And there are May and Algy Meade;
  How proud she looks on her promotion!
The ring must be amused indeed,
  And edified by such devotion!
I wonder if she ever guessed! —
  I wonder if he'll call on Friday! —
I often wonder which is best! —
  I only hope my hair is tidy!

Some girls repine, and some rejoice,
  And some get bored, but I'm contented
To make my destiny my choice,
  I'll never dream that I've repented.
There's something sad in *loved and cross'd*,
  For all the fond, fond hope that rings it:
There's something sweet in 'Loved and Lost';
  And Oh, how sweetly Alfred sings it!

I'll own I'm bored with *handicaps!*
  Bluerocks! (they always are '*bluerock*'-ing!) —
With May, a little bit, perhaps, —
  And yon Faust's *teufelshund* is shocking!
Bang . . . bang . . .! That's Willy! There's his bird,
  Blithely it cleaves the skies above me!
He's miss'd all ten! He's too absurd! —
  I hope he'll always, always love me!

We've lost! To tea, then back to town;
  The crowd is laughing, eating, drinking:
The Moon's eternal eyes look down, —
  Of what can yon pale Moon be thinking?
Oh, but for some good fairy's wand!
  This *Pigeoncide* is worse than silly,
But still I'm very, very fond
  Of Hurlingham, and tea, — and Willy.

Charles Stuart Calverley

A, B, C.

Charles Stuart Calverley (1831–84) had that quality of sheer cleverness which seems even more suspect in the twentieth century than in the nineteenth. An accomplished parodist and author of light verse, he was a natural wit and a scholar. In the present poem he makes a wry assessment of the social scene.

A   is an Angel of blushing eighteen:
B   is the Ball where the Angel was seen:
C   is her Chaperone, who cheated at cards:
D   is the Deuxtemps, with Frank of the Guards:
E   is the Eye which those dark lashes cover:
F   is the Fan it peeped wickedly over:
G   is the Glove of superlative kid:
H   is the Hand which it spitefully hid:
I   is the Ice which spent nature demanded:
J   is the Juvenile who hurried to hand it:
K   is the Kerchief, a rare work of art:
L   is the Lace which composed the chief part.
M   's the old Maid who watch'd the girls dance:
N   is the Nose she turned up at each glance:
O   is the Olga (just then in its prime):
P   is the Partner who wouldn't keep time:
Q   's a Quadrille, put instead of the Lancers:
R   the Remonstrances made by the dancers:
S   is the Supper, where all went in pairs:
T   is the Twaddle they talked on the stairs:
U   is the Uncle who 'thought we'd be going':
V   is the Voice which his niece replied 'No' in:
W   is the Waiter, who sat up till eight:
X   is his Exit, not rigidly straight:
Y   is a Yawning fit caused by the Ball:
Z   stands for Zero, or nothing at all.

Thomas Hardy
THE RUINED MAID

Thomas Hardy (1840–1928) spans at least two ages of English verse. Though better known for his later poems, he was also a poet as a young man. 'The Ruined Maid' was written in 1866, when he was living in London at Westbourne Park Villas. After so much sermonising and solemn debate on 'The Great Social Evil' of prostitution, Hardy's laconic observation suggests that some of the 'victims' destined to be 'saved' are content as they are and doing rather well in their profession by contrast with their sisters in other walks of life.

'O 'melia, my dear, this does everything crown!
Who could have supposed I should meet you in Town?
And whence such fair garments, such prosperi-ty?' —
'O didn't you know I'd been ruined?' said she.

— 'You left us in tatters, without shoes or socks,
Tired of digging potatoes, and spudding up docks;
And now you've gay bracelets and bright feathers three!' —
'Yes: that's how we dress when we've ruined,' said she.

— 'At home in the barton you said "thee" and "thou",
Aud "thik oon", and "theäs oon", and "t'other"; but now
Your talking quite fits 'ee for high compa-ny!' —
'Some polish is gained with one's ruin,' said she.

— 'Your hands were like paws then, your face blue and bleak
But now I'm bewitched by your delicate cheek,
And your little gloves fit as on any la-dy!' —
'We've never do work when we're ruined,' said she.

— 'You used to call home-life a hag-ridden dream,
And you'd sigh, and you'd sock; but at present you seem
To know not of megrims or melancho-ly!' —
'True. One's pretty lively when ruined,' said she.

— 'I wish I had feathers, a fine sweeping gown,
And a delicate face, and could strut about Town!' —
'My dear — a raw country girl, such as you be,
Cannot quite expect that. You ain't ruined,' said she.

Anonymous
VILIKINS AND HIS DINAH

No sample of Victorian verse on the subject of love and marriage is complete without reference to the most popular form of all, enjoyed by readers and the illiterate alike. From the 1840s onwards, the music-hall had developed in the so-called 'Penny Gaffs' of converted shops, the Coal Hole and 'chanting cribs', the taverns where a chairman superintended the entertainment. Amateur dancing and singing was the staple of the performance and most songs were written with a chorus for the audience to join in. 'Vilikins and his Dinah' was one of the most popular, the story of love blighted by parental tyranny but with not a solemn moment in the song. It was said to have been written by Henry Mayhew, author of *London Labour and the London Poor*, but it exists in no definitive version. Between each verse, the singer speaks a line of commentary as an encouragement to the chorus of 'Too-ral-loo, too-ral-loo, too-ral-loo-ay'.

> Oh! 'tis of a rich merchant,
> In London did dwell,
> He had but one daughter,
> An uncommon nice young gal!
> Her name it was Dinah,
> Scarce sixteen years old,
> She had a large fortune,
> In silver and gold.
> > Singing Too-ral-loo, etc.
>
> As Dinah was valking
> In the garden vun day,
> SPOKEN (*It was the front garden, not the back garden.*)
> Her papa came up to her,
> And thus he did say,
> Go, dress yourself, Dinah,
> In gor-ge-ous array,
> And I'll get you a husband,
> Both val-ly-ant and gay.
> > Singing Too-ral-loo, etc.

SPOKEN (*This is what the infant progeny said to the author of her being.*)

> Oh, papa! oh, papa!
> I've not made up my mind,
> To marry just yet
> I do not feel inclined,
> And all my large fortune,
> I'll freely give o'er,
> If you'll let me stay single
> A year or two more.
>> Singing Too-ral-loo, etc.

SPOKEN (*This is what the indignant parient replied — I represent the father.*)

> Then go, boldest daughter,
> The parient replied,
> If you don't consent to be
> This here young man's bride,
> I'll leave your large fortune
> To the nearest of kin,
> And you shan't have the benefit
> Of one single pin.
>> Singing Too-ral-loo, etc.

SPOKEN (*Now comes the epiflabbergastrinum of the lovier.*)

> As Vilikins vas valking
> The garden around —

SPOKEN (*The aforesaid front garden*)

> He spied his dear Dinah
> Lying dead on the ground,
> A cup of cold pison
> It laid by her side,
> And a billy dux stating
> By pison she died.

SPOKEN (*Taken inwardly,* Singing Too-ral-loo, etc.)

SPOKEN (*This is what the lovier did.*)

> Then he kissed her cold corpus
> A thousand times o'er,
> He called her his Dinah —
> Though she was no more!
> He swallowed the pison
> Like a true lovier brave,
> And Vilikins and his Dinah
> Lie a-buried in one grave.

SPOKEN (*Both on 'em*) Singing Too-ral-loo, etc.

MORAL

Now all you young vimmen,
Take a warning by her,
And never by any means
Disobey the guv'ner:
And all you young fellers,
Mind who you clap eyes on,
Think of Vilikins and Dinah
And the cup of cold pison.

SPOKEN (*Else you'll be singing*) Too-ral-loo, etc.

Anonymous
POLLY PERKINS

Of all the songs of early music-hall, none was more popular than
'Polly Perkins', the jollity of its music comically at odds with the
lament of the rejected lover. For concision and vividness of descrip-
tion, its verse is hard to match. A story that might have filled a
three-volume romantic novel is more graphically told in seven short
verses.

I am a broken-hearted milkman, in grief I'm arrayed,
Through keeping of the company of a young servant maid,
Who lived on board and wages the house to keep clean
In a gentleman's family near Paddington Green.

Chorus:
     She was as beautiful as a butterfly
       And as proud as a Queen
     Was pretty little Polly Perkins of
       Paddington Green.

She'd an ankle like an antelope and a step like a deer,
A voice like a blackbird, so mellow and clear,
Her hair hung in ringlets so beautiful and long,
I thought that she loved me but I found I was wrong.

Chorus:
     She was as beautiful as a butterfly
       And as proud as a Queen
     Was pretty little Polly Perkins of
       Paddington Green.

When I'd rattle in a morning and cry 'milk below',
At the sound of my milk-cans her face she would show
With a smile upon her countenance and a laugh in her eye,
If I thought she'd have loved me, I'd have laid down to die.

Chorus:
> She was as beautiful as a butterfly
>> And as proud as a Queen
> Was pretty little Polly Perkins of
>> Paddington Green.

When I asked her to marry me she said 'Oh! what stuff',
And told me to 'drop it, for she had quite enough
Of my nonsense' — at the same time I'd been very kind,
But to marry a milkman she didn't feel inclined.

Chorus:
> She was as beautiful as a butterfly
>> And as proud as a Queen
> Was pretty little Polly Perkins of
>> Paddington Green.

'Oh, the man that has me must have silver and gold,
A chariot to ride in and be handsome and bold,
His hair must be curly as any watch spring,
And his whiskers as big as a brush for clothing.'

Chorus:
> She was as beautiful as a butterfly
>> And as proud as a Queen
> Was pretty little Polly Perkins of
>> Paddington Green.

The words that she uttered went straight through my heart,
I sobbed, I sighed, and straight did depart;
With a tear on my eyelid as big as a bean,
Bidding good-bye to Polly and Paddington Green.

Chorus:
> She was as beautiful as a butterfly
>> And as proud as a Queen
> Was pretty little Polly Perkins of
>> Paddington Green.

In six months she married, — this hard-hearted girl, —
But it was not a Wi-count, and it was not a Nearl,
It was not a 'Baronite', but a shade or two wuss,
It was a bow-legged conductor of a twopenny bus.

Chorus:
> She was as beautiful as a butterfly
>   And as proud as a Queen
> Was pretty little Polly Perkins of
>   Paddington Green.

John Clare
I AM

In the whole of English poetry few voices are more distinct than
that of John Clare (1793–1864). A herdboy, militiaman, vagrant
and unsuccessful farmer, he spent almost all the last twenty-eight
years of his life in a lunatic asylum. His testament was unique and
disturbing, the poems of his madness unwelcome enough to delay
publication for half a century after his death. He was threatened by
terrors in the dark; 'thin, death-like shadows and goblins with
saucer-eyes were continually shaping on the darkness from my
haunted imagination.' Yet from his madness Clare's poetry presents
a vision of the poet and his world, powerful in its simplicity and
unimpeded in its directness of perception.

I am: yet what I am none cares or knows
    My friends forsake me like a memory lost,
I am the self-consumer of my woes —
    They rise and vanish in oblivious host,
Like shadows in love's frenzied, stifled throes: —
And yet I am, and live — like vapours tost

Into the nothingness of scorn and noise,
    Into the living sea of waking dreams,
Where there is neither sense of life or joys,
    But the vast shipwreck of my life's esteems;
Even the dearest, that I love the best,
Are strange — nay, rather stranger than the rest.

I long for scenes, where man hath never trod,
    A place where woman never smiled or wept —
There to abide with my Creator, God,
    And sleep as I in childhood sweetly slept,
Untroubling, and untroubled where I lie,
The grass below — above the vaulted sky.

THE PEASANT POET

As in so many of his poems, Clare takes a subject that might have
led to mawkishness in the hands of most of his contemporaries and
controls it by his strength and directness of writing.

He loved the brook's soft sound,
    The swallow swimming by
He loved the daisy-covered ground,
    The cloud-bedappled sky.
To him the dismal storm appeared
    The very voice of God;
And when the evening rock was reared
    Stood Moses with his rod.
And everything his eyes surveyed,
    The insects i' the brake,
Were creatures God Almighty made.
    He loved them for his sake —
A silent man in life's affairs,
    A thinker from a boy,
A peasant in his daily cares,
    A poet in his joy.

WRITTEN IN PRISON

Written in Northampton Asylum, this is perhaps Clare's most
poignant personal testimony. Those who believed that he had come
to terms with his confinement and had grown content, saw little of
the truth.

I envy e'en the fly its gleams of joy
In the green woods; from being but a boy
Among the vulgar and the lowly bred,
I envied e'en the hare her grassy bed.
Inured to strife and hardship from a child,

I traced with lonely step the desert wild,
Sighed o'er bird pleasures, but no nest destroyed,
With pleasure felt the singing they enjoyed,
Saw nature smile on all and shed no tears,
A slave through ages, though a child in years —
The mockery and scorn of those more old,
An Æsop in the world's extended fold.
The fly I envy settling in the sun
On the green leaf, and wish my goal was won.

John Warren, Lord de Tabley
THE STUDY OF A SPIDER

John Warren Byrne Leicester, Baron de Tabley (1835–95), was a
botanist whose observation of nature was far removed from the
sentimental or the indulgent. In this case, the cruelty of the spider is
seen as a parallel to the failings of the human species.

From holy flower to holy flower
Thou weavest thine unhallowed bower.
The harmless dewdrops, beaded thin,
Ripple along thy ropes of sin.
Thy house a grave, a gulf thy throne
Affright the fairies every one.
Thy winding sheets are grey and fell,
Imprisoning with nets of hell
The lovely births that winnow by,
Winged sisters of the rainbow sky:
Elf-darlings, fluffy, bee-bright things,
And owl-white moths with mealy wings,
And tiny flies, as gauzy thin
As e'er were shut electrum in.
These are thy death spoils, insect ghoul,
With their dear life thy fangs are foul.
Thou felon anchorite of pain
Who sittest in a world of slain.
Hermit, who tunest song unsweet
To heaving wing and writhing feet.
A glutton of creation's sighs,
Miser of many miseries.

Toper, whose lonely feasting chair
Sways in inhospitable air.
The board is bare, the bloated host
Drinks to himself toast after toast.
His lips require no goblet brink,
But like a weasel must he drink.
The vintage is as old as time
And bright as sunset, pressed and prime.

Ah venom mouth and shaggy thighs
And paunch grown sleek with sacrifice,
Thy dolphin back and shoulders round
Coarse-hairy as some goblin hound
Whom a hag rides to sabbath on,
While shuddering stars in fear grow wan.
Thou palace priest of treachery,
Thou type of selfish lechery,
I break the toils around thy head
And from their gibbets take thy dead.

Eugene Lee-Hamilton
WOOD SONG

Eugene Lee-Hamilton (1845–1907) was an invalid, bedridden for
the greater part of his life. Much of his poetry is marked by a
macabre and violent imagery, sharing with Browning a certain
interest in 'morbid anatomy', though vivid in metaphor and with
an easy lyricism. 'Wood Song' is a Victorian reflection on the
unconsoled intimations of mortality.

When we are gone, love,
    Gone as the breeze,
Woods will be sweet, love,
    Even as these.

Sunflecks will dance, love,
    Even as now,
Here on the moss, love,
    Under the bough.

Others unborn, love,
    Maybe will sit
Here in the wood, love,
    Leafily lit;

Hearking as now, love,
    Treble of birds;
Breathing as we, love,
    Wondering words.

Others will sigh, love,
    Even as we:
'Only a day, love,'
    Murmurs the bee.

THE EAGLES OF TIBERIUS

In its barbaric imagery, Lee-Hamilton's sonnet is a reminder of the extent to which his body, crippled by a spinal disease, was 'shackled' for many years to the bed on which he lay.

They say at Capri that Tiberius bound
    His slaves to eagles, ere he had them flung
    In the abysses, from the rocks that hung
Beetling above the sea and the sea's sound.

Slowly the eagle, struggling round and round
    With the gagged slave that from his talons swung,
    Sank through the air, to which he fiercely clung,
Until the sea caught both, and both were drowned.

O Eagle of the Spirit, hold thy own;
    Work thy great wings, and grapple to the sky;
Let not this shackled body drag thee down.

Into that stagnant sea where, by-and-by,
    The ethereal and the clayey both must drown,
Bound by a link that neither can untie!

Matthew Arnold
THE LAST WORD

Resignation and stoicism, like the courage of the defeated in some far colonial battle, are the prescription of Matthew Arnold (1822–88) in the personal skirmishes of mid-century. Appropriately for Arnold, it is the valour of the Greek or the Roman which is recommended, rather than a Christian submission to Providence.

Creep into thy narrow bed,
Creep, and let no more be said!
Vain thy onset! all stands fast;
Thou thyself must break at last.

Let the long contention cease!
Geese are swans, and swans are geese.
Let them have it how they will!
Thou art tired; best be still!

They out-talk'd thee, hiss'd thee, tore thee
Better men fared thus before thee;
Fired their ringing shot and pass'd,
Hotly charged — and broke at last.

Charge once more, then, and be dumb!
Let the victors, when they come,
When the forts of folly fall,
Find thy body by the wall.

'ENGLAND,
MY ENGLAND'

John Keble

NOVEMBER

John Keble (1792–1866) is so bound up with the history of the
Oxford Movement and the writing of religious verse that the extent
to which his poetry may describe nature with only a glance at moral
teaching may be overlooked. In 'November' he might be taken for
an early Thomas Hardy.

Red o'er the forest peers the setting sun;
   The line of yellow light dies fast away
That crown'd the eastern copse; and chill and dun
   Falls on the moor the brief November day.

Now the tired hunter winds a parting note,
   And Echo bids good-night from every glade;
Yet wait awhile and see the calm leaves float
   Each to his rest beneath their parent shade.

How like decaying life they seem to glide
   And yet no second spring have they in store;
But where they fall, forgotten to abide
   Is all their portion, and they ask no more.

Soon o'er their heads blithe April airs shall sing,
   A thousand wild-flowers round them shall unfold,
The green buds glisten in the dews of Spring,
   And all be vernal rapture as of old.

Unconscious they in waste oblivion lie,
   In all the world of busy life around
No thought of them — in all the bounteous sky
   No drop, for them, of kindly influence found.

Man's portion is to die and rise again:
   Yet he complains, while these unmurmuring part
With their sweet lives, as pure from sin and stain
   As his when Eden held his virgin heart.

John Clare
THE WINTER'S COME

Clare's tribute to the pleasures of winter is characteristically a poem about human activity rather than nature in itself. Winter is the season of comfort before the fire with Dante or Milton, or Burton's *Anatomy of Melancholy*.

Sweet chestnuts brown, like soling leather, turn,
   The larch-trees, like the colour of the sun,
That paled sky in the autumn seem'd to burn.
   What a strange scene before us now does run —
Red, brown, and yellow, russet, black, and dun,
   Whitethorn, wild cherry, and the poplar bare;
The sycamore all withered in the sun.
    No leaves are now upon the birch-tree there:
    All now is stript to the cold wintry air.

See, not one tree but what has lost its leaves —
   And yet the landscape wears a pleasing hue.
The winter chill on his cold bed receives
   Foliage which once hung o'er the waters blue.
Naked and bare the leafless trees repose,
   Blue-headed titmouse now seeks maggots rare,
Sluggish and dull the leaf-strewn river flows;
    That is not green, which was so through the year —
    Dark chill November draweth to a close.

'Tis winter and I love to read indoors,
   When the moon hangs her crescent up on high;
While on the window shutters the wind roars,
   And storms like furies pass remorseless by,
How pleasant on a feather-bed to lie,
   Or sitting by the fire, in fancy soar
With Dante or with Milton to regions high,
    Or read fresh volumes we've not seen before,
    Or o'er old Burton's *Melancholy* pore.

Elizabeth Barrett Browning
ON A PORTRAIT OF WORDSWORTH
BY B. R. HAYDON

Benjamin Robert Haydon (1786–1846) was admired by both Keats and Wordsworth, who wrote a sonnet on him. Returning the compliment, Haydon painted Wordsworth's portrait. Elizabeth Barrett Browning's sonnet is a reminder of how often the ideal of English landscape is fashioned by the vision of Wordsworth or his kind.

> Wordsworth upon Helvellyn! Let the cloud
> Ebb audibly along the mountain-wind,
> Then break against the rock, and show behind
> The lowland valleys floating up to crowd
> The sense with beauty. He with forehead bowed
> And humble-lidded eyes, as one inclined
> Before the sovran thought of his own mind
> And very meek with inspirations proud,
> Takes here his rightful place as poet-priest
> By the high altar, singing prayer and prayer
> To the higher Heavens. A noble vision free
> Our Haydon's hand has flung out from the mist!
> No portrait this, with Academic air!
> This is the poet and his poetry.

ADEQUACY

As in her previous sonnet, Elizabeth Barrett Browning lays emphasis not on nature alone but on nature as observed by humanity and the process of such observation.

> Now by the verdure on thy thousand hills,
> Belovèd England, — doth the earth appear
> Quite good enough for men to overbear
> The will of God in, with rebellious wills!
> We cannot say the morning sun fulfils
> Ingloriously its course, nor that the clear
> Strong stars without significance insphere
> Our habitation. We, meantime, our ills

Heap up against this good, and lift a cry
Against this work-day world, this ill-spread feast,
As if ourselves were better certainly
Than what we come to. Maker and High Priest,
I ask Thee not my joys to multiply, —
Only to make me worthier of the least.

T. E. Brown
THE BRISTOL CHANNEL

A good deal of Victorian writing about the natural scene was pure
enjoyment of it, shorn of the philosophical or aesthetic significance
which the Romantics indulged. T. E. Brown (1830–97) was second
master at Clifton College for almost thirty years. In these eight lines
of symbolism and word-painting he depicts a memorable sunset
where the Bristol Channel widens towards the Atlantic.

This sea was Lazarus, all day
At Dives' gate he lay,
   And lapped the crumbs:
   Night comes;
   The beggar dies —
Forthwith the Channel, coast to coast,
   Is Abraham's bosom; and the beggar lies
A lovely ghost.

Jean Ingelow
FOR EXMOOR

Jean Ingelow (1820–97) was a Lincolnshire poetess whose work
has something of the idealised rural life of a genre painting. Exmoor
in her poem is recognisably Exmoor but the cherry-seller is a rather
decorative production of the studio, an agreeable vision of how the
new reading public of the cities wished the countryside might be
rather than a description of social reality.

For Exmoor —
For Exmoor, where the red deer run, my weary heart doth cry:

She that will a rover wed, far her feet shall hie.
Narrow, narrow, shows the street, dull the narrow sky.
   — *Buy my cherries, whiteheart cherries, good my masters,*
    buy!

For Exmoor —
O he left me, left alone, aye to think and sigh —
'Lambs feed down yon sunny coombe, hind and yearling shy
Mid the shrouding vapours walk now like ghosts on high.'
   — *Buy my cherries, blackheart cherries, lads and lasses, buy!*

For Exmoor —
Dear my dear, why did ye so? Evil day have I;
Mark no more the antler'd stag, hear the curlew cry,
Milking at my father's gate while he leans anigh.
   — *Buy my cherries, whiteheart, blackheart, golden girls, O*
    buy!

Robert Stephen Hawker
A CROON ON HENNACLIFF

Robert Stephen Hawker (1803–75) is one of the more intriguing
figures of Victorian literature, the subject of Sabine Baring-Gould's
biography *The Vicar of Morwenstow* (1876). A High Church priest
educated at Pembroke College, Oxford, Hawker became a Roman
Catholic shortly before his death. For most of his life, however, he
was Vicar of Morwenstow, a remote parish on the north coast of
Cornwall, no land between it and North America. With Hartland
Point and Lundy Island on the northern horizon, Tintagel to the
south-west, his little church was equally within sight of storm,
shipwreck and Arthurian symbol. In imagination at least, Hawker
was to glimpse at Tintagel the Holy Grail which had served as
Christ's cup at the Last Supper and in which Joseph of Arimathea
had collected Christ's blood at the Cross. Hawker devoted much of
his energy to collecting the bodies or fragments of drowned sailors,
the 'gobbets' of flesh as they were called, and giving them Christian
burial in his churchyard. As the seaman's rhyme put it,

> From Padstow Point to Lundy Light,
> Is a watery grave by day or night.

'A Croon on Hennacliff' is the banquet-song of two ravens hoping
to feast on corpses before they reach land and are interred.

Thus said the rushing raven,
　　Unto his hungry mate:
　　'Ho! gossip! for Bude Haven:
　　There be corpses six or eight.
Cawk! cawk! the crew and skipper
　　Are wallowing in the sea:
So there's a savoury supper
　　For my old dame and me.'

'Cawk! gaffer! thou art dreaming,
　　The shore hath wreckers bold;
Would rend the yelling seamen
　　From the clutching billows' hold.
Cawk! cawk! they'd bound for booty
　　Into the dragon's den:
And shout, for "death or duty,"
　　If the prey were drowning men.'

Loud laughed the listening surges,
　　At the guess our grandame gave:
You might call them Boanerges,
　　From the thunder of their wave.
And mockery followed after
　　The sea-bird's jeering brood:
That filled the skies with laughter,
　　From Lundy Light to Bude.

'Cawk! cawk!' then said the raven,
　　'I am fourscore years and ten:
Yet never in Bude Haven
　　Did I croak for rescued men. —
They will save the Captain's girdle,
　　And shirt, if shirt there be:
But leave their blood to curdle,
　　For my old dame and me.'

So said the rushing raven
　　Unto his hungry mate:
'Ho! gossip! for Bude Haven:
　　There be corpses six or eight.
Cawk! cawk! the crew and skipper
　　Are wallowing in the sea:
O what a savoury supper
　　For my old dame and me.'

Charles Tennyson Turner
THE WHITE HORSE OF WESTBURY

Charles Tennyson Turner (1808–79) was the elder brother of
Alfred, Lord Tennyson, with whom he collaborated in their first
published volume, *Poems by Two Brothers* (1827). In his own
right, Tennyson Turner published a number of volumes of sonnets
between 1830 and his death, many of them describing country
scenes or events. In 'The White Horse of Westbury' he combines a
view of the prehistoric horse carved in the hill above Westbury,
Wiltshire, with a characteristically Victorian enthusiasm, the evoc-
ation of the English, or British, past.

As from the Dorset shore I travelled home,
I saw the charger of the Wiltshire wold;
A far-seen figure, stately to behold,
Whose groom the shepherd is, the hoe his comb;
His wizard-spell even sober daylight owned;
That night I dreamed him into living will;
He neighed — and, straight, the chalk poured down the hill;
He shook himself, and all beneath was stoned;
Hengist and Horsa shouted o'er my sleep,
Like fierce Achilles; while that storm-blanched horse
Sprang to the van of all the Saxon force,
And pushed the Britons to the Western deep;
Then, dream-wise, as it were a thing of course,
He floated upwards, and regained the steep.

AFTER THE SCHOOL FEAST

By contrast with a twentieth-century aversion to the discussion or
contemplation of individual death, perhaps in the hope that it may
be long delayed even if not avoidable, the Victorians had reason to
meditate on early mortality. In an era when the average age at death
was forty, and in some areas seventeen, it was certainly possible
that the pastor at this year's school feast might not live to see the
next one. A simple case of appendicitis would be fatal, as for the
diarist Francis Kilvert in 1879 at the age of thirty-nine. With such
expectations, Tennyson Turner infuses a village scene with a little
light melancholy.

The Feast is o'er — the music and the stir —
The sound of bat and ball, the mimic gun;
The lawn grows darker, and the setting sun
Has stolen the flash from off the gossamer,
And drawn the midges westward; youth's glad cry —
The smaller children's fun-exacting claims,
The merry raids across the graver games,
Their ever-crossing paths of restless joy,
Have ceased — and, ere a new Feast day shall shine,
Perchance my soul to other worlds may pass;
Another head in childhood's cause may plot,
Another Pastor muse in this same spot,
And the fresh dews, that gather on the grass
Next morn, may gleam in every track but mine!

W. C. Monkhouse
THE NIGHT EXPRESS

William Cosmo Monkhouse's (1840–1901) poem of the railway
age is almost interchangeable with Stephen Spender's poem *The
Express*, written early in the 1930s.

> After the first powerful, plain manifesto
> The black statement of pistons, without more fuss
> But gliding like a queen, she leaves the station ...

The modernity of Monkhouse's panorama of England raises some
doubt as to whether we should customarily talk of the Victorian
period rather than of a century which began in the 1830s with
Dickens and *Sketches by Boz*, ending in the 1930s with George
Orwell and *The Road to Wigan Pier*.

> With three great snorts of strength,
> Stretching my mighty length,
> Like some long dragon stirring in his sleep,
> Out from the glare of gas
> Into the night I pass,
> And plunge alone into the silence deep.
>
> Little I know or care
> What be the load I bear,

Why thus compell'd, I seek not to divine;
    At man's command I stir,
      I, his stern messenger!
Does he his duty well as I do mine?

    Straight on my silent road,
    Flank'd by no man's abode,
No foe I parley with, no friend I greet;
    On like a bolt I fly
    Under the starry sky,
Scorning the current of the sluggish street.

    Onward from South to North,
    Onward from Thames to Forth,
On — like a comet — on, unceasingly;
    Faster and faster yet
    On — where far boughs of jet
Stretch their wild woof against the pearly sky.

    Faster and faster still —
    Dive I through rock and hill,
Starting the echoes with my shrill alarms;
    Swiftly I curve and bend;
    While, like an eager friend,
The distance runs to clasp me in its arms.

    Ne'er from my path I swerve
    Rattling around a curve
Not vainly trusting to my trusty bars;
    On through the hollow night,
    While, or to left or right,
A city glistens like a clump of stars.

    On through the night I steer;
    Never a sound I hear
Save the strong beating of my steady stroke —
    Save when the circling owl
    Hoots, or the screaming fowl
Rise from the marshes like a sudden smoke.

    Now o'er a gulf I go:
    Dark is the depth below,
Smites the slant beam the shoulder of the height —
    Now through a lane of trees —
    Past sleeping villages,
Their white walls whiter in the silver light.

Be the night foul or fair,
Little I reck or care,
Bandy with storms, and with the tempests jest;
Little I care or know
What winds may rage or blow,
But charge the whirlwind with a dauntless breast.

Now through the level plain,
While, like a mighty mane,
Stretches my endless breath in cloudy miles;
Now o'er a dull lagoon
While the broad beamèd moon
Lights up its sadness into sickly smiles.

O, 'tis a race sublime!
I, neck and neck with Time, —
I, with my thews of iron and heart of fire, —
Run without pause for breath,
While all the earth beneath
Shakes with the shocks of my tremendous ire!

On — till the race be won;
On — till the coming sun
Blinds moon and stars with his excessive light;
On — till the earth be green,
And the first lark be seen
Shaking away with songs the dews of night.

Sudden my speed I slack —
Sudden all force I lack —
Without a struggle yield I up my breath;
Numb'd are my thews of steel,
Wearily rolls each wheel,
My heart cools slowly to the sleep of death.

Why for so brief a length
Dower'd with such mighty strength?
Man is my God — I seek not to divine:
At his command I stir,
I, his stern messenger; —
Does he his duty well as I do mine?

Henry S. Leigh
ROTTEN ROW

Henry Sambrooke Leigh (1837–1883) was a dramatist and poet who adapted French comic operas for the English Stage. His England was that of cheerful metropolitan society. Nowhere was this more evident in the 1860s than where the 'pretty horsebreakers' and their admirers rode through Hyde Park, along Rotten Row. Leigh's poem was published in Frederick Locker's *Lyra Elegantarium*.

There's a tempting bit of greenery — of *rus in urbe* scenery —
  That's haunted by the London 'upper ten;'
Where, by exercise on horseback, an equestrian may force back
  Little fits of *tedium vitæ* now and then.

Oh! the times that I have been there, and the types that I have seen
    there
  Of that gorgeous Cockney animal, the 'swell;'
And the scores of pretty riders (both patricians and outsiders)
  Are considerably more than I can tell.

When first the warmer weather brought these people all together,
  And the crowds began to thicken through the Row,
I reclined against the railing on a sunny day, inhaling
  All the spirits that the breezes could bestow.

And the riders and the walkers and the thinkers and the talkers
  Left me lonely in the thickest of the throng,
Not a touch upon my shoulder — not a nod from one beholder —
  As the stream of Art and Nature went along.

But I brought away one image, from that fashionable scrimmage,
  Of a figure and a face — ah, *such* a face!
Love has photograph'd the features of that loveliest of creatures
  On my memory, as Love alone can trace.

Did I hate the little dandy in the whiskers, (they were sandy,)
  Whose absurd salute was honour'd by a smile?
Did I marvel at his rudeness in presuming on her goodness,
  When she evidently loathed him all the while?

Oh the hours that I have wasted, the regrets that I have tasted,
  Since the day (it seems a century ago)

When my heart was won *instanter* by a lady in a canter,
  On a certain sunny day in Rotten Row!

Gerard Manley Hopkins
A WINDY DAY IN SUMMER

Gerard Manley Hopkins (1844–89) is one of the few major figures in Victorian poetry between the 1860s and the 1890s. Though he was thought of as a technical innovator, this is less apparent in an age which has absorbed much of his influence. His reputation as a poet of religion was easily established after the eventual publication of his poems in 1918. He is also one of the finest Victorian poets of country and city. 'A Windy Day in Summer' is one of his earliest poems, written at Highgate School when he was eighteen.

> The vex'd elm-heads are pale with the view
> Of a mastering heaven utterly blue;
> Swoll'n is the wind that in argent billows
> Rolls across the labouring willows;
> The chestnut-fans are loosely flirting,
> And bared is the aspen's silky skirting;
> The sapphire pools are smit with white
> And silver-shot with gusty light;
> While the breeze by rank and measure
> Paves the clouds on the swept azure.

PENMAEN POOL

'Penmaen Pool' was written in 1876, while Hopkins was studying theology at St Beuno's college in North Wales. The students were to spend a fortnight's holiday at Barmouth on the coast of Cardigan Bay, during which they would row up the Mawddach estuary to Penmaen Pool and lunch at the George Inn. Hopkins wrote his poem for the Visitors' Book at the Inn.

> Who long for rest, who look for pleasure
> Away from counter, court, or school
> O where live well your lease of leisure
> But here at, here at Penmaen Pool?

You'll dare the Alp? you'll dart the skiff? —
Each sport has here its tackle and tool:
Come, plant the staff by Cadair cliff;
Come, swing the sculls on Penmaen Pool.

What's yonder? — Grizzled Dyphwys dim:
The triple-hummocked Giant's stool,
Hoar messmate, hobs and nobs with him
To halve the bowl of Penmaen Pool.

And all the landscape under survey,
At tranquil turns, by nature's rule,
Rides repeated topsyturvy
In frank, in fairy Penmaen Pool.

And Charles's Wain, the wondrous seven,
And sheep-flock clouds like worlds of wool,
For all they shine so, high in heaven,
Shew brighter shaken in Penmaen Pool.

The Mawddach, how she trips! though throttled
If floodtide teeming thrills her full,
And mazy sands all water-wattled
Waylay her at ebb, past Penmaen Pool.

But what's to see in stormy weather,
When grey showers gather and gusts are cool? —
Why, raindrop-roundels looped together
That lace the face of Penmaen Pool.

Then even in weariest wintry hour
Of New Year's month or surly Yule
Furred snows, charged tuft above tuft, tower
From darksome darksome Penmaen Pool.

And ever, if bound here hardest home,
You've parlour-pastime left and (who'll
Not honour it?) ale like goldy foam
That frocks an oar in Penmaen Pool.

Then come who pine for peace or pleasure
Away from counter, court, or school,
Spend here your measure of time and treasure
And taste the treats of Penmaen Pool.

BINSEY POPLARS

'Binsey Poplars' was written while Hopkins was at Oxford in 1879. The poplars lined the banks of the Thames as it flowed through the wide pastureland of Port Meadow west of the city, near the little church of St Margaret's, Binsey. Hopkins' sadness in finding that these companions of a favourite walk had been felled is edged by a chill warning against the uncalculating damage that progress inflicts on nature.

My aspens dear, whose airy cages quelled,
Quelled or quenched in leaves the leaping sun,
All felled, felled, are all felled;
    Of a fresh and following folded rank
        Not spared, not one
        That dandled a sandalled
     Shadow that swam or sank
On meadow and river and wind-wandering weed-winding bank.

  O if we but knew what we do
     When we delve or hew —
  Hack and rack the growing green!
    Since country is so tender
  To touch, her being só slender,
  That, like this sleek and seeing ball
  But a prick will make no eye at all,
Where we, even where we mean
     To mend her we end her,
    When we hew or delve:
After-comers cannot guess the beauty been.
  Ten or twelve, only ten or twelve
    Strokes of havoc únselve
     The sweet especial scene,
    Rural scene, a rural scene,
    Sweet especial rural scene.

DUNS SCOTUS'S OXFORD

Another poem of 1879 warns against the effects of change, evident to Hopkins in Oxford since he had been a Balliol undergraduate in 1863–7. In recalling Oxford as Duns Scotus knew it in the fourteenth century, Hopkins indulges in no mere nostalgia of Arnold's *Scholar-Gipsy* but a celebration of the intellectual strength and spiritual dedication seen in Duns Scotus' belief in 'realty' or philosophic realism, the existence of objective universals and absolute truth.

Towery city and branchy between towers;
Cuckoo-echoing, bell-swarmèd, lark-charmèd, rook-racked, river-
    rounded;
The dapple-eared lily below thee; that country and town did
Once encounter in, here coped and poisèd powers;

Thou hast a base and brickish skirt there, sours
That neighbour-nature thy grey beauty is grounded
Best in; graceless growth, thou hast confounded
Rural rural keeping — folk, flocks, and flowers.

Yet ah! this air I gather and I release
He lived on; these weeds and waters, these walls are what
He haunted who of all men most sways my spirits to peace;

Of realty the rarest-veinèd unraveller; a not
Rivalled insight, be rival Italy or Greece;
Who fired France for Mary without spot.

Thomas Hardy
SNOW IN THE SUBURBS

Homely, vivid, strongly written, this city poem of Hardy's dates from the late 1870s. In its final lines there is a spare and impressionistic modernity.

        Every branch big with it,
        Bent every twig with it;
    Every fork like a white web-foot;
    Every street and pavement mute:
Some flakes have lost their way, and grope back upward, when
Meeting those meandering down they turn and descend again.
    The palings are glued together like a wall,
    And there is no waft of wind with the fleecy fall.

A sparrow enters the tree,
Whereon immediately
A snow-lump thrice his own slight size
Descends on him and showers his head and eyes,
And overturns him,
And near inurns him,
And lights on a nether twig, when its brush
Starts off a volley of other lodging lumps with a rush.

The steps are a blanched slope,
Up which, with feeble hope,
A black cat comes, wide-eyed and thin;
And we take him in.

THE LAST SIGNAL

Hardy's tribute to his fellow Dorset poet, William Barnes, was
written at the time of the older poet's death in 1886 and bears the
subscription 'Winterborne Came Path', close to the parish where
Barnes was rector. In the best tradition of the English elegy it
combines landscape, mood, and commemoration.

Silently I footed by an uphill road
That led from my abode to a spot yew-boughed;
Yellowly the sun sloped low down to westward,
And dark was the east with cloud.

Then, amid the shadow of that livid sad east,
Where the light was least, and a gate stood wide,
Something flashed the fire of the sun that was facing it,
Like a brief blaze on that side.

Looking hard and harder I knew what it meant —
The sudden shine sent from the livid east scene;
It meant the west mirrored by the coffin of my friend there,
Turning to the road from his green,

To take his last journey forth — he who in his prime
Trudged so many a time from that gate athwart the land!
Thus a farewell to me he signalled on his grave-way,
As with a wave of his hand.

AT MIDDLE-FIELD GATE IN FEBRUARY

Hardy's poem of 1889 falls into a period of more mature writing
and into his main area of writing about the rural scene.

The bars are thick with drops that show
    As they gather themselves from the fog
Like silver buttons ranged in a row,
And as evenly spaced as if measured, although
    They fall at the feeblest jog.

They load the leafless hedge hard by,
    And the blades of last year's grass,
While the fallow ploughland turned up nigh
In raw rolls, clammy and clogging lie —
    Too clogging for feet to pass.

How dry it was on a far-back day
    When straws hung the hedge and around,
When amid the sheaves in amorous play
In curtained bonnets and light array
    Bloomed a bevy now underground!

Wilfred Scawen Blunt
ST VALENTINE'S DAY

Wilfrid Scawen Blunt (1840–1922) was a poet, patrician and
political supporter of nationalism in Ireland, Egypt and India. He
travelled a good deal in Arabia. In England, he was a lover of
Catherine Walters ('Skittles'), sharing her favours with the Prince
of Wales. Despite his Byronic pretensions and political radicalism,
his poetry shows an attachment to the prevailing social order.

To-day, all day, I rode upon the down,
With hounds and horsemen, a brave company,
On this side in its glory lay the sea,
On that the Sussex weald, a sea of brown.
The wind was light, and brightly the sun shone,
And still we gallop'd on from gorse to gorse:
And once, when check'd, a thrush sang, and my horse
Prick'd his quick ears as to a sound unknown.

I knew the Spring was come. I knew it even
Better than all by this, that through my chase
In bush and stone and hill and sea and heaven
I seem'd to see and follow still your face.
Your face my quarry was. For it I rode,
My horse a thing of wings, myself a god.

Andrew Lang
TWILIGHT ON TWEED

Andrew Lang (1844–1912) was a minor poet of the period as well
as the translator of Homer, an essayist and historian. A good deal
of his interest is in Scottish history and literature.

Three crests against the saffron sky,
   Beyond the purple plain,
The kind remember'd melody
   Of Tweed once more again.

Wan water from the border hills,
   Dear voice from the old years,
Thy distant music lulls and stills,
   And moves to quiet tears.

Like a loved ghost thy fabled flood
   Fleets through the dusky land;
Where Scott, come home to die, has stood,
   My feet returning stand.

A mist of memory broods and floats,
   The Border waters flow;
The air is full of ballad notes,
   Borne out of long ago.

Old songs that sung themselves to me,
   Sweet through a boy's day-dream,
While trout below the blossom'd tree
   Flash'd in the golden stream.

*

Twilight, and Tweed, and Eildon Hill,
   Fair and too fair you be;
You tell me that the voice is still
   That should have welcomed me.

Robert Louis Stevenson
WISHES

Robert Louis Stevenson (1850–94) remains far better known for his novels, including *Treasure Island* (1883), *The Strange Case of Dr Jekyll and Mr Hyde* (1886) and *Kidnapped* (1886), than for his poetry. However, *A Child's Garden of Verses* (1885) was an influential collection and in this short poem he sums up the good things of material existence as they appeared to many middle-class Victorians.

> Go, little book, and wish to all
> Flowers in the garden, meat in the hall,
> A bin of wine, a spice of wit,
> A house with lawns enclosing it,
> A living river by the door,
> A nightingale in the sycamore.

A. E. Housman
from A SHROPSHIRE LAD

Although A. E. Housman (1859–1936) published *A Shropshire Lad* in 1896, its style was not that of the decade. He belongs to the Victorian tradition of writing about landscape and character. As the following sections of *A Shropshire Lad* may indicate, the simplicity and accessibility of Housman's style has something in common with Hardy's rural scenes and something with Kipling's portrayal of the common man.

i
1887

> From Clee to heaven the beacon burns,
>   The shires have seen it plain,
> From north and south the sign returns
>   And beacons burn again.
>
> Look left, look right, the hills are bright,
>   The dales are light between,
> Because 'tis fifty years to-night
>   That God has saved the Queen.

Now, when the flame they watch not towers
   About the soil they trod,
Lads, we'll remember friends of ours
   Who shared the work with God.

To skies that knit their heartstrings right,
   To fields that bred them brave,
The saviours come not home to-night:
   Themselves they could not save.

It dawns in Asia, tombstones show·
   And Shropshire names are read;
And the Nile spills his overflow
   Beside the Severn's dead.

We pledge in peace by farm and town
   The Queen they served in war,
And fire the beacons up and down
   The land they perished for.

'God save the Queen' we living sing,
   From height to height 'tis heard;
And with the rest your voices ring,
   Lads of the Fifty-third.

Oh, God will save her, fear you not:
   Be you the men you've been,
Get you the sons your fathers got,
   And God will save the Queen.

ii

Loveliest of trees, the cherry now
Is hung with bloom along the bough,
And stands about the woodland ride
Wearing white for Eastertide.

Now, of my threescore years and ten,
Twenty will not come again,
And take from seventy springs a score,
It only leaves me fifty more.

And since to look at things in bloom
Fifty springs are little room,
About the woodlands I will go
To see the cherry hung with snow.

vii

When smoke stood up from Ludlow,
  And mist blew off from Teme,
And blithe a field to ploughing
  Against the morning beam
  I strode beside my team,

The blackbird in the coppice
  Looked out to see me stride,
And hearkened as I whistled
  The trampling team beside,
  And fluted and replied:

'Lie down, lie down, young yeoman;
  What use to rise and rise?
Rise man a thousand mornings
  Yet down at last he lies,
  And then the man is wise.'

I heard the tune he sang me,
  And spied his yellow bill;
I picked a stone and aimed it
  And threw it with a will:
  Then the bird was still.

Then my soul within me
  Took up the blackbird's strain,
And still beside the horses
  Along the dewy lane
  It sang the song again:

'Lie down, lie down, young yeoman;
  The sun moves always west;
The road one treads to labour
  Will lead one home to rest,
  And that will be the best.'

viii

'Farewell to barn and stack and tree,
  Farewell to Severn shore.
Terence, look your last at me,
  For I come home no more.

'The sun burns on the half-mown hill,
    By now the blood is dried;
And Maurice amongst the hay lies still
    And my knife is in his side.

'My mother thinks us long away;
    'Tis time the field were mown.
She had two sons at rising day,
    To-night she'll be alone.

'And here's a bloody hand to shake,
    And oh, man, here's good-bye;
We'll sweat no more on scythe and rake,
    My bloody hands and I.

'I wish you strength to bring you pride,
    And a love to keep you clean,
And I wish you luck, come Lammastide,
    At racing on the green.

'Long for me the rick will wait,
    And long will wait the fold,
And long will stand the empty plate,
    And dinner will be cold.'

ix

On moonlit heath and lonesome bank
    The sheep beside me graze;
And yon the gallows used to clank
    Fast by the four cross ways.

A careless shepherd once would keep
    The flocks by moonlight there,
And high amongst the glimmering sheep
    The dead man stood on air.*

They hang us now in Shrewsbury jail:
    The whistles blow forlorn,
And trains all night groan on the rail
    To men that die at morn.

There sleeps in Shrewsbury jail to-night,
    Or wakes, as may betide,

* A condemned man who was hanged in chains and his body left to rot was said to be 'keeping flocks by moonlight'.

A better lad, if things went right,
   Than most that sleep outside.

And naked to the hangman's noose
   The morning clocks will ring
A neck God made for other use
   Than strangling in a string.

And sharp the link of life will snap,
   And dead on air will stand
Heels that held up as straight a chap
   As treads upon the land.

So here I'll watch the night and wait
   To see the morning shine,
When he will hear the stroke of eight
   And not the stroke of nine;

And wish my friend as sound a sleep
   As lads' I did not know,
That shepherded the moonlit sheep
   A hundred years ago.

x
March

The Sun at noon to higher air,
Unharnessing the silver Pair
That late before his chariot swam,
Rides on the gold wool of the Ram.

So braver notes the storm-cock sings
To start the rusted wheel of things,
And brutes in field and brutes in pen
Leap that the world goes round again.

The boys are up the woods with day
To fetch the daffodils away,
And home at noonday from the hills
They bring no dearth of daffodils.

Afield for palms the girls repair,
And sure enough the palms are there,
And each will find by hedge or pond
Her waving silver-tufted wand.

In farm and field through all the shire
The eye beholds the heart's desire;

Ah, let not only mine be vain,
For lovers should be loved again.

xii

When I watch the living meet,
    And the moving pageant file
Warm and breathing through the street
    Where I lodge a little while,

If the heats of hate and lust
    In the house of flesh are strong,
Let me mind the house of dust
    Where my sojourn shall be long.

In the nation that is not
    Nothing stands that stood before;
There revenges are forgot,
    And the hater hates no more;

Lovers lying two and two
    Ask not whom they sleep beside,
And the bridegroom all night through
    Never turns him to the bride.

xxi
Bredon Hill

In summertime on Bredon
    The bells they sound so clear;
Round both the shires they ring them
    In steeples far and near,
    A happy noise to hear.

Here of a Sunday morning
    My love and I would lie,
And see the coloured counties,
    And hear the larks so high
    About us in the sky.

The bells would ring to call her
    In valleys miles away:
'Come all to church, good people;
    Good people, come and pray.'
    But here my love would stay.

And I would turn and answer
    Among the springing thyme,
'Oh, peal upon our wedding,

And we will hear the chime,
And come to church in time.'

But when the snows at Christmas
On Bredon top were strown,
My love rose up so early
And stole out unbeknown
And went to church alone.

They tolled the one bell only,
Groom there was none to see,
The mourners followed after,
And so to church went she,
And would not wait for me.

The bells they sound on Bredon,
And still the steeples hum.
'Come all to church, good people,' —
Oh, noisy bells, be dumb;
I hear you, I will come.

xxviii
The Welsh Marches

High the vanes of Shrewsbury gleam
Islanded in Severn stream;
The bridges from the steepled crest
Cross the water east and west.

The flag of morn in conqueror's state
Enters at the English gate:
The vanquished eve, as night prevails,
Bleeds upon the road to Wales.

Ages since the vanquished bled
Round my mother's marriage-bed;
There the ravens feasted far
About the open house of war:

When Severn down to Buildwas ran
Coloured with the death of man,
Couched upon her brother's grave
The Saxon got me on the slave.

The sound of fight is silent long
That began the ancient wrong;
Long the voice of tears is still
That wept of old the endless ill.

In my heart it has not died,
The war that sleeps on Severn side;
They cease not fighting, east and west,
On the marches of my breast.

Here the truceless armies yet
Trample, rolled in blood and sweat;
They kill and kill and never die;
And I think that each is I.

None will part us, none undo
The knot that makes one flesh of two,
Sick with hatred, sick with pain,
Strangling — When shall we be slain?

When shall I be dead and rid
Of the wrong my father did?
How long, how long, till spade and hearse
Put to sleep my mother's curse?

xxxix

'Tis time, I think, by Wenlock town
   The golden broom should blow;
The hawthorn sprinkled up and down
   Should charge the land with snow.

Spring will not wait the loiterer's time
   Who keeps so long away;
So others wear the broom and climb
   The hedgerows heaped with may.

Oh tarnish late on Wenlock Edge,
   Gold that I never see;
Lie long, high snowdrifts in the hedge
   That will not shower on me.

lix
The Isle of Portland

The star-filled seas are smooth to-night
   From France to England strown;
Black towers above the Portland light
   The felon-quarried stone.

On yonder island, not to rise,
   Never to stir forth free,
Far from his folk a dead lad lies
   That once was friends with me.

Lie you easy, dream you light,
   And sleep you fast for aye;
And luckier may you find the night
   Than ever you found the day.

THE WAY
OF THE CROSS

Emily Brontë

LAST LINES

Emily Brontë (1818–48) was part-author with her sisters Anne and Charlotte of *Poems by Currer, Ellis, and Acton Bell* (1846). She is best known for 'Last Lines' and 'Remembrance'. According to her sister Charlotte, this was Emily's last poem, written in January 1846, almost three years before her death.

> No coward soul is mine,
> No trembler in the world's storm-troubled sphere:
>   I see Heaven's glories shine,
> And faith shines equal, arming me from fear.
>
>   O God within my breast,
> Almighty, ever-present Deity!
>   Life — that in me has rest,
> As I — undying Life — have power in Thee!
>
>   Vain are the thousand creeds
> That move men's hearts: unutterably vain;
>   Worthless as wither'd weeds,
> Or idlest froth amid the boundless main,
>
>   To waken doubt in one
> Holding so fast by thine infinity;
>   So surely anchor'd on
> The steadfast rock of immortality.
>
>   With wide-embracing love
> Thy Spirit animates eternal years,
>   Pervades and broods above,
> Changes, sustains, dissolves, creates, and rears.
>
>   Though earth and man were gone,
> And suns and universes ceased to be,
>   And Thou were left alone,
> Every existence would exist in Thee.
>
>   There is not room for Death,
> Nor atom that his might could render void:
>   Thou — Thou art Being and Breath,
> And what Thou art may never be destroy'd.

John Henry Newman
from THE DREAM OF GERONTIUS

As a poet, John Henry Newman (1801–90) remains best known for his long verse sequence of death and judgment in *The Dream of Gerontius* (1866) and his short poem 'The Pillar of the Cloud' written in 1833. The latter with its opening lines,

> Lead, Kindly Light, amid the encircling gloom,
>   Lead Thou me on!
> The night is dark, and I am far from home —
>   Lead Thou me on!

has a certain resemblance to a Pre-Raphaelite painting like Holman Hunt's 'Light of the World', where Christ stands with a lantern at the open door.

Like 'The Pillar of the Cloud', the best known passage of *The Dream of Gerontius*, 'The Chorus of Angelicals', was to become famous as a hymn. Indeed, Newman's poem was to be set to music by Sir Edward Elgar as an oratorio in 1900.

> Praise to the Holiest in the height,
>   And in the depths be praise:
> In all His words most wonderful;
>   Most sure in all His ways.
>
> O loving wisdom of our God!
>   When all was sin and shame,
> A second Adam to the fight
>   And to the rescue came.
>
> O wisest love! that flesh and blood
>   Which did in Adam fail,
> Should strive afresh against their foe,
>   Should strive and should prevail;
>
> And that a higher gift than grace
>   Should flesh and blood refine,
> God's presence and His very Self,
>   And Essence all-divine.
>
> O generous love! that He who smote
>   In man for man the foe,

The double agony in man
  For man should undergo;

And in the garden secretly
  And on the cross on high,
Should teach His brethren and inspire
  To suffer and to die.

John Ellerton
THE DAY THOU GAVEST, LORD, IS ENDED

Among the great undogmatic hymns of the Victorian period, 'The Day Thou Gavest, Lord, Is Ended' by John Ellerton (1826–93) is a good example of a hymn which is more than it might appear to be. Its popularity has never been in doubt yet it belongs characteristically to the mid-Victorians. In its third verse, it comes close to proclaiming an empire on which the sun never sets, only to subordinate that in the last verse to an eternal kingdom.

The day Thou gavest, Lord, is ended,
  The darkness falls at Thy behest;
To Thee our morning hymns ascended,
  Thy praise shall sanctify our rest.

We thank Thee that Thy Church unsleeping,
  While earth rolls onward into light,
Through all the world her watch is keeping,
  And rests not now by day or night.

As o'er each continent and island
  The dawn leads on another day,
The voice of prayer is never silent,
  Nor dies the strain of praise away.

The sun that bids us rest is waking
  Our brethren 'neath the western sky,
And hour by hour fresh lips are making
  Thy wondrous doings heard on high.

So be it, Lord; Thy throne shall never,
  Like earth's proud empires, pass away;

Thy kingdom stands, and grows for ever,
Till all Thy creatures own Thy sway.

Sabine Baring-Gould
ONWARD! CHRISTIAN SOLDIERS

Many of the best known hymns sung on public occasions, 'O God,
Our Help in Ages Past', 'Rock of Ages', 'Abide With Me', or 'Cwm
Rhondda', for example, pre-date the nineteenth century. Perhaps
the most characteristic of all Victorian hymns is this song of triumph
by Sabine Baring-Gould (1834–1924), novelist, clergyman and
biographer. Poetry might deal in religious doubt but there was no
place for faint-heartedness in hymns. Subsequently, Sabine-Gould's
famous verses contrived to annoy pacifists, who thought the Church
had no business donning the rhetoric of war, and opponents of
High Church or 'Anglo-Catholic' tendencies in the Church of
England, who felt the lines had a certain odour of incense, proces-
sions, and ritual. Hence the parody, 'Onward! Christian soldiers,/
Marching as to war,/ With the Cross of Jesus/ Left behind the door'.
Such critics remained a minority, however, among thousands who
would recognise Baring-Gould's lines, as set to music by Sir Arthur
Sullivan, even if they knew few other hymns.

Onward! Christian soldiers,
  Marching as to war,
With the Cross of Jesus
  Going on before.
Christ, the royal Master,
  Leads against the foe;
Forward into battle,
  See! His banners go.

Onward! Christian soldiers,
  Marching as to war,
With the Cross of Jesus
  Going on before.

At the sign of triumph
  Satan's host doth flee;
On then, Christian soldiers,
  On to victory!

Hell's foundations quiver
    At the shout of praise;
Brothers lift your voices,
    Loud your anthems raise.

Onward! Christian soldiers,
    Marching as to war,
With the Cross of Jesus
    Going on before.

Like a mighty army
    Moves the Church of God;
Brothers, we are treading
    Where the saints have trod.
We are not divided,
    All one body we,
One in hope, in doctrine,
    One in charity.

Onward! Christian soldiers,
    Marching as to war,
With the Cross of Jesus
    Going on before.

Crowns and thrones may perish,
    Kingdoms rise and wane,
But the Church of Jesus
    Constant will remain.
Gates of hell can never
    'Gainst that Church prevail;
We have Christ's own promise,
    And that cannot fail.

Onward! Christian soldiers,
    Marching as to war,
With the Cross of Jesus
    Going on before.

Onward then, ye people!
    Join our happy throng;
Blend with ours your voices
    In the triumph song:
Glory, laud, and honour
    Unto Christ the King!
This through countless ages
    Men and angels sing.

Onward! Christian soldiers,
Marching as to war,
With the Cross of Jesus
Going on before.

James Thomson

from THE CITY OF DREADFUL NIGHT

James Thomson (1834–82) was the son of poor parents and was
educated at the Royal Caledonia Asylum. Dismissed from his post
as an army schoolmaster in 1862, he lived a solitary life in London.
An alcoholic and insomniac, Thomson produced in *The City of
Dreadful Night* an urban vision of atheistic despair. It is the far
extreme to the triumphant song of Baring-Gould's hymn or the
expectant mysticism of Robert Stephen Hawker's glimpse of the
Holy Grail. Religious imagery when it occurs in these lines of
Thomson's poem serves only to deepen the despair.

A river girds the city west and south,
The main north channel of a broad lagoon,
Regurging with the salt tides from the mouth;
Waste marshes shine and glister to the moon
For leagues, then moorland black, then stony ridges;
Great piers and causeways, many noble bridges,
Connect the town and islet suburbs strewn.

Upon an easy slope it lies at large,
And scarcely overlaps the long curved crest
Which swells out two leagues, from the river marge.
A trackless wilderness rolls north and west,
Savannahs, savage woods, enormous mountains,
Bleak uplands, black ravines with torrent fountains;
And eastwards rolls the shipless sea's unrest.

The city is not ruinous, although
Great ruins of an unremembered past,
With others of a few short years ago
More sad, are found within its precincts vast.
The street-lamps always burn; but scarce a casement
In house or palace from roof to basement
Doth glow a gleam athwart the mirk air cast.

The street-lamps burn amidst the baleful glooms,
Amidst the soundless solitudes immense
Of rangèd mansions dark and still as tombs.
The silence which benumbs or strains the sense
Fulfils with awe the soul's despair unweeping:
Myriads of habitants are ever sleeping,
Or dead, or fled from nameless pestilence!

Yet as in some necropolis you find
Perchance one mourner to a thousand dead,
So there; worn faces that look deaf and blind
Like tragic masks of stone. With weary tread,
Each wrapt in his own doom, they wander, wander,
Or sit foredone and desolately ponder
Through sleepless hours with heavy drooping head.

*

Although lamps burn along the silent streets;
Even when moonlight silvers empty squares
The dark holds countless lanes and close retreats;
But when the night its sphereless mantle wears
The open spaces yawn with gloom abysmal,
The sombre mansions loom immense and dismal,
The lanes are black as subterranean lairs.

And soon the eye a strange new vision learns:
The night remains for it as dark and dense,
Yet clearly in this darkness it discerns
As in the daylight with its natural sense;
Perceives a shade in shadow not obscurely,
Pursues a stir of black in blackness surely,
Sees spectres also in the gloom intense.

The ear, too, with the silence vast and deep
Becomes familiar though unreconciled;
Hears breathings as of hidden life asleep,
And muffled throbs as of pent passions wild,
Far murmurs, speech of pity or derision;
But all more dubious than the things of vision,
So that it knows not when it is beguiled.

No time abates the first despair and awe,
But wonder ceases soon; the weirdest thing
Is felt least strange beneath the lawless law

Where Death-in-Life is the eternal king;
Crushed impotent beneath this reign of terror.
Dazed with such mysteries of woe and error,
The soul is too outworn for wondering.

*

The mansion stood apart in its own ground;
In front thereof a fragrant garden-lawn.
High trees about it, and the whole walled round:
The massive iron gates were both withdrawn;
And every window of its front shed light,
Portentous in that City of the Night.

But though thus lighted it was deadly still
As all the countless bulks of solid gloom:
Perchance a congregation to fulfil
Solemnities of silence in this doom,
Mysterious rites of dolour and despair
Permitting not a breath of chant or prayer?

Broad steps ascended to a terrace broad
Whereon lay still light from the open door;
The hall was noble, and its aspect awed,
Hung round with heavy black from dome to floor;
And ample stairways rose from left and right
Whose balustrades were also draped with night.

I paced from room to room, from hall to hall,
Nor any life throughout the maze discerned;
But each was hung with its funereal pall.
And held a shrine, around which tapers burned,
With picture or with statue or with bust,
All copied from the same fair form of dust:

A woman very young and very fair;
Beloved by bounteous life and joy and youth,
And loving these sweet lovers, so that care
And age and death seemed not for her in sooth:
Alike as stars, all beautiful and bright,
These shapes lit up that mausoléan night.

At length I heard a murmur as of lips,
And reached an open oratory hung
With heaviest blackness of the whole eclipse;
Beneath the dome a fuming censer swung;

And one lay there upon a low white bed,
With tapers burning at the foot and head:

The Lady of the images: supine,
Deathstill, lifesweet, with folded palms she lay:
And kneeling there as at a sacred shrine
A young man wan and worn who seemed to pray:
A crucifix of dim and ghostly white
Surmounted the large altar left in night: —

The chambers of the mansion of my heart,
In every one whereof thine image dwells,
Are black with grief eternal for thy sake.

The inmost oratory of my soul,
Wherein thou ever dwellest quick or dead,
Is black with grief eternal for thy sake.

I kneel beside thee and I clasp the cross,
With eyes for ever fixed upon that face,
So beautiful and dreadful in its calm.

I kneel here patient as thou liest there;
As patient as a statue carved in stone,
Of adoration and eternal grief.

Whilst thou dost not awake I cannot move;
And something tells me thou wilt never wake
And I alive feel turning into stone.

Most beautiful were Death to end my grief,
Most hateful to destroy the sight of thee,
Dear vision better than all death or life.
But I renounce all choice of life or death,
For either shall be ever at thy side,
And thus in bliss or woe be ever well. —

He murmured thus and thus in monotone,
Intent upon that uncorrupted face,
Entranced except his moving lips alone:
I glided with hushed footsteps from the place.
This was the festival that filled with light
That palace in the City of the Night.

*

How the moon triumphs through the endless nights!
How the stars throb and glitter as they wheel
Their thick processions of supernal lights
Around the blue vault obdurate as steel!

And men regard with passionate awe and yearning
The mighty marching and the golden burning,
And think the heavens respond to what they feel.

Boats gliding like dark shadows of a dream,
Are glorified from vision as they pass
The quivering moonbridge on the deep black stream;
Cold windows kindle their dead glooms of glass
To restless crystals; cornice, dome and column
Emerge from chaos in the splendour solemn;
Like faëry lakes gleam lawns of dewy grass.

With such a living light these dead eyes shine,
These eyes of sightless heaven, that as we gaze
We read a pity, tremulous, divine,
Or cold majestic scorn in their pure rays:
Fond man! they are not haughty, are not tender;
There is no heart or mind in all their splendour,
They thread mere puppets all their marvellous maze.

If we could near them with the flight unflown,
We should but find them worlds as sad as this,
Or suns all self-consuming like our own
Enringed by planet worlds as much amiss:
They wax and wane through fusion and confusion;
The spheres eternal are a grand illusion,
The empyréan is a void abyss.

Robert Stephen Hawker
from THE QUEST OF THE SANGRAAL

Of all accounts of the quest for the Holy Grail in Victorian poetry,
none is more individual than Hawker's mystical vision of Tintagel,
a few miles away from his parish of Morwenstow. *The Quest of
the Sangraal* was written on the Atlantic coast in the winter days of
grief following the death of his wife in February 1863. It precedes
Tennyson's poem on the subject by seven years and excels it in
freshness of vision. Sabine Baring-Gould suggested that readers
would 'prefer the masterpiece of the Cornish poet to a piece in
which Lord Tennyson scarcely rises to his true level'.

Hawker's poem ends with Merlin's vision of the future, the Holy
Grail seen again at Tintagel — 'Dundagel' in the poem. The word

'Sangraal' is of doubtful origin, the usual assumptions being that it derived from 'Sang-réal' — 'True Blood', collected in a gold vessel by Joseph of Arimathea at the foot of the Cross; or from the Provençal 'Sanc-Grazal' — 'Holy Cup', used by Christ at the Last Supper and subsequently containing the True Blood. Of Hawker's more unusual words, 'libbard' is an archaic term for leopard, 'hin' was a Hebrew liquid measure coming to little more than a gallon. 'Igdarsil', the mystic tree, is the ash tree of Celtic ritual. The 'Raun' or rowan tree is a mountain ash with similar properties. Abarim is a mountain range in the east of Jordan, where St Michael, commanding the heavenly host, defeated Satan. Gennesaret is the Lake of Galilee.

In this latter half of the poem, Arthur addresses his knights, Lancelot, Perceval, Tristan and Galahad, as they set off to the points of the compass on their quest. That night at Tintagel, Merlin evokes a vision of the finding of the Sangraal and its appearance at Tintagel, before it is lost again in a northern invasion. Mythology though it may be, the life and landscape of Cornwall is never far from the surface of Hawker's poem.

> They stand — and hush their hearts to hear the King.
> Then said he, like a prince of Tamar-land —
> Around his soul, Dundagel and the sea —
>
> 'Ha! Sirs — ye seek a noble crest to-day,
> To win and wear the starry Sangraal,
> The link that binds to God a lonely land.
> Would that my arm went with you, like my heart
> But the true shepherd must not shun the fold:
> For in this flock are crouching grievous wolves,
> And chief among them all, my own false kin.
> Therefore I tarry by the cruel sea,
> To hear at eve the treacherous mermaid's song,
> And watch the wallowing monsters of the wave, —
> 'Mid all things fierce, and wild, and strange, alone!
>
> 'Ay! all beside can win companionship:
> The churl may clip his mate beneath the thatch,
> While his brown urchins nestle at his knees:
> The soldier give and grasp a mutual palm,
> Knit to his flesh in sinewy bonds of war:
> The knight may seek at eve his castle-gate,

Mount the old stair, and lift the accustom'd latch,
To find, for throbbing brow and weary limb,
That paradise of pillows, one true breast:
But he, the lofty ruler of the land,
Like yonder Tor, first greeted by the dawn,
And wooed the latest by the lingering day,
With happy homes and hearths beneath his breast,
Must soar and gleam in solitary snow.
The lonely one is, evermore, the King.
So now farewell, my lieges, fare ye well,
And God's sweet Mother be your benison!
Since by grey Merlin's gloss, this wondrous cup
Is, like the golden vase in Aaron's ark,
A fount of manna for a yearning world,
As full as it can hold of God and heaven,
Search the four winds until the balsam breathe,
Then grasp, and fold it in your very soul!

'I have no son, no daughter of my loins,
To breathe, 'mid future men, their father's name:
My blood will perish when these veins are dry;
Yet am I fain some deeds of mine should live —
I would not be forgotten in this land:
I yearn that men I know not, men unborn,
Should find, amid these fields, King Arthur's fame!
Here let them say, by proud Dundagel's walls —
'They brought the Sangraal back by his command,
They touched these rugged rocks with hues of God:'
So shall my name have worship, and my land.

'Ah! native Cornwall! throned upon the hills,
Thy moorland pathways worn by Angel feet,
Thy streams that march in music to the sea
'Mid Ocean's merry noise, his billowy laugh!
Ah me! a gloom falls heavy on my soul —
The birds that sung to me in youth are dead;
I think, in dreamy vigils of the night,
It may be God is angry with my land,
Too much athirst for fame, too fond of blood;
And all for earth, for shadows, and the dream
To glean an echo from the winds of song!

'But now, let hearts be high! the Archangel held
A tournay with the fiend on Abarim,
And good Saint Michael won his dragon-crest!

'Be this our cry! the battle is for God!
If bevies of foul fiends withstand your path,
Nay! if strong angels hold the watch and ward,
Plunge in their midst, and shout, "A Sangraal!"'

He ceased; the warriors bent a knightly knee,
And touched, with kiss and sign, Excalibur;
Then turned, and mounted for their perilous way!

That night Dundagel shuddered into storm —
The deep foundations shook beneath the sea:
Yet there they stood, beneath the murky moon,
Above the bastion, Merlin and the King.
Thrice waved the sage his staff, and thrice they saw
A peopled vision throng the rocky moor.

First fell a gloom, thick as a thousand nights,
A pall that hid whole armies; and beneath
Stormed the wild tide of war; until on high
Gleamed red the dragon, and the Keltic glaive
Smote the loose battle of the roving Dane!
Then yelled a fiercer fight: for brother blood
Rushed mingling, and twin dragons fought the field!
The grisly shadows of his faithful knights
Perplext their lord: and in their midst, behold!
His own stern semblance waved a phantom brand,
Drooped, and went down the war. Then cried the King,

'Ho! Arthur to the rescue!' and half drew
Excalibur; but sank, and fell entranced.

A touch aroused the monarch: and there stood
He, of the billowy beard and awful eye,
The ashes of whole ages on his brow —
Merlin the bard, son of a demon-sire!
High, like Ben Amram at the thirsty rock,
He raised his prophet staff: that runic rod,
The stem of Igdrasil — the crutch of Raun —
And wrote strange words along the conscious air.

Forth gleamed the east, and yet it was not day!
A white and glowing horse outrode the dawn;
A youthful rider ruled the bounding rein,

And he, in semblance of Sir Galahad shone:
A vase he held on high; one molten gem,
Like massive ruby or the chrysolite:
Thence gushed the light in flakes; and flowing, fell
As though the pavement of the sky brake up,
And stars were shed to sojourn on the hills,
From grey Morwenna's stone to Michael's tor,
Until the rocky land was like a heaven.

Then saw they that the mighty Quest was won!
The Sangraal swoon'd along the golden air:
The sea breathed balsam, like Gennesaret:
The streams were touched with supernatural light:
And fonts of Saxon rock, stood, full of God!
Altars arose, each like a kingly throne,
Where the royal chalice, with its lineal blood,
The Glory of the Presence, ruled and reigned.
This lasted long: until the white horse fled,
The fierce fangs of the libbard in his loins:
Whole ages glided in that blink of time,
While Merlin and the King, looked, wondering, on.

But see! once more the wizard-wand arise,
To cleave the air with signals, and a scene.

Troops of the demon-north, in yellow garb,
The sickly hue of vile Iscariot's hair,
Mingle with men, in unseen multitudes!
Unscared, they throng the valley and the hill;
The shrines were darkened and the chalice void:
That which held God was gone: Maran-atha!
The awful shadows of the Sangraal, fled!
Yet giant-men arose, that seemed as gods,
Such might they gathered from the swarthy kind:
The myths were rendered up: and one by one,
The Fire — the Light — the Air — were tamed and bound
Like votive vassals at their chariot-wheel.
Then learnt they War: yet not that noble wrath,
That brings the generous champion face to face
With equal shield, and with a measured brand,
To peril life for life, and do or die;
But the false valour of the lurking fiend

To hurl a distant death from some deep den:
To wing with flame the metal of the mine:
And, so they rend God's image, reck not who!

'Ah! haughty England! lady of the wave!'
Thus said pale Merlin to the listening King,
'What is thy glory in the world of stars?
To scorch and slay: to win demoniac fame,
In arts and arms; and then to flash and die!
Thou art the diamond of the demon-crown,
Smitten by Michael upon Abarim,
That fell; and glared, an island of the sea.
Ah! native England! wake thine ancient cry;
Ho! for the Sangraal! vanish'd Vase of Heaven,
That held, like Christ's own heart, an hin of blood!'

He ceased; and all around was dreamy night:
There stood Dundagel, throned: and the great sea
Lay, a strong vassal at his master's gate,
And, like a drunken giant, sobb'd in sleep!

Gerard Manley Hopkins
THE HABIT OF PERFECTION

Written in 1866, before he became a Catholic, this is Hopkins'
lyrical expression of physical dedication to a spiritual vision.

Elected Silence, sing to me
And beat upon my whorlèd ear,
Pipe me to pastures still and be
The music that I care to hear.

Shape nothing, lips; be lovely-dumb:
It is the shut, the curfew sent
From there where all surrenders come
Which only makes you eloquent.

Be shellèd, eyes, with double dark
And find the uncreated light:
This ruck and reel which you remark
Coils, keeps, and teases simple sight.

Palate, the hutch of tasty lust,
Desire not to be rinsed with wine:
The can must be so sweet, the crust
So fresh that come in fasts divine!

Nostrils, your careless breath that spend
Upon the stir and keep of pride,
What relish shall the censers send
Along the sanctuary side!

O feel-of-primrose hands, O feet
That want the yield of plushy sward,
But you shall walk the golden street
And you unhouse and house the Lord.

And, Poverty, be thou the bride
And now the marriage feast begun,
And lily-coloured clothes provide
Your spouse not laboured-at nor spun.

THE WRECK OF THE DEUTSCHLAND

Hopkins's grandest and most famous poem was written in 1875–6 and subtitled 'To the happy memory of five Franciscan Nuns, exiles by the Falk Laws, drowned between midnight and morning of Dec. 7th 1875.' Bismarck's so-called *kulturkampf* against the Papacy, following the proclamation of papal infallibility by Pius IX in 1870, led to the exiling of religious communities from Germany under the anti-clerical laws administered by Adalbert Falk. The steamer *Deutschland*, bound from Bremerhaven to New York with the five nuns on board, went aground on a sandbank in atrocious weather during the night. The rising tide on the second day flooded the ship, forcing some survivors into the rigging, from which they fell into the sea as cold and exhaustion overtook them. The weather was so bad that neither the men of the Kentish Knock lightship nor the Harwich lifeboat could reach the steamer. Though there were survivors, the five nuns were not among them.

Hopkins, not yet a priest, had entered the Society of Jesus seven years earlier and had written no poetry since. He broke his silence on hearing of the *Deutschland's* fate, though this may merely have been an opportunity to do something that would have happened in any case. He wrote to Richard Watson Dixon, a minor Pre-Raphaelite poet and assistant master at Highgate School when

Hopkins was a boy, 'I had long had haunting my ear the echo of a new rhythm which I now realized on paper'.

According to Hopkins, in a letter to Robert Bridges, 'this poem is an ode and not primarily a narrative ... the principal business is lyrical.' The result is one of the most splendid religious poems that England had seen since the seventeenth century. Whether one reads it as an exercise in 'Sprung Rhythm', or devotional rhetoric of the first order must be a matter of taste. The first part of the poem is a personal meditation by its author, the second part describes the wreck and expresses a hope for the blossoming of the Catholic faith in Britain. In response to Robert Bridges, Hopkins wrote of his poem, 'I cannot think of altering anything. Why should I? I do not write for the public. You are my public and I hope to convert you.'

To the
happy memory of five Franciscan Nuns
exiles by the Falk Laws
drowned between midnight and morning of
Dec. 7th, 1875

Part the First

1

Thou mastering me
    God! giver of breath and bread;
World's strand, sway of the sea;
    Lord of living and dead;
Thou has bound bones and veins in me, fastened me flesh,
And after it almost unmade, what with dread,
        Thy doing: and dost thou touch me afresh?
Over again I feel thy finger and find thee.

2

I did say yes
    O at lightning and lashed rod;
Thou heardst me truer than tongue confess
    Thy terror, O Christ, O God;
Thou knowest the walls, altar and hour and night;
The swoon of a heart that the sweep and the hurl of thee trod
        Hard down with a horror of height:
And the midriff astrain with leaning of, laced with fire of stress.

3

The frown of his face
Before me, the hurtle of hell
Behind, where, where was a, where was a place?
I whirled out wings that spell
And fled with a fling of the heart to the heart of the Host.
My heart, but you were dovewinged, I can tell,
Carrier-witted, I am bold to boast,
To flash from the flame to the flame then, tower from the grace to
the grace.

4

I am soft sift
In an hourglass — at the wall
Fast, but mined with a motion, a drift,
And it crowds and it combs to the fall;
I steady as a water in a well, to a poise, to a pane,
But roped with, always, all the way down from the tall
Fells or flanks of the voel, a vein
Of the gospel proffer, a pressure, a principle, Christ's gift.

5

I kiss my hand
To the stars, lovely-asunder
Starlight, wafting him out of it; and
Glow, glory in thunder;
Kiss my hand to the dappled-with-damson west:
Since, tho' he is under the world's splendour and wonder,
His mystery must be instressed, stressed;
For I greet him the days I meet him, and bless when I understand.

6

Not out of his bliss
Springs the stress felt
Nor first from heaven (and few know this)
Swings the stroke dealt —
Stroke and a stress that stars and storms deliver,
That guilt is hushed by, hearts are flushed by and melt —
But it rides time like riding a river
(And here the faithful waver, the faithless fable and miss).

7

It dates from day
Of his going in Galilee;
Warm-laid grave of a womb-life grey;

Manger, maiden's knee;
The dense and the driven Passion, and frightful sweat;
Thence the discharge of it, there its swelling to be,
　　Though felt before, though in high flood yet —
What none would have known of it, only the heart, being hard at
　　bay,

8

　　Is out with it! Oh,
　　We lash with the best or worst
Word last! How a lush-kept plush-capped sloe
　　Will, mouthed to flesh-burst,
Gush! — flush the man, the being with it, sour or sweet
Brim, in a flash, full! — Hither then, last or first,
　　To hero of Calvary, Christ's feet —
Never ask if meaning it, wanting it, warned of it — men go.

9

　　Be adored among men,
　　God, three-numberèd form;
Wring thy rebel, dogged in den,
　　Man's malice, with wrecking and storm.
Beyond saying sweet, past telling of tongue,
Thou are lightning and love, I found it, a winter and warm;
　　Father and fondler of heart thou hast wrung:
Hast thy dark descending and most art merciful then.

10

　　With an anvil-ding
　　And with fire in him forge thy will
Or rather, rather then, stealing as Spring
　　Through him, melt him but master him still:
Whether at once, as once at a crash Paul,
Or as Austin, a lingering-out swéet skill,
　　Make mercy in all of us, out of us all
Mastery, but be adored, but be adored King.

Part the Second

11

　　'Some find me a sword; some
　　The flange and the rail; flame,
Fang, or flood' goes Death on drum,
　　And storms bugle his fame.
But wé dream we are rooted in earth — Dust!

Flesh falls within sight of us, we, though our flower the same,
    Wave with the meadow, forget that there must
The sour scythe cringe, and the blear share come.

12

    On Saturday sailed from Bremen,
      American-outward-bound,
  Take settler and seamen, tell men with women,
      Two hundred souls in the round —
O Father, not under thy feathers nor ever as guessing
The goal was a shoal, of a fourth the doom to be drowned;
    Yet did the dark side of the bay of thy blessing
Not vault them, the millions of rounds of thy mercy not reeve even
    them in?

13

    Into the snows she sweeps,
      Hurling the haven behind,
  The Deutschland, on Sunday; and so the sky keeps,
      For the infinite air is unkind,
And the sea flint-flake, black-backed in the regular blow,
Sitting Eastnortheast, in cursed quarter, the wind;
    Wiry and white-fiery and whirlwind-swivellèd snow
Spins to the widow-making unchilding unfathering deeps.

14

    She drove in the dark to leeward,
      She struck — not a reef or a rock
  But the combs of a smother of sand: night drew her
      Dead to the Kentish Knock;
And she beat the bank down with her bows and the ride of her
    keel:
The breakers rolled on her beam with ruinous shock;
    And canvas and compass, the whorl and the wheel
Idle for ever to waft her or wind her with, these she endured.

15

  Hope had grown grey hairs,
    Hope had mourning on,
Trenched with tears, carved with cares,
    Hope was twelve hours gone;
And frightful a nightfall folded rueful a day
Nor rescue, only rocket and lightship, shone,

And lives at last were washing away:
To the shrouds they took, — they shook in the hurling and
  horrible airs.

16

One stirred from the rigging to save
  The wild woman-kind below,
With a rope's end round the man, handy and brave —
  He was pitched to his death at a blow,
For all his dreadnought breast and braids of thew:
They could tell him for hours, dandled the to and fro
  Through the cobbled foam-fleece, what could he do
With the burl of the fountains of air, buck and the flood of the
  wave?

17

They fought with God's cold —
  And they could not and fell to the deck
(Crushed them) or water (and drowned them) or rolled
  With the sea-romp over the wreck.
Night roared, with the heart-break hearing a heart-broke
  rabble,
The woman's wailing, the crying of a child without check —
  Till a lioness arose breasting the babble,
A prophetess towered in the tumult, a virginal tongue told.

18

Ah, touched in your bower of bone
  Are you! turned for an exquisite smart,
Have you! make words break from me here all alone,
  Do you! — mother of being in me, heart.
O unteachably after evil, but uttering truth,
Why tears! is it? tears; such a melting, a madrigal start!
  Never-eldering revel and river of youth,
What can it be, this glee? the good you have there of your
  own?

19

Sister, a sister calling
  A master, her master and mine! —
And the inboard seas run swirling and hawling;
  The rash smart sloggering brine
Blinds her; but she that weather sees one thing, one;
Has one fetch in her: she rears herself to divine

Ears, and the call of the tall nun
To the men in the tops and the tackle rode over the storm's
    brawling.

20

She was first of a five and came
    Of a coifèd sisterhood.
(O Deutschland, double a desperate name!
    O world wide of its good!
But Gertrude, lily, and Luther, are two of a town,
Christ's lily and beast of the waste wood:
    From life's dawn it is drawn down,
Abel is Cain's brother and breasts they have sucked the same.)

21

Loathed for a love men knew in them,
    Banned by the land of their birth,
Rhine refused them. Thames would ruin them;
    Surf, snow, river and earth
Gnashed: but thou art above, thou Orion of light;
Thy unchancelling poising palms were weighing the worth,
    Thou martyr-master: in thy sight
Storm flakes were scroll-leaved flowers, lily showers — sweet
    heaven was astrew in them.

22

Five! the finding and sake
    And cipher of suffering Christ.
Mark, the mark is of man's make
    And the word of it Sacrificed.
But he scores it in scarlet himself on his own bespoken,
Before-time-taken, dearest prizèd and priced —
    Stigma, signal, cinquefoil token
For lettering of the lamb's fleece, ruddying of the rose-flake.

23

Joy fall to thee, father Francis,
    Drawn to the Life that died;
With the gnarls of the nails in thee, niche of the lance, his
    Lovescape crucified
And seal of his seraph-arrival! and these thy daughters
And five-livèd and leavèd favour and pride,
    Are sisterly sealed in wild waters,

To bathe in his fall-gold mercies, to breathe in his all-fire
  glances.

24
Away in the loveable west,
  On a pastoral forehead of Wales,
I was under a roof here, I was at rest,
  And they the prey of the gales;
She to the black-about air, to the breaker, the thickly
Falling flakes, to the throng that catches and quails
  Was calling 'O Christ, Christ, come quickly':
The cross to her she calls Christ to her, christens her wild-worst
  Best.

25
The majesty! what did she mean?
  Breathe, arch and original Breath.
Is it love in her of the being as her lover had been?
  Breathe, body of lovely Death.
They were else-minded then, altogether, the men
Woke thee with a *we are perishing* in the weather of
  Gennesareth.
  Or is it that she cried for the crown then,
The keener to come at the comfort for feeling the combating
  keen?

26
For how to the heart's cheering
  The down-dugged ground-hugged grey
Hovers off, the jay-blue heavens appearing
  Of pied and peeled May!
Blue-beating and hoary-glow height; or night, still higher,
With belled fire and the moth-soft Milky Way,
  What by your measure is the heaven of desire,
The treasure never eyesight got, nor was ever guessed what for the
  hearing?

27
No, but it was not these.
  The jading and jar of the cart,
Time's tasking, it is fathers that asking for ease
  Of the sodden-with-its-sorrowing heart,
Not danger, electrical horror; then further it finds
The appealing of the Passion is tenderer in prayer apart:

Other, I gather, in measure her mind's
Burden, in wind's burly and beat of endragonèd seas.

28

But how shall I . . . make me room there:
Reach me a . . . Fancy, come faster —
Strike you the sight of it? look at it loom there,
Thing that she . . . there then! the Master,
Ipse, the only one, Christ, King, Head:
He was to cure the extremity where he had cast her;
Do, deal, lord it with living and dead;
Let him ride, her pride, in his triumph, despatch and have done
with his doom there.

29

Ah! there was a heart right!
There was single eye!
Read the unshapeable shock night
And knew the who and the why;
Wording it how but by him that present and past,
Heaven and earth are word of, worded by? —
The Simon Peter of a soul! to the blast
Tarpeian-fast, but a blown beacon of light.

30

Jesu, heart's light,
Jesu, maid's son,
What was the feast followed the night
Thou hadst glory of this nun? —
Feast of the one woman without stain.
For so conceivèd, so to conceive thee is done;
But here was heart-throe, birth of a brain,
Word, that heard and kept thee and uttered thee outright.

31

Well, she has thee for the pain, for the
Patience; but pity of the rest of them!
Heart, go and bleed at a bitterer vein for the
Comfortless unconfessed of them —
No not uncomforted: lovely-felicitous Providence
Finger of a tender of, O of a feathery delicacy, the breast of the
Maiden could obey so, be a bell to, ring of it, and
Startle the poor sheep back! is the shipwrack then a harvest, does
tempest carry the grain for thee?

32

I admire thee, master of the tides,
    Of the Yore-flood, of the year's fall;
The recurb and the recovery of the gulf's sides,
    The girth of it and the wharf of it and the wall;
Stanching, quenching ocean of a motionable mind;
Ground of being, and granite of it: past all
    Grasp God, throned behind
Death with a sovereignty that heeds but hides, bodes but abides;

33

    With a mercy that outrides
    The all of water, an ark
For the listener; for the lingerer with a love glides
    Lower than death and the dark;
A vein for the visiting of the past-prayer, pent in prison,
The-last-breath penitent spirits — the uttermost mark
    Our passion-plungèd giant risen,
The Christ of the Father compassionate, fetched in the storm of his
    strides.

34

    Now burn, new born to the world,
    Doubled-naturèd name,
The heaven-flung, heart-fleshed, maiden-furled
    Miracle-in-Mary-of-flame,
Mid-numbered He in three of the thunder-throne!
Not a dooms-day dazzle in his coming nor dark as he came;
    Kind, but royally reclaiming his own;
A released shower, let flash to the shire, not a lightning of fire
    hard-hurled.

35

    Dame, at our door
    Drowned, and among our shoals,
    Remember us in the roads, the heaven-haven of the
    Reward:
        Our King back, oh, upon English souls!
Let him easter in us, be a dayspring to the dimness of us, be a
    crimson-cresseted east,
More brightening her, rare-dear Britain, as his reign rolls,
    Pride, rose, prince, hero of us, high-priest,
Our hearts' charity's hearth's fire, our thoughts' chivalry's throng's
    Lord.

THE WINDHOVER

To Christ our Lord

Written in 1877, this poem combines a characteristic intensity of religious feeling and sense of natural beauty. Its conclusion is symbolic of Crucifixion and sacrifice.

I caught this morning morning's minion, kingdom of daylight's
    dauphin, dapple-dawn-drawn Falcon, in his riding
  Of the rolling level underneath him steady air, and striding
High there, how he rung upon the rein of a wimpling wing
In his ecstasy! then off, off forth on swing,
    As a skate's heel sweeps smooth on a bow-bend: the hurl and
      gliding
  Rebuffed the big wind. My heart in hiding
Stirred for a bird, — the achieve of, the mastery of the thing!

Brute beauty and valour and act, oh, air, pride, plume here
  Buckle! AND the fire that breaks from thee then, a billion
Times told lovelier, more dangerous, O my chevalier!

  No wonder of it: shéer plód makes plough down sillion
Shine, and blue-beak embers, ah my dear,
  Fall, gall themselves, and gash gold-vermilion.

PIED BEAUTY

Written in the summer of 1877, this is a curtal or shortened sonnet.

Glory be to God for dappled things —
  For skies of couple-colour as a brinded cow;
    For rose-moles all in stipple upon trout that swim;
Fresh-firecoal chestnut-falls; finches' wings;
  Landscape plotted and pieced — fold, fallow, and plough;
    And áll trádes, their gear and tackle and trim.

All things counter, original, spare, strange;
  Whatever is fickle, freckled (who knows how?)
    With swift, slow; sweet, sour; adazzle, dim;
He fathers-forth whose beauty is past change:
            Praise him.

NO WORST, THERE IS NONE

'No Worst, There is None' is one of the five 'Sonnets of Desolation', as they became known, written in 1885. In 1884 Hopkins had been appointed Fellow in Classics and Professor at University College, Dublin. Though the more depressing aspects of academic life, unreceptive students and inordinate examination marking, were not solely responsible for his state of mind, Hopkins was little suited to the tedium of such teaching. The sonnets came to him 'against my will', he wrote to Robert Bridges on 1 September 1885, describing his academic life to Bridges as 'one of a continually jaded and harassed mind'.

The sestet of this sonnet is particularly powerful in its representation of the intellectual precipice by which the mind may be threatened. In certain aspects, this recalls Browning's reference to 'the dangerous edge of things' in 'Bishop Blougram's Apology'.

No worst, there is none. Pitched past pitch of grief,
More pangs will, schooled at forepangs, wilder wring.
Comforter, where, where is your comforting?
Mary, mother of us, where is your relief?
My cries heave, herds-long; huddle in a main, a chief
Woe, wórld-sorrow; on an áge-old anvil wince and sing —
Then lull, then leave off. Fury had shrieked 'No ling-
    ering!
Let me be fell: force I must be brief'.

  O the mind, mind has mountains; cliffs of fall
Frightful, sheer, no-man-fathomed. Hold them cheap
May who ne'er hung there. Nor does long our small
Durance deal with that steep or deep. Here! creep,
Wretch, under a comfort serves in a whirlwind: all
Life death does end and each day dies with sleep.

I WAKE AND FEEL THE FELL OF DARK

The third 'Sonnet of Desolation' is an account of waking at night,
the 'fell' of dark combining the meanings of the word, bitterness, a
blow, and fleece or skin most prominent among them. The only
comfort, at the end of the poem, may be that the damned are
theologically more wretched than the poet.

> I wake and feel the fell of dark, not day.
> What hours, O what black hoürs we have spent
> This night! what sights you, heart, saw; ways you went!
> And more must, in yet longer light's delay.
>   With witness I speak this. But where I say
> Hours I mean years, mean life. And my lament
> Is cries countless, cries like dead letters sent
> To dearest him that lives alas! away.
>
>   I am gall, I am heartburn. God's most deep decree
> Bitter would have me taste: my taste was me;
> Bones built in me, flesh filled, blood brimmed the curse.
>   Selfyeast of spirit a dull dough sours. I see
> The lost are like this, and their scourge to be
> As I am mine, their sweating selves; but worse.

'THOU ART INDEED JUST, LORD'

*Justus quidem tu es, Domine, si disputem tecum: verumtamen
justa loquar ad te: Quare via impiorum prosperatur? &c.*

Hopkins died of typhoid in 1889, at the age of forty-five, his poetry
not destined to be published until 1918. In this quiet sonnet, written
in the last year of his life, he argues gently with God about the
apparent futility of all that he attempts. The epigraph to the sonnet
is from the Vulgate version of Jeremiah, xii, 1. 'Thou indeed, O
Lord, art just if I plead with Thee, but yet I will speak what is just
to Thee: Why doth the way of the wicked prosper?' In the previous
year, Hopkins told Bridges that he was producing nothing by way
of poetry. 'Nothing comes: I am a eunuch — but it is for the
kingdom of heaven's sake.' The reference in the sonnet to 'fretty
chervil' is to cow parsley with its serrated leaves.

Thou art indeed just, Lord, if I contend
With thee; but, sir, so what I plead is just.
Why do sinners' ways prosper? and why must
Disappointment all I endeavour end?
    Wert thou my enemy, O thou my friend,
How wouldst thou worse, I wonder, than thou dost
Defeat, thwart me? Oh, the sots and thralls of lust
Do in spare hours more thrive than I that spend,
Sir, life upon thy cause. See, banks and brakes
Now, leavèd how thick! lacèd they are again
With fretty chervil, look, and fresh wind shakes
Them; birds build — but not I build; no, but strain,
Time's eunuch, and not breed one work that wakes.
Mine, O thou lord of life, send my roots rain.

Francis Thompson
THE HOUND OF HEAVEN

Francis Thompson (1859–1907) failed through ill-health in his attempts to be either a priest or a doctor. He suffered from tuberculosis and, in consequence of medical treatment, became addicted to opium. He was more or less destitute on the streets of London when rescued by the poet Alice Meynell. Thompson's Catholicism is the mainspring of 'The Hound of Heaven', though its religious and spiritual appeal was among the most widespread and popular of any in the Victorian period. It was not published until 1893, yet its haunting and haunted stanzas belong more appropriately to a select body of late-Victorian verse on religious themes. 'Since Gabriel's *Blessed Damozel*,' said Edward Burne-Jones wistfully, 'no mystical words have so touched me as *The Hound of Heaven*.' Elsewhere, Thompson was compared to his celebrated Catholic predecessor of the seventeenth century, Richard Crashaw. To a later age, his poem may seem to have an element of the melodramatic or cinematic in its personal drama.

I fled Him, down the nights and down the days;
    I fled Him, down the arches of the years;
I fled Him, down the labyrinthine ways
    Of my own mind; and in the mist of tears
I hid from Him, and under running laughter.
        Up vistaed hopes, I sped;
        And shot, precipitated,

Adown Titanic glooms of chasmèd fears,
  From those strong Feet that followed, followed after.

      But with unhurrying chase,
      And unperturbèd pace,
Deliberate speed, majestic instancy,
      They beat — and a Voice beat
      More instant than the Feet —
'All things betray thee, who betrayest Me.'

      I pleaded, outlaw-wise,
By many a hearted casement, curtained red,
  Trellised with intertwining charities
(For, though I knew His love Who followèd,
      Yet was I sore adread
Lest, having Him, I must have naught beside);
But, if one little casement parted wide,
  The gust of His approach would clash it to.
  Fear wist not to evade as Love wist to pursue.
Across the margent of the world I fled,
  And troubled the gold gateways of the stars,
  Smiting for shelter on their clangèd bars;
      Fretted to dulcet jars
And silvern chatter the pale ports o' the moon.
I said to dawn: Be sudden; to eve: Be soon —
  With thy young skyey blossoms heap me over
      From this tremendous Lover!
Float thy vague veil about me, lest He see!
  I tempted all His servitors, but to find
My own betrayal in their constancy,
In faith to Him their fickleness to me,
  Their traitorous trueness, and their loyal deceit.
To all swift things for swiftness did I sue;
  Clung to the whistling mane of every wind.
      But whether they swept, smoothly fleet,
      The long savannahs of the blue;
      Or whether, Thunder-driven,
      They clanged His chariot 'thwart a heaven,
Plashy with flying lightnings round the spurn o' their feet:
Fear wist not to evade as Love wist to pursue.

      Still with unhurrying chase,
      And unperturbèd pace,
  Deliberate speed, majestic instancy,
      Came on the following Feet,

And a Voice above their beat —
'Naught shelters thee, who wilt not shelter Me.'

I sought no more that after which I strayed
      In face of man or maid;
But still within the little children's eyes
      Seems something, something that replies,
They at least are for me, surely for me!
I turned me to them very wistfully;
But just as their young eyes grew sudden fair
      With dawning answers there,
Their angel plucked them from me by the hair.
'Come then, ye other children, Nature's — share
With me' (said I) 'your delicate fellowship;
      Let me greet you lip to lip,
      Let me twine with you caresses,
          Wantoning
      With our Lady-Mother's vagrant tresses,
          Banqueting
      With her in her wind-walled palace,
      Underneath her azured daïs,
      Quaffing, as your taintless way is,
          From a chalice
Lucent-weeping out of the dayspring.'
      So it was done:
I in their delicate fellowship was one —
Drew the bolt of Nature's secrecies.
      I knew all the swift importings
      On the wilful face of skies;
      I knew how the clouds arise,
      Spumèd of the wild sea-snortings;
         All that's born or dies
      Rose and drooped with; made them shapers
Of mine own moods, or wailful or divine —
      With them joyed and was bereaven.
      I was heavy with the even,
    When she lit her glimmering tapers
      Round the day's dead sanctities.
      I laughed in the morning's eyes.
I triumphed and I saddened with all weather,
      Heaven and I wept together,
And its sweet tears were salt with mortal mine;
Against the red throb of its sunset-heart

> I laid my own to beat,
>   And share commingling heat;
> But not by that, by that, was eased my human smart.
> In vain my tears were wet on Heaven's grey cheek.
> For ah! we know not what each other says,
>   These things and I; in sound *I* speak —
> *Their* sound is but their stir, they speak by silences.
> Nature, poor stepdame, cannot slake my drouth;
>   Let her, if she would owe me,
> Drop yon blue bosom-veil of sky, and show me
>   The breasts o' her tenderness:
> Never did any milk of hers once bless
>   My thirsting mouth.

> Nigh and nigh draws the chase,
>   With unperturbèd pace,
> Deliberate speed, majestic instancy,
>   And past those noisèd Feet
>   A voice comes yet more fleet —
> 'Lo! naught contents thee, who content'st not Me.'

Naked I wait Thy love's uplifted stroke!
My harness piece by piece Thou has hewn from me,
    And smitten me to my knee;
    I am defenceless utterly.
    I slept, methinks, and woke.
And, slowly gazing, find me stripped in sleep.
In the rash lustihead of my young powers,
    I shook the pillaring hours
And pulled my life upon me; grimed with smears,
I stand amid the dust o' the mounded years —
My mangled youth lies dead beneath the heap.
My days have crackled and gone up in smoke,
Have puffed and burst as sun-starts on a stream.
    Yea, faileth now even dream
The dreamer, and the lute the lutanist;
Even the linked fantasies, in whose blossomy twist
I swung the earth a trinket at my wrist,
Are yielding; cords of all too weak account
For earth, with heavy griefs so overplussed.
    Ah! is Thy love indeed
A weed, albeit an amaranthine weed,
Suffering no flowers except its own to mount?
    Ah! must —

      Designer infinite! —
Ah! must Thou char the wood ere Thou canst limn with it?
My freshness spent its wavering shower i' the dust;
And now my heart is as a broken fount,
Wherein tear-drippings stagnate, spilt down ever
      From the dank thoughts that shiver
Upon the sighful branches of my mind.
      Such is; what is to be?
The pulp so bitter, how shall taste the rind?
I dimly guess what Time in mists confounds;
Yet ever and anon a trumpet sounds
From the hid battlements of Eternity:
Those shaken mists a space unsettle, then
Round the half-glimpsèd turrets slowly wash again;

      But not ere him who summoneth
      I first have seen, enwound
With glooming robes purpureal, cypress-crowned;
His name I know, and what his trumpet saith.
Whether man's heart or life it be which yields
      Thee harvest, must Thy harvest fields
      Be dunged with rotten death?

      Now of that long pursuit
      Comes on at hand the bruit;
   That Voice is round me like a bursting sea:
      'And is thy earth so marred,
      Shattered in shard on shard?
   Lo, all things fly thee, for thou fliest Me!
      Strange, piteous, futile thing,
Wherefore should any set thee love apart?
Seeing none but I makes much of naught' (He said),
'And human love needs human meriting:
      How hast thou merited —
Of all man's clotted clay the dingiest clot?
      Alack, thou knowest not
How little worthy of any love thou art!
Whom wilt thou find to love ignoble thee,
      Save Me, save only Me?
All which I took from thee I did but take,
      Not for thy harms,
But just that thou might'st seek it in My arms.
      All which thy child's mistake

Fancies as lost, I have stored for thee at home:
　Rise, clasp My hand, and come.'

　Halts by me that footfall:
　Is my gloom, after all,
Shade of His hand, outstretched caressingly?
　'Ah, fondest, blindest, weakest,
　I am He Whom thou seekest!
Thou dravest love from thee, who dravest Me.'

ARMY AND EMPIRE

Sir Francis Doyle
THE PRIVATE OF THE BUFFS

Sir Francis Hastings Doyle (1810–1888) published a number of
volumes of poetry on contemporary events and succeeded Matthew
Arnold as Professor of Poetry at Oxford in 1867. The present poem
commemorates the death of Private John Moyse who was taken
prisoner in the Third China War of 1856–60 and executed when
he refused to 'kow-tow' to a Tartar mandarin. Humble in rank, he
shows a pride and nobility that might have graced Lord Elgin,
British envoy with the expedition which was led by General Sir
Robert Napier. The poem is one of many in which the Victorians
celebrated the courage of ordinary soldiers in the face of death or
defeat.

Last night, among his fellow roughs,
   He jested, quaff'd, and swore;
A drunken private of the Buffs,
   Who never look'd before.
To-day, beneath the foeman's frown,
   He stands in Elgin's place,
Ambassador from Britain's crown
   And type of all her race.

Poor, reckless, rude, low-born, untaught,
   Bewilder'd, and alone,
A heart with English instinct fraught
   He yet can call his own.
Aye, tear his body limb from limb,
   Bring cord, or axe, or flame:
He only knows, that not through him
   Shall England come to shame.

Far Kentish hop-fields round him seem'd,
   Like dreams, to come and go;
Bright leagues of cherry-blossom gleam'd,
   One sheet of living snow;
The smoke above his father's door
   In grey soft eddyings hung:
Must he then watch it rise no more,
   Doom'd by himself, so young?

Yes, honour calls! — with strength like steel
    He put the vision by.
Let dusky Indians whine and kneel;
    An English lad must die.
And thus, with eyes that would not shrink,
    With knee to man unbent,
Unfaltering on its dreadful brink,
    To his red grave he went.

Vain, mightiest fleets of iron framed;
    Vain, those all-shattering guns;
Unless proud England keep, untamed,
    The strong heart of her sons.
So, let his name through Europe ring —
    A man of mean estate,
Who died, as firm as Sparta's king,
    Because his soul was great.

G. H. Boker
DIRGE FOR A SOLDIER

By no means all poems on the fate of the private soldier required a
Kiplingesque hero. G. H. Boker (1823–90) offers a lament for the
unknown Victorian soldier of so many battlefields of the Sikh Wars
or the China campaigns.

Close his eyes; his work is done.
    What to him is friend or foeman,
Rise of moon or set of sun,
    Hand of man or kiss of woman?

Lay him low, lay him low,
In the clover or the snow!
What cares he? He cannot know:
    Lay him low!

As man may, he fought his fight,
    Proved his truth by his endeavour:
Let him sleep in solemn night,
    Sleep for ever and for ever.

Fold him in his country's stars,
    Roll the drum and fire the volley!
What to him are all our wars?
    What but death bemocking folly?

Leave him to God's watching eye:
    Trust him to the hand that made him.
Mortal love weeps idly by:
    God alone has power to aid him.

Lay him low, lay him low,
In the clover or the snow!
What cares he? He cannot know:
    Lay him low!

Slade Murray

OH! 'TIS A FAMOUS STORY OF BALACLAVA

The Charge of the Light Brigade at Balaclava on 25 October 1854 was an emotive event in Victorian life. A large Russian army menaced the British Crimean expeditionary force at Balaclava. Early that day, the Russians took the Turkish guns on a flank of the position. Lord Raglan, from the heights above, ordered their recapture. The order was received in the valley by men who saw only the main Russian artillery across the far end. The Light Cavalry Brigade rode at the most powerful armament of the industrial age, the Earl of Cardigan at their head in dress uniform of the 11th Hussars. The 17th Lancers carried only bamboo shafts, metal-tipped. As the guns opened up, the slaughter was appalling. Of 670 men, 193 returned twenty minutes later. With most of their officers dead, ordinary troopers rallied survivors. But against all odds they overran the Russian guns. Questions were asked about the 'blunder' of command, none about the courage of the men who obeyed. Tennyson's poem was more famous but Slade Murray's music-hall ballad caught the mood of national pride. To read accounts of the action unmoved, is a task reserved for the literary critic.

Six hundred stalwart warriors of England's pride the best,
Did grasp the lance and sabre on Balaclava's crest,
And with their trusty leader, Earl Cardigan the brave,
Dashed through the Russian valley to glory or a grave.

Their foemen stood in thousands, a dark and awful mass,
Beneath their famous strongholds resolved to guard the pass,
Their guns with fierce defiance belched thunders up the vale,
Where sat our English horsemen firm beneath the iron gale.

Oh! 'tis a famous story, proclaim it far and wide,
And let your children's children re-echo it with pride,
How Cardigan the fearless, his name immortal made,
When he crossed that Russian valley with the famous Light
    Brigade.

Brave Nolan brought the order, Good God can it be true,
Cried Cardigan the fearless, and my Brigade so few,
To take those awful cannon from yonder teeming mass,
'Tis madness, sir, where shall we charge — what guns bring from
    the pass?
The messenger with hauteur looked once at the brave Earl,
Then pointing to the enemy, his lip began to curl.
There, there, my lord, there are your guns and there your foemen
    too,
Then turned his charger's head away, and bade the Earl adieu.

Oh! 'tis a famous story, proclaim it far and wide,
And let your children's children re-echo it with pride,
How Cardigan the fearless, his name immortal made,
When he crossed that Russian valley with the famous Light
    Brigade.

And they were but six hundred, 'gainst two score thousand foes,
Hemmed in with furious cannon, and crushed with savage blows.
Yet fought they there like heroes, for our noble England's fame,
Oh glorious charge! Heroic deed! What honour crowns thy name!
Four hundred of those soldiers fell, fighting where they stood,
And thus that fatal death vale they enriched with English blood.
Four hundred of those soldiers bequeathed their lives away,
To the England they had fought for on that wild October day.

Oh! 'tis a famous story, proclaim it far and wide,
And let your children's children re-echo it with pride,
How Cardigan the fearless, his name immortal made,
When he crossed that Russian valley with the famous Light
    Brigade.

Mary E. Leslie
MASSACRE AT CAWNPORE, 1857

In the whole of British imperial experience, there were few events that haunted the public imagination more poignantly than the massacre of women and children at Cawnpore on 15 July 1857, during the opening months of the Indian Mutiny. When the insurgents took Cawnpore, it was first agreed that the women and children should be evacuated under safe conduct on 27 June. When this was attempted, there was a moment of panic, an exchange of shots, and the Nana Sahib's forces opened fire, killing many of the evacuees. The surviving women and children were taken to the so-called House of Women. On 15 July, several men who were butchers by trade entered the house and systematically slaughtered every woman and child, their remains filling a well fifty feet deep. The news provoked public grief, anger, and revulsion when it reached England. Mary Leslie's poem, published in *Sorrows, Aspirations, and Legends from India* (1858) once again captures the public mood.

They range themselves to die, hand clasping hand —
That mournful brotherhood in death and woe —
While one with saddened voice, yet calm and slow,
Read holy words about yon better land,
Upon whose ever-blushing summer strand
Comes never shadow of a fiendish foe,
Nor hellish treachery like to that below
Is with malignant hatred coldly planned —
Then prayed. O Crucified, didst Thou not stoop
Down from above with Thy deep sympathy,
Soothing the suffering, bleeding, huddled group,
While the fierce vollies poured in hurriedly,
And with uplifted swords the yelling troop
Rushed to complete their deed of perfidy?

But all is over — the fierce agony
Of men who could not their beloveds save
From unheard tortures, and a common grave
Heaped high with quivering, crushed humanity —
The frantic woe of women forced to see
Their tiny infants, unto whom they clave
With love which could all fear and torment brave,

Dashed down upon the ground unpityingly:
And nought remains but the wet, bloody floor,
And little rings of soft, white baby-hair
Mingled with long, dark tresses, dimmed with gore,
In hopeless tangles scattered here and there,
And God's own blessed Book of holy lore,
Sole comforter amid that deep despair.

Sir Alfred Lyall
STUDIES AT DELHI

After the suppression of the mutiny, the Victorian period was never again to see a threat to British rule in India. Economic, educational and political development took the place of the less enlightened commercialism of the East India Company. Viceroys of India now ruled in the Queen's name. A new and more agreeable social life took its lead from the viceregal court in Calcutta or the viceregal lodge in the cool hills of Simla. This change is reflected in the poetry of Sir Alfred Lyall (1835–1911), an administrator who became Lieutenant-Governor of the North-West Provinces and Oudh in 1882–7.

(i) The Hindu Ascetic
Here as I sit by the Jumna bank,
    Watching the flow of the sacred stream,
Pass me the legions, rank on rank,
    And the cannon roar, and the bayonets gleam.

Is it a god or a king that comes?
    Both are evil, and both are strong;
With women and worshipping, dancing and drums,
    Carry your gods and your kings along.

Fanciful shapes of a plastic earth,
    These are the visions that weary the eye;
These I may 'scape by a luckier birth,
    Musing, and fasting, and hoping to die.

When shall these phantoms flicker away
    Like the smoke of the guns on the wind-swept hill,
Like the sounds and colours of yesterday:
    And the soul have rest, and the air be still?

(ii) Badminton

Hardly a shot from the gate we storm'd,
  Under the Moree battlement's shade;
Close to the glacis our game was form'd,
  There had the fight been, and there we play'd.

Lightly the demoiselles titter'd and leapt,
  Merrily caper'd the players all;
North, was the garden where Nicholson slept,
  South, was the sweep of a batter'd wall.

Near me a Musalmán, civil and mild,
  Watch'd as the shuttlecocks rose and fell;
And he said, as he counted his beads and smiled,
  'God smite their souls to the depths of hell.'

A NIGHT IN THE RED SEA

Until the opening of the Suez Canal in 1869, the short route to
India was by train across France to Marseille, ship to Port Said, a
dash in a type of horse-bus across the Isthmus of Suez and then ship
down the Red Sea, across the Indian Ocean to Bombay. Even after
the opening of the canal, the Red Sea still marked the meridian of
the journey. In Lyall's poem, the Exile's Gate is the strait of Bab-el-
Mandeb or the Gate of Tears, linking the Red Sea and the Gulf of
Aden.

The strong hot breath of the land is lashing
  The wild sea-horses, they rear and race;
The plunging bows of our ships are dashing
  Full in the fiery south wind's face.

She rends the water, it foams and follows,
  And the silvery jet of the towering spray,
And the phosphor sparks in the deep wave hollows,
  Lighten the line of our midnight way.

The moon above, with its full-orbed lustre,
  Lifting the veil of the slumberous land,
Gleams o'er a desolate island cluster,
  And the breakers white on the lonely sand.

And a bare hill-range in the distance frowning
    Dim wrapt in haze like a shrouded ghost,
With its jagged peaks the horizon crowning,
    Broods o'er the stark Arabian coast.

See, on the edge of the waters leaping,
    The lamp, far flashing, of Perim's strait
Glitters and grows, as the ship goes sweeping
    Fast on its course for the Exile's Gate.

And onward still to the broadening ocean
    Out of the narrow and perilous seas,
Till we rock with a large and listless motion
    In the moist soft air of the Indian breeze.

And the Southern Cross, like a standard flying,
    Hangs in the front of the tropic night,
But the Great Bear sinks, like a hero dying,
    And the Pole-star lowers its signal light;

And the round earth rushes toward the morning,
    And the waves grow paler and wan the foam,
Misty and dim, with a glance of warning,
    Vanish the stars of my northern home.

Let the wide waste sea for a space divide me,
    Till the close-coiled circles of time unfold,
Till the stars rise westward to greet and guide me,
    When the exile ends, and the years are told.

Walter Yeldham
FOR ENGLAND HO!

Walter Yeldham wrote under the pseudonym of 'Aliph Cheem' and his poem appeared in *Lays of Ind*, published in Calcutta in 1875. Despite the myth of the rapacious and greedy coloniser, India was not a popular posting. Wealthy officers paid other men to do their tours of duty there, tours which might last for ten or eleven years. The death rate from disease and drink was high. Yeldham's regiment, which had seen half its six hundred men die, would in truth probably have left England eleven years before, leaving also its wives and families. As the *Naval and Military Gazette* put it,

'none but needy adventurers and seedy boys' were eager for Indian
service. The greatest prize for most men was a passage back to
England.

The morning sun is shining o'er the harbour of Bombay,
And the gallant trooper *Crocodile* is getting under weigh;
Her snowy sides give shelter to a thousand men or so,
My regiment and another; and the word's 'For England Ho!'

We've worked our foreign service out, our full apportioned time;
Eleven lagging years we've spent in India's sunny clime —
Eleven years — a goodish hole to knock out of a life,
A change-effecting term on soil where cholera is rife

Yes, change indeed! We left old England full six hundred strong;
And scarce three hundred faces to the ancient roll belong.
Three hundred comrades blotted out! The tribute that we pay
To death and sickness as the price of Oriental sway!

No part we've played in battle scenes, no glory have we won.
We've done our duty quietly, as nowadays 'tis done;
Ours certainly has been the uneventfullest of trades —
A round of drills, diversified with funeral parades . . .

Still, as I cheer I can't expel the sorrow from my mind,
I cannot drown the memory of those we leave behind.
I wave my cap to India, fast sinking in the blue,
But the shadows of my comrades seem to wave me their adieu.

Good-bye, my friends: although the bullet did not lay you low,
A thought, a tear upon your graves, at least your brothers owe;
Ye died for England, though ye died not 'mid the cannon's boom,
Nor any 'mention in despatches' glorified your tomb.

The breeze is fair, the sails are spread, the screw goes grinding
        round,
The hills beyond Bombay are dwindling to a little mound.
One last long look! Farewell, farewell, thou region of the sun!
Old England is before us, and our exile it is done!

Rudyard Kipling
A CODE OF MORALS

Few major Victorian writers were prepared to spend much time on imperial themes, which they regarded as being beneath their notice. Rudyard Kipling (1865–1936) was an exception, though he belongs to that later Victorian period when life in India had become more relaxed and self-regarding for the Raj. The energy and imagination of certain Viceroys, notably Lord Curzon who held office from 1899 to 1905, had certainly made life more physically agreeable for Indians and English alike. Kipling's is the India of this later and more relaxed culture, when many Indians as well as Englishmen were to become Anglo-Indian in culture and education. In some of his earlier and less well-known poems, Kipling cast a sardonic glance at the social comedy of imperial life. The present poem is a good example.

> Lest you should think this story true
> I merely mention I
> Evolved it lately. 'Tis a most
> Unmitigated misstatement.

Now Jones had left his new-wed bride to keep his house in order,
And hied away to the Hurrum Hills above the Afghan border,
To sit on a rock with a heliograph; but ere he left he taught
His wife the working of the Code that sets the miles at naught.

And Love had made him very sage, as Nature made her fair;
So Cupid and Apollo linked, *per* heliograph, the pair.
At dawn, across the Hurrum Hills, he flashed her counsel wise —
At e'en, the dying sunset bore her husband's homilies.

He warned her 'gainst seductive youths in scarlet clad and gold,
As much as 'gainst the blandishments paternal of the old;
But kept his gravest warnings for (hereby the ditty hangs)
That snowy-haired Lothario, Lieutenant-General Bangs.

'Twas General Bangs, with Aide and Staff, who tittupped on the
    way,
When they beheld a heliograph tempestuously at play.
They thought of Border risings, and of stations sacked and
    burnt —
So stopped to take the message down — and this is what they
    learnt —

'Dash dot dot dot, dot dash, dot dash dot' twice. The General
  swore.
'Was ever General Officer addressed as "dear" before?
'"My Love," i' faith! "My Duck," Gadzooks! "My darling popsy-
  wop!"
'Spirit of great Lord Wolseley, *who* is on that mountain-top?'

The artless Aide-de-camp was mute; the gilded Staff were still,
As, dumb with pent-up mirth, they booked that message from the
  hill;
For clear as summer lightning-flare, the husband's warning ran: —
'Don't dance or ride with General Bangs — a most immoral man.'

[At dawn, across the Hurrum Hills, he flashed her counsel wise —
But, howsoever Love be blind, the world at large hath eyes.]
With damnatory dot and dash he heliographed his wife
Some interesting details of the General's private life.

The artless Aide-de-camp was mute, the shining Staff were still,
And red and ever redder grew the General's shaven gill.
And this is what he said at last (his feelings matter not): —
'I think we've tapped a private line. Hi! Threes about there! Trot!'

All honour unto Bangs, for ne'er did Jones thereafter know
By word or act official who read off that helio.
But the tale is on the Frontier, and from Michni to Mool*tan*
They know the worthy General as 'that most immoral man.'

THE POST THAT FITTED

Kipling's comedy was sometimes close to slapstick and, in the
present case, the effect may be exaggerated. What he achieves,
however, is nonetheless a reflection of the social taboos and
anxieties of expatriate society.

Though tangled and twisted the course of true love
    This ditty explains,
No tangle's so tangled it cannot improve
    If the Lover has brains.

Ere the steamer bore him Eastward, Sleary was engaged to marry
An attractive girl at Tunbridge, whom he called 'my little Carrie.'

Sleary's pay was very modest; Sleary was the other way.
Who can cook a two-plate dinner on eight poor rupees a day?

Long he pondered o'er the question in his scantly furnished
    quarters —
Then proposed to Minnie Boffkin, eldest of Judge Boffkin's
    daughters.
Certainly an impecunious Subaltern was not a catch,
But the Boffkins knew that Minnie mightn't make another match.

So they recognised the business and, to feed and clothe the bride,
Got him made a Something Something somewhere on the Bombay
    side.
Anyhow, the billet carried pay enough for him to marry —
As the artless Sleary put it: — 'Just the thing for me and Carrie.'

Did he, therefore, jilt Miss Boffkin — impulse of a baser mind?
No! He started epileptic fits of an appalling kind.
[Of his *modus operandi* only this much I could gather: —
'Pears's shaving sticks will give you little taste and lots of lather.']

Frequently in public places his affliction used to smite
Sleary with distressing vigour — always in the Boffkins' sight.
Ere a week was over Minnie weepingly returned his ring,
Told him his 'unhappy weakness' stopped all thought of marrying.

Sleary bore the information with a chastened holy joy, —
Epileptic fits don't matter in Political employ, —
Wired three short words to Carrie — took his ticket, packed his
    kit —
Bade farewell to Minnie Boffkin in one last, long, lingering fit.

Four weeks later, Carrie Sleary read — and laughed until she
    wept —
Mrs Boffkin's warning letter on the 'wretched epilept.' . . .
Year by year, in pious patience, vengeful Mrs Boffkin sits
Waiting for the Sleary babies to develop Sleary's fits.

PAGETT MP

The most disliked person in India was that man or woman in
England who exploited the hardships of the Indians or the Raj for
his or her own ends. In the following poem, the fatuous Member of
Parliament, Pagett, comes to India and gets exactly what he
deserves. 'Chota Bursat' are the early rains.

> The toad beneath the harrow knows
> Exactly where each tooth-point goes;
> The butterfly upon the road
> Preaches contentment to that toad.

Pagett, MP, was a liar, and a fluent liar therewith, —
He spoke of the heat of India as 'The Asian Solar Myth';
Came on a four months' visit, to 'study the East' in November,
And I got him to make an agreement vowing to stay till September.

March came in with the *köil*. Pagett was cool and gay,
Called me a 'bloated Brahmin,' talked of my 'princely pay.'
March went out with the roses. 'Where is your heat?' said he.
'Coming,' said I to Pagett. 'Skittles!' said Pagett, MP.

April began with the punkah, coolies, and prickly-heat, —
Pagett was dear to mosquitoes, sandflies found him a treat.
He grew speckled and lumpy — hammered, I grieve to say,
Aryan brothers who fanned him, in an illiberal way.

May set in with a dust-storm, — Pagett went down with the sun.
All the delights of the season tickled him one by one.
Imprimis — ten days' 'liver' — due to his drinking beer;
Later, a dose of fever — slight, but he called it severe.

Dysent'ry touched him in June, after the *Chota Bursat* —
Lowered his portly person — made him yearn to depart.
He didn't call me a 'Brahmin,' or 'bloated,' or 'overpaid,'
But seemed to think it a wonder that any one ever stayed.

July was a trifle unhealthy, — Pagett was ill with fear,
Called it the 'Cholera Morbus,' hinted that life was dear.
He babbled of 'Eastern exile,' and mentioned his home with tears;
But I hadn't seen *my* children for close upon seven years.

We reached a hundred and twenty once in the Court at noon,
[I've mentioned Pagett was portly] Pagett went off in a swoon.
That was an end to the business. Pagett, the perjured, fled
With a practical, working knowledge of 'Solar Myths' in his head.

And I laughed as I drove from the station, but the mirth died out
    on my lips
As I thought of the fools like Pagett who write of their 'Eastern
    trips,'
And the sneers of the travelled idiots who duly misgovern the land,
And I prayed to the Lord to deliver another one into my hand.

DANNY DEEVER

At their best, Kipling's poems are once read and never forgotten. This is true of 'Danny Deever', the execution by hanging of a private soldier in the presence of his regiment for shooting a comrade. The grim ritual, the whispers in the ranks, the condemned man's coffin in its place beside him, are all graphically suggested in Kipling's ballad.

'What are the bugles blowin' for?' said Files-on-Parade.
'To turn you out, to turn you out,' the Colour-Sergeant said.
'What makes you look so white, so white?' said Files-on-Parade.
'I'm dreadin' what I've got to watch,' the Colour-Sergeant said.
 For they're hangin' Danny Deever, you can hear the Dead
  March play,
  The regiment's in 'ollow square — they're hangin' him to-day;
  They've taken of his buttons off an' cut his stripes away,
  An' they're hangin' Danny Deever in the mornin'.

'What makes the rear-rank breathe so 'ard?' said Files-on-Parade.
'It's bitter cold, it's bitter cold,' the Colour-Sergeant said.
'What makes that front-rank man fall down?' said Files-on-Parade.
'A touch o' sun, a touch o' sun,' the Colour-Sergeant said.
 They are hangin' Danny Deever, they are marchin' of 'im round,
  They 'ave 'alted Danny Deever by 'is coffin on the ground;
  An' 'e'll swing in 'arf a minute for a sneakin' shootin' hound —
  O they're hangin' Danny Deever in the mornin'!

''Is cot was right-'and cot to mine,' said Files-on-Parade.
''E's sleepin' out an' far to-night,' the Colour-Sergeant said.
'I've drunk 'is beer a score o' times,' said Files-on-Parade.
''E's drinkin' bitter beer alone,' the Colour-Sergeant said.
 They are hangin' Danny Deever, you must mark 'im to 'is place,
  For 'e shot a comrade sleepin' — you must look 'im in the face;
  Nine 'undred of 'is county an' the Regiment's disgrace,
  While they're hangin' Danny Deever in the mornin'.

'What's that so black agin the sun?' said Files-on-Parade.
'It's Danny fightin' 'ard for life,' the Colour-Sergeant said.
'What's that that whimpers over'ead?' said Files-on-Parade.
'It's Danny's soul that's passin' now,' the Colour-Sergeant said.
 For they're done with Danny Deever, you can 'ear the quickstep
  play,
  The regiment's in column, an' they're marchin' us away;

Ho! the young recruits are shakin', an' they'll want their beer to-
day,
After hangin' Danny Deever in the mornin'!

THE SERGEANT'S WEDDIN'

A great attraction in Kipling is the humanity with which he presents
the life of the 'other ranks'. He never did so with greater effect than
in 'The Sergeant's Weddin'' with the muttered insults of the
reluctant guard of honour. Kipling is too reticent to complete the
final line of the refrain, 'And a rogue is married to a whore', but it
can have no other completion nor rhyme.

'E was warned agin 'er —
   That's what made 'im look;
She was warned agin' 'im —
   That is why she took.
'Wouldn't 'ear no reason,
   'Went an' done it blind;
We know all about 'em,
   They've got all to find!

Cheer for the Sergeant's weddin' —
   Give 'em one cheer more!
Grey gun-'orses in the lando,
   An' a rogue is married to, etc.

What's the use o' tellin'
   'Arf the lot she's been?
'E's a bloomin' robber,
   An' 'e keeps canteen.
'Ow did 'e get 'is buggy?
   Gawd, you needn't ask!
'Made 'is forty gallon
   Out of every cask!

Watch 'im, with 'is 'air cut,
   Count us filin' by —
Won't the colonel praise 'is
   Pop — u — lar — i — ty!

We 'ave scores to settle —
    Scores for more than beer;
She's the girl to pay 'em —
    That is why we're 'ere!

See the Chaplain thinkin'?
    See the women smile?
Twig the married winkin'
    As they take the aisle?
Keep your side-arms quiet,
    Dressin' by the Band.
Ho! You 'oly beggars,
    Cough be'ind your 'and!

Now it's done an' over,
    'Ear the organ squeak,
"Voice that breathed o'er Eden" —
    Ain't she got the cheek!
White an' laylock ribbons,
    Think yourself so fine!
I'd pray Gawd to take yer
    'Fore I made yer mine!

Escort to the kerridge,
    Wish 'im luck, the brute!
Chuck the slippers after —
    [Pity 't ain't a boot!]
Bowin' like a lady,
    Blushin' like a lad —
'Oo would say to see 'em
    Both is rotten bad?

Cheer for the Sergeant's weddin' —
    Give 'em one cheer more!
Grey gun-'orses in the lando,
    An' a rogue is married to, etc.

THE ABSENT-MINDED BEGGAR

This sketch of late-imperial Victorian England commemorates the
outbreak of the Boer War — known at the time as the Second South
African War — in 1899. A considerable British army was shipped

out to evict the Boer farmers from Natal and pacify South Africa.
In England, there remained the soldiers' women and the children
they had borne. As the 'absent-minded beggar' sails with his
regiment for Table Bay and Cape Town to fight Paul Kruger's
riflemen, his woman shakes her tambourine, begging on the streets
of London or Portsmouth. The reference to 'kharki' is significant.
This was the first war in which the British army had worn khaki as
camouflage on the open spaces of the veldt.

When you've shouted 'Rule Britannia,' when you've sung 'God
    save the Queen,'
  When you've finished killing Kruger with your mouth,
Will you kindly drop a shilling in my little tambourine
    For a gentleman in *kharki* ordered South?
He's an absent-minded beggar, and his weaknesses are great —
    But we and Paul must take him as we find him —
He is out on active service, wiping something off a slate —
    And he's left a lot of little things behind him!
    Duke's son — cook's son — son of a hundred kings —
    (Fifty thousand horse and foot going to Table Bay!)
Each of 'em doing his country's work
    (and who's to look after their things?)
Pass the hat for your credit's sake,
               and pay — pay — pay!

There are girls he married secret, asking no permission to,
    For he knew he wouldn't get it if he did.
There is gas and coals and vittles, and the house-rent falling due,
    And it's more than rather likely there's a kid.
There are girls he walked with casual. They'll be sorry now he's
    gone,
    For an absent-minded beggar they will find him,
But it ain't the time for sermons with the winter coming on.
    We must help the girl that Tommy's left behind him!
Cook's son — duke's son — son of a belted earl —
    Son of a Lambeth publican — it's all the same to-day!
Each of 'em doing his country's work
    (and who's to look after the girl?)
Pass the hat for your credit's sake,
               and pay — pay — pay!

There are families by thousands, far too proud to beg or speak,
    And they'll put their sticks and bedding up the spout,
And they'll live on half o' nothing, paid 'em punctual once a week

'Cause the man that earns the wage is ordered out.
He's an absent-minded beggar, but he heard his country call,
　　And his reg'ment didn't need to send to find him!
He chucked his job and joined it — so the job before us all
　　Is to help the home that Tommy's left behind him!
Duke's job — cook's job — gardener, baronet, groom
　　Mews or palace or paper-shop, there's someone gone away!
Each of 'em doing his country's work
　　(and who's to look after the room?)
Pass the hat for your credit's sake,
　　　　　　　any pay — pay — pay!

Let us manage so as, later, we can look him in the face,
　　And tell him — what he'd very much prefer —
That, while he saved the Empire, his employer saved his place
　　And his mates (that's you and me) looked out for *her*.
He's an absent-minded beggar and he may forget it all,
　　But we do not want his kiddies to remind him
That we sent 'em to the workhouse while their daddy hammered
　　Paul,
　　So we'll help the homes that Tommy left behind him!
Cook's home — Duke's home — home of a millionaire,
　　(Fifty thousand horse and foot going to Table Bay!)
Each of 'em doing his country's work
　　(and what have you got to spare?)
Pass the hat for your credit's sake,
　　　　　　　and pay — pay — pay!

Sir Henry Newbolt
VITAÏ LAMPADA

Sir Henry Newbolt (1862–1938) was the most uncompromising
patriot among late Victorian poets, perhaps a Cecil Rhodes of
literature. 'Vitaï Lampada' is his hymn of praise to the ethic of the
public school, cricket, and imperial service. The boy whose charac-
ter is moulded on the cricket pitch by the rules of the game will be
the hero in colonial victory or defeat.

　　There's a breathless hush in the Close to-night —
　　　　Ten to make and the match to win —

A bumping pitch and a blinding light,
　An hour to play and the last man in.
And it's not for the sake of a ribboned coat,
　Or the selfish hope of a season's fame,
But his Captain's hand on his shoulder smote —
　'Play up! play up! and play the game!'

The sand of the desert is sodden red, —
　Red with the wreck of a square that broke; —
The Gatling's jammed and the Colonel dead,
　And the regiment blind with dust and smoke.
The river of death has brimmed his banks,
　And England's far, and Honour a name,
But the voice of a schoolboy rallies the ranks:
　'Play up! play up! and play the game!'

This is the word that year by year,
　While in her place the School is set,
Every one of her sons must hear,
　And none that hears it dare forget.
This they all with a joyful mind
　Bear through life like a torch in flame,
And falling fling to the host behind —
　'Play up! play up! and play the game!'

CLIFTON CHAPEL

Of all the great Victorian public schools, Clifton was perhaps best
known for its concentration on producing the future leaders of
army and empire. The present poem, in the form of a lesson given
to a schoolboy among the memorials of the chapel, is a recital of
Newbolt's creed — and that of many of his contemporaries — at
its most simple. The sense of tradition and fellowship is self-
sustaining. In Newbolt's lines, the noblest Latin epitaph is reserved
for one who perished far away and before his time, but as a soldier
and for his country.

This is the Chapel: here, my son,
　Your father thought the thoughts of youth,
And heard the words that one by one
　The touch of Life has turned to truth.

Here in a day that is not far,
   You too may speak with noble ghosts
Of manhood and the vows of war
   You made before the Lord of Hosts.

To set the Cause above renown,
   To love the game beyond the prize,
To honour, while you strike him down,
   The foe that comes with fearless eyes;
To count the life of battle good,
   And dear the land that gave you birth,
And dearer yet the brotherhood
   That binds the brave of all the earth —

My son, the oath is yours: the end
   Is His, Who built the world of strife,
Who gave His children Pain for friend,
   And Death for surest hope of life.
To-day and here the fight's begun,
   Of the great fellowship you're free;
Henceforth the School and you are one,
   And what You are, the race shall be.

God send you fortune: yet be sure,
   Among the lights that gleam and pass,
You'll live to follow none more pure
   Than that which glows on yonder brass.
'*Qui procul hinc*,' the legend's writ, —
   The frontier-grave is far away —
'*Qui ante diem periit:*
   Sed miles, sed pro patriâ.'

HE FELL AMONG THIEVES

'He Fell Among Thieves' might almost seem a continuation and
conclusion of 'Clifton Chapel', the fate of a British officer facing
death at the hands of his captors. He is, however, a hero rather
than a victim in Newbolt's view. The images recall the life of the
man about to die. In the vestigial outlines of character, there is
something of Lawrence of Arabia and perhaps a little of Conrad's
Lord Jim. The thieves are the Englishman's Afghan captors, though

why they should be thieves is not plain. Certainly a good many
Victorian soldiers had met their deaths in Afghan campaigns from
1838 onwards.

'Ye have robbed,' said he, 'ye have slaughtered and made
    an end,
    Take your ill-got plunder, and bury the dead:
What will ye more of your guest and sometime friend?'
    'Blood for our blood,' they said.

He laughed: 'If one may settle the score for five,
    I am ready; but let the reckoning stand till day:
I have loved the sunlight as dearly as any alive.'
    'You shall die at dawn,' said they.

He flung his empty revolver down the slope,
    He climbed alone to the Eastward edge of the trees;
All night long in a dream untroubled of hope
    He brooded, clasping his knees.

He did not hear the monotonous roar that fills
    The ravine where the Yassin river sullenly flows;
He did not see the starlight on the Laspur hills,
    Or the far Afghan snows.

He saw the April noon on his books aglow,
    The wistaria trailing in at the window wide;
He heard his father's voice from the terrace below
    Calling him down to ride.

He saw the gray little church across the park,
    The mounds that hide the loved and honoured dead;
The Norman arch, the chancel softly dark,
    The brasses black and red.

He saw the School Close, sunny and green,
    The runner beside him, the stand by the parapet wall,
The distant tape, and the crowd roaring between,
    His own name over all.

He saw the dark wainscot and timbered roof,
    The long tables, and the faces merry and keen;
The College Eight and their trainer dining aloof,
    The Dons on the daïs serene.

He watched the liner's stem ploughing the foam,
   He felt her trembling speed and the thrash of her screw;
He heard her passengers' voices talking of home,
   He saw the flag she flew.

And now it was dawn. He rose strong on his feet,
   And strode to his ruined camp below the wood;
He drank the breath of the morning cool and sweet;
   His murderers round him stood.

Light on the Laspur hills was broadening fast,
   The blood-red snow-peaks chilled to a dazzling white:
He turned, and saw the golden circle at last,
   Cut by the Eastern height.

'O glorious Life, Who dwellest in earth and sun,
   I have lived, I praise and adore Thee.'
                     A sword swept.
Over the pass the voices one by one
   Faded, and the hill slept.

THE CHILD'S WORLD

John Clare

INFANTS' GRAVES

Death came early to many Victorian children and the subject was
one easily bungled in verse. John Clare's poem, written in Nor-
thampton Asylum in 1844, is suffused with his characteristic clarity
and simplicity. A subject which would have booby-trapped Words-
worth or Tennyson provides a vehicle for Clare's thought and
imagery at their most persuasive.

Infants' graves are steps of angels, where
Earth's brightest gems of innocence repose.
God is their parent, and they need no tear,
He takes them to his bosom from earth's woes,
A bud their lifetime and a flower their close.
Their spirits are an Iris of the skies,
Needing no prayers; a sunset's happy close,
Gone are the bright rays of their soft blue eyes;
Flowers weep in dewdrops o'er them, and the gale gently sighs.

Their lives were nothing but a sunny shower,
Melting on flowers as tears melt from the eye,
Their deaths were dewdrops on heaven's amaranth bower,
And tolled on flowers as summer gales went by.
They bowed and trembled, and they left no sigh,
And the sun smiled to show their end was well.
Infants have naught to weep for ere they die;
All prayers are needless, beads they need not tell,
White flowers their mourners are, nature their passing-bell.

F. T. Palgrave

EUTOPIA

The Victorian age was perhaps the last to believe in childhood
innocence. F. T. Palgrave (1824–97), famous as the compiler of
The Golden Treasury of Songs and Lyrics (1861), here laments a
lost and perfect world of infancy, the true Utopia.

There is a garden where lilies
And roses are side by side;

And all day between them in silence
    The silken butterflies glide.

I may not enter the garden,
    Tho' I know the road thereto;
And morn by morn to the gateway
    I see the children go.

They bring back light on their faces;
    But they cannot bring back to me
What the lilies say to the roses,
    Or the songs of the butterflies be.

Anonymous
EPITAPH OF DIONYSIA

Every age has its own prudery and there are, perhaps, few poets at
the end of the twentieth century who would hurry into public print
with this elegy to an eight-year-old girl, her 'childhood's dawning
sex' and 'warm gusts of womanhood'. On the other hand, when the
average age of death was seventeen in some areas of England, the
race would either procreate young or not at all. Not surprisingly,
the age of consent was twelve until 1876, when it was raised to
thirteen.

Here doth Dionysia lie:
    She whose little wanton foot
Tripping (ah, too carelessly!)
    Touch'd this tomb and fell into 't.

Trip no more shall she, nor fall,
    And her trippings were so few!
Summers only eight in all
    Had the sweet child wander'd through.

But already life's few suns
    Love's strong seeds had ripen'd warm,
All her ways were winning ones,
    All her cunning was to charm.

And the fancy, in the flower
    While the flesh wast in the blood,
Childhood's dawning sex did dower
    With warm gusts of womanhood.

O what joys by hope begun,
  O what kisses kiss'd by thought,
What love-deeds by fancy done,
  Death to endless dust hath wrought!

Had the Fates been kind as thou,
  Who, till now, was never cold,
Once Love's aptest scholar, now
  Thou hadst been his teacher bold.

But if buried seeds upthrow
  Fruits and flowers; if flower and fruit
By their nature fitly show
  What the seeds are whence they shoot;

Dionysia, o'er this tomb,
  Where thy buried beauties be,
From their dust shall spring and bloom
  Loves and graces like to thee.

Edward Lear

BY WAY OF PREFACE

Of the two most celebrated writers for children in the Victorian
period, the more amiable is Edward Lear (1812–88). His 'nonsense'
combines wit and wistfulness, melancholy and incongruity. He
seems to reveal himself as Lewis Carroll does not. A more censo-
rious age might find much in his verse unsuitable for children.
Children would probably not find it so.

'How pleasant to know Mr Lear!'
  Who has written such volumes of stuff!
Some think him ill-tempered and queer,
  But a few think him pleasant enough.

His mind is concrete and fastidious,
  His nose is remarkably big;
His visage is more or less hideous,
  His beard it resembles a wig.

He has ears, and two eyes, and ten fingers,
  Leastways if you reckon two thumbs;

Long ago he was one of the singers,
　　But now he is one of the dumbs.

He sits in a beautiful parlour,
　　With hundreds of books on the wall;
He drinks a great deal of Marsala,
　　But never gets tipsy at all.

He has many friends, laymen and clerical,
　　Old Foss is the name of his cat:
His body is perfectly spherical,
　　He weareth a runcible hat.

When he walks in a waterproof white,
　　The children run after him so!
Calling out, 'He's come out in his night-
　　gown, that crazy old Englishman, oh!'

He weeps by the side of the ocean,
　　He weeps on the top of the hill;
He purchases pancakes and lotion,
　　And chocolate shrimps from the mill.

He reads but he cannot speak Spanish,
　　He cannot abide ginger-beer:
Ere the days of his pilgrimage vanish,
　　How pleasant to know Mr Lear!

THE OWL AND THE PUSSY-CAT

Lear's best-known whimsy is one of the few Victorian pieces for
children to have remained perennially popular. It suggests that pure
fantasy for children is the only form to escape censorship under one
moral fashion or another.

The Owl and the Pussy-Cat went to sea
　　In a beautiful pea-green boat.
They took some honey, and plenty of money
　　Wrapped up in a five-pound note.
The Owl looked up to the stars above,
　　And sang to a small guitar,
'O lovely Pussy! O Pussy, my love,
What a beautiful Pussy you are,
　　　　　You are,

You are!
What a beautiful Pussy you are!'

Pussy said to the Owl, 'You elegant fowl!
  How charmingly sweet you sing!
O let us be married! too long we have tarried:
  But what shall we do for a ring?'
They sailed away, for a year and a day,
  To the land where the Bong-Tree grows,
And there in a wood a Piggy-wig stood,
With a ring at the end of his nose,
      His nose,
      His nose!
With a ring at the end of his nose.

'Dear Pig, are you willing to sell for one shilling
  Your ring?' Said the Piggy, 'I will.'
So they took it away, and were married next day
  By the Turkey who lives on the hill.
They dinèd on mince, and slices of quince,
  Which they ate with a runcible spoon;
And hand in hand, on the edge of the sand
  They danced by the light of the moon,
      The moon,
      The moon,
They danced by the light of the moon.

INCIDENTS IN THE LIFE
OF MY UNCLE ARLY

The fate of innocent and amiable Uncle Arly is a compelling and perhaps a disturbing tale told on a far edge of humour. He is a comic outcast from society, a wanderer in a world that perhaps only children may understand. An uneasy balance of melancholy and self-mockery seems as plain here as in Lear's 'Preface'. Uncle Arly dies and it appears important in the scheme of the poem that he should. The tightness of his shoes represents a phobia or neurosis only to be guessed at.

i

O My aged Uncle Arly!
Sitting on a heap of Barley
Thro' the silent hours of night, —

Close beside a leafy thicket: —
On his nose there was a Cricket, —
In his hat a Railway-Ticket
(But his shoes were far too tight).

ii

Long ago, in youth, he squander'd
All his goods away, and wander'd
To the Tiniskoop-hills afar.
There on golden sunsets blazing,
Every evening found him gazing, —
Singing, — 'Orb! you're quite amazing!
How I wonder what you are!'

iii

Like the ancient Medes and Persians,
Always by his own exertions
He subsisted on those hills; —
Whiles, — by teaching children spelling, —
Or at times by merely yelling, —
Or at intervals by selling
'Propter's Nicodemus Pills'.

iv

Later, in his morning rambles
He perceived the moving brambles —
Something square and white disclose; —
'Twas a First-class Railway-Ticket;
But, on stooping down to pick it
Off the ground, — a pea-green Cricket
Settled on my Uncle's Nose.

v

Never — Never more, — oh! never,
Did that Cricket leave him ever, —
Dawn or evening, day or night; —
Clinging as a constant treasure, —
Chirping with a cheerious measure, —
Wholly to my uncle's pleasure
(Though his shoes were far too tight).

vi

So for three and forty winters,
Till his shoes were worn to splinters,
All those hills he wanders o'er, —

Sometimes silent; — sometimes yelling; —
Till he came to Borley-Melling,
Near his old ancestral dwelling
(But his shoes were far too tight).

vii
On a little heap of Barley
Died my aged Uncle Arly,
And they buried him one night; —
Close beside the leafy thicket; —
There, — his hat and Railway-Ticket; —
There, — his ever-faithful Cricket
(But his shoes were far too tight).

LIMERICKS

Those who expect to find Edward Lear's limericks instantly funny
— or funny at all — are disappointed. Amusing for some technical-
ity or other, they present a world in which Old Men are chased or
smashed up and only the Young Lady is universally admired.

There was an Old Man in a boat,
Who said, 'I'm afloat! I'm afloat!'
    When they said, 'No, you ain't!'
    He was ready to faint,
That unhappy Old Man in a boat.

There was an Old Person of Basing,
Whose presence of mind was amazing;
    He purchased a steed,
    Which he rode at full speed,
And escaped from the people of Basing.

There was an Old Man who said, 'How
Shall I flee from that horrible cow?
    I will sit on this stile,
    And continue to smile,
Which may soften the heart of that cow.'

There was an Old Man of Whitehaven,
Who danced a quadrille with a raven;
    But they said, 'It's absurd
    To encourage this bird!'
So they smashed that Old Man of Whitehaven.

There was a Young Lady of Tyre,
Who swept the loud chords of a lyre;
   At the sound of each sweep
   She enraptured the deep,
And enchanted the city of Tyre.

Lewis Carroll

YOU ARE OLD, FATHER WILLIAM

By contrast with Edward Lear, who seems to have ill-prepared his
defences against the world, Lewis Carroll (1832–98) appears
assured and well-protected by his style. He is the voice of authority,
when Lear is the supplicant. He also has a fashionable 'grown-up'
dimension. In England his books may be presents for children. In
France he appears with Swift, Sade, and the surrealists in André
Breton's *Anthologie de l'Humour Noir* (1939). Father William,
from *Alice in Wonderland*, is more simply a poem about childish
curiosity over elders.

'You are old, Father William,' the young man said
   'And your hair has become very white;
And yet you incessantly stand on your head —
   Do you think, at your age, it is right?'

'In my youth', Father William replied to his son,
   'I feared it might injure the brain;
But, now that I'm perfectly sure I have none,
   Why, I do it again and again.'

'You are old,' said the youth, 'as I mentioned before.
   And have grown most uncommonly fat;
Yet you turned a back-somersault in at the door —
   Pray, what is the reason of that?'

'In my youth', said the sage, as he shook his grey locks,
   'I kept all my limbs very supple
By the use of this ointment — one shilling the box —
   Allow me to sell you a couple?'

'You are old', said the youth, 'and your jaws are too weak
   For anything tougher than suet;
Yet you finished the goose, with the bones and the beak —
   Pray, how did you manage to do it?'

'In my youth', said his father, 'I took to the law,
   And argued each case with my wife;
And the muscular strength, which it gave to my jaw
   Has lasted the rest of my life.'

'You are old,' said the youth, 'one would hardly suppose
   That your eye was as steady as ever;
Yet you balanced an eel on the end of your nose —
   What made you so awfully clever?'

'I have answered three questions, and that is enough,'
   Said his father, 'Don't give yourself airs!
Do you think I can listen all day to such stuff?
   Be off, or I'll kick you down-stairs!'

JABBERWOCKY

'Jabberwocky' from *Through the Looking-Glass* is the most accomplished nonsense. Many of its words have no obvious meaning and yet the thread of meaning in the poem is never in doubt. The dream or nightmare landscape is, once again, like a surrealist vision devised by Max Ernst or Jean Cocteau.

'Twas brillig, and the slithy toves
   Did gyre and gimble in the wabe:
All mimsy were the borogoves,
   And the mome raths outgrabe.

'Beware the Jabberwock, my son!
   The jaws that bite, the claws that catch!
Beware the Jubjub bird, and shun
   The frumious Bandersnatch!'

He took his vorpal sword in hand:
   Long time the manxome foe he sought —
So rested he by the Tumtum tree,
   And stood awhile in thought.

And, as in uffish thought he stood,
   The Jabberwock, with eyes of flame,
Came whiffling through the tulgey wood,
   And burbled as it came!

One, two! One, two! And through and through
   The vorpal blade went snicker-snack!
He left it dead, and with its head
   He went galumphing back.

'And hast thou slain the Jabberwock?
   Come to my arms, my beamish boy!
O frabjous day! Callooh! Callay!'
   He chortled in his joy.

'Twas brillig, and the slithy toves
   Did gyre and gimble in the wabe:
All mimsy were the borogoves,
   And the mome raths outgrabe.

A BOAT, BENEATH A SUNNY SKY

How the Alice stories came to be told is almost as intriguing as the
stories themselves. The Oxford idyll of river afternoons and summer
picnics among the Godstow haycocks is a lost Eden to modern
readers. No account of those days could improve upon the poem
which Carroll himself placed at the end of the second story. Wistful
and elegaic, it looks towards exile from the enchanted garden. The
initial letters of its lines, unsurprisingly, spell the name 'Alice
Pleasance Liddell', as if secretly carved upon a tree by a lover.

    A boat, beneath a sunny sky
    Lingering onward dreamily
    In an evening of July —

    Children three that nestle near,
    Eager eye and willing ear,
    Pleased a simple tale to hear —

    Long has paled that sunny sky:
    Echoes fade and memories die:
    Autumn frosts have slain July.

    Still she haunts me, phantomwise.
    Alice moving under skies
    Never seen by waking eyes.

Children yet, the tale to hear,
Eager eye and willing ear,
Lovingly shall nestle near.

In a Wonderland they lie,
Dreaming as the days go by,
Dreaming as the summers die:

Ever drifting down the stream —
Lingering in the golden gleam —
Life, what is it but a dream?

Eugene Lee-Hamilton
THE DEATH OF PUCK

Shakespeare, not least those more agreeable scenes and characters
which had been adapted for children in *Lamb's Tales from Shake-
speare* (1807), remained central to childhood reading. Eugene Lee-
Hamilton invests this world with mythology, story-book animals,
and death.

i

I fear that Puck is dead, — it is so long
    Since men last saw him; — dead with all the rest
    Of that sweet elfin crew that made their nest
In hollow nuts, where hazels sing their song;
Dead and for ever, like the antique throng
    The elves replaced: the Dryad that you guess'd
    Behind the leaves; the Naiad weed-bedress'd;
The leaf-ear'd Faun that loved to lead you wrong.

Tell me, thou hopping Robin, hast thou met
    A little man, no bigger than thyself,
Whom they call Puck, where woodland bells are wet?
    Tell me, thou Wood-Mouse, hast thou seen an elf
Whom they call Puck, and is he seated yet,
    Capp'd with a snail-shell, on his mushroom shelf?

ii

The Robin gave three hops, and chirp'd, and said:
    'Yes, I knew Puck, and loved him; though I trow
    He mimick'd oft my whistle, chuckling low;

Yes, I knew cousin Puck; but he is dead.
We found him lying on his mushroom bed —
    The Wren and I, — half cover'd up with snow,
    As we were hopping where the berries grow.
We think he died of cold. Ay, Puck is fled.'

And then the Wood-Mouse said: 'We made the Mole
    Dig him a little grave beneath the moss,
And four big Dormice placed him in the hole.
    The Squirrel made with sticks a little cross;
Puck was a Christian elf, and had a soul;
    And all we velvet jackets mourn his loss.'

Robert Louis Stevenson
MY BED IS A BOAT

Robert Louis Stevenson was not exclusively a children's writer. Yet
many of his novels and their characters became children's classics,
as did his *Child's Garden of Verses*. By contrast with Eugene Lee-
Hamilton, his poems are bedtime poems, though Stevenson in
sickness and exile was the first to derive from them the comfort of
nostalgia.

My bed is like a little boat;
    Nurse helps me in when I embark;
She girds me in my sailor's coat
    And starts me in the dark.

At night, I go on board and say
    Good-night to all my friends on shore;
I shut my eyes and sail away
    And see and hear no more.

And sometimes things to bed I take,
    As prudent sailors have to do;
Perhaps a slice of wedding-cake,
    Perhaps a toy or two.

All night across the dark we steer:
    But when the day returns at last,
Safe in my room, beside the pier,
    I find my vessel fast.

DREAMS OF ELSEWHERE

John Henry Newman
HEATHEN GREECE

The Victorian imagination cherished images of the ancient world as a place of beauty, rationality and escape. From Byron to Rupert Brooke, English classicism was a pervasive influence, reinforced by a widespread classical education among readers and writers. Neither the reality of ancient Greece, whose archaeological remains led to Schliemann's discoveries at Mycenae in 1876, nor modern Greece in the aftermath of its independence from Turkey, held such riches as the visions and legends of the past. In Newman's poem, Peneus is a river of Thessaly and Phlegethon a river of the underworld. The land of the Tauri, to which Iphigenia escaped in Euripides' *Iphigenia in Tauris*, is identified with the Crimea.

Where are the Islands of the Blest?
They stud the Ægean Sea;
And where the deep Elysian rest?
It haunts the vale where Peneus strong
Pours his incessant stream along,
While craggy ridge and mountain bare
Cut keenly through the liquid air,
And, in their own pure tints array'd,
Scorn earth's green robes which change and fade,
And stand in beauty undecay'd,
Guards of the bold and free.

For what is Afric, but the home
Of burning Phlegethon?
What the low beach and silent gloom,
And chilling mists of that dull river,
Along whose banks the thin ghosts shiver, —
The thin wan ghosts that once were men, —
But Tauris, isle of moor and fen,
Or, dimly traced by seamen's ken,
The pale-cliff'd Albion.

William Johnson Cory
ANTERÓS

William Johnson (1823–92), who wrote as William Cory, was
assistant master at Eton 1845–72. He published several volumes of
verse, the best-known being *Ionica* (1858). Though his subject may
be Grecian, it owes a good deal to the water-meadows of the
Thames and the Eton landscape. In the present poem, the name
Anterós is the Greek word for 'love-for-love' or 'love-in-return'.
Narcissus, absorbed by his own reflection and Echo are appropriate
to such a theme. In contemplating the river scene, the reader may
feel more of the Thames than of ancient Greece. This is not
surprising, since Cory was better-known as the author of 'The Eton
Boating Song'.

> Naiad, hid beneath the bank
>   By the willowy river-side,
> Where Narcissus gently sank,
>   Where unmarried Echo died,
> Unto thy serene repose
> Waft the stricken Anterós.
>
> Where the tranquil swan is borne,
>   Imaged in a watery glass,
> Where the sprays of fresh pink thorn
>   Stoop to catch the boats that pass,
> Where the earliest orchis grows,
> Bury thou fair Anterós.
>
> Glide we by, with prow and oar:
>   Ripple shadows off the wave,
> And reflected on the shore
>   Haply play about the grave.
> Folds of summer-light enclose
> All that once was Anterós.
>
> On a flickering wave we gaze,
>   Not upon his answering eyes:
> Flower and bird we scarce can praise,
>   Having lost his sweet replies;
> Cold and mute the rive flows
> With our tears for Anterós.

HERACLITUS

Of all Cory's poems, this remains the most read. It is in fact a translation of an elegy by Callimachus, the Greek poet of the third century B.C. His friend is Heraclitus of Halicarnassus, who is not to be confused with the earlier Heraclitus of Ephesus, the philosopher of change. Halicarnassus, on the south-west coast of modern Turkey, was the capital of Mausolus, tyrant of Caria, hence 'Carian guest'.

They told me, Heraclitus, they told me you were dead,
They brought me bitter news to hear and bitter tears to shed.
I wept as I remember'd how often you and I
Had tired the sun with talking and sent him down the sky.

And now that thou art lying, my dear old Carian guest,
A handful of grey ashes, long, long ago at rest,
Still are thy pleasant voices, thy nightingales, awake;
For Death, he taketh all away, but them he cannot take.

Andrew Lang
THE ODYSSEY

Andrew Lang, part-author of the famous 'Butcher and Lang' translation of Homer's *Odyssey*, transforms his model into dream, symbol, and ornament.

As one that for a weary space has lain
    Lull'd by the song of Circe and her wine
    In gardens hear the pale of Proserpine,
Where that Æean isle forgets the main,
And only the low lutes of love complain,
    And only shadows of wan lovers pine —
    As such an one were glad to know the brine
Salt on his lips, and the large air again, —
So gladly, from the songs of modern speech
    Men turn, and see the stars, and feel the free
        Shrill wind beyond the close of heavy flowers,
        And through the music of the languid hours
They hear like Ocean on the western beach
    The surge and thunder of the Odyssey.

Eugene Lee-Hamilton
IDLE CHARON and
WHAT THE SONNET IS

Eugene Lee-Hamilton's two sonnets bring together the ancient and modern worlds. The first describes how the advent of Christianity had put an end to the trade of Charon, the boatman who ferried the souls of the dead across the Styx to the underworld. In the second poem Lee-Hamilton devises a mythology of the sonnet-form, linking Homer's figures from the *Odyssey* with poets as modern as Dante Gabriel Rossetti.

Idle Charon

The shores of Styx are lone for evermore,
    And not one shadowy form upon the steep
    Looms through the dusk, as far as eyes can sweep,
To call the ferry over as of yore;
But tintless rushes, all about the shore,
    Have hemm'd the old boat in, where, lock'd in sleep,
    Hoar-bearded Charon lies; while pale weeds creep
With tightening grasp all round the unused oar.

For in the world of Life strange rumours run
    That now the Soul departs not with the breath,
But that the Body and the Soul are one;
    And in the loved one's mouth, now, after death,
The widow puts no obol, nor the son,
    To pay the ferry in the world beneath.

What the Sonnet is

Fourteen small broider'd berries on the hem
    Of Circe's mantle, each of magic gold;
    Fourteen of lone Calypso's tears that roll'd
Into the sea, for pearls to come to them;
Fourteen clear signs of omen in the gem
    With which Medea human fate foretold;
    Fourteen small drops, which Faustus, growing old,
Craved of the Fiend, to water Life's dry stem.

It is the pure white diamond Dante brought
   To Beatrice; the sapphire Laura wore
When Petrarch cut it sparkling out of thought;
   The ruby Shakespeare hew'd from his heart's core;
The dark deep emerald that Rossetti wrought
   For his own soul, to wear for evermore.

Rosamund Marriott Watson
A SOUTH COAST IDYLL

A good many Victorian visions of the ancient world transported
Arcadia or Thessaly to Sussex or Devon. Rosamund Marriott
Watson's landscapes are characteristically English and her South
Coast scarcely has the sound of the Mediterranean. For her readers,
this detracted little from the pleasant neo-classicism of the land-
scape, mingling English summer with classical myth. They might
have recalled that even the dreamy sub-tropical vision of Tennyson's
'Lotos-Eaters' had been inspired by a day trip to Torquay.

Beneath these sun-warm'd pines among the heather,
A white goat, bleating, strains his hempen tether,
   A purple stain dreams on the broad blue plain,
The waters and the west wind sing together.

The soft grey lichen creeps o'er the ridge and hollow,
Where swift and sudden skims the slim sea swallow;
   The hid cicalas play their viols all the day,
Merry of heart, although they may not follow.

Beyond yon slope, out-wearied with his reaping,
With vine-bound brows, young Daphnis lies a-sleeping;
   Stolen from the sea on feet of ivory,
The white nymphs whisper, through the pine stems peeping.

We hear their steps, yet turn to seek them never,
Nor scale the sunny slope in fond endeavour;
   It may not be, too swiftly would they flee
Our world-stain'd gaze and come no more for ever.

Pan, Pan is piping in the noontide golden,
Let us lie still, as in a dream enfolden,
   Hear by the sea the airs of Arcady,
And feel the wind of tresses unbeholden.

Charles Stuart Calverley
DOVER TO MUNICH

Charles Stuart Calverley's account of his journey from Dover to
Munich, via the Rhine, is one of the best Victorian odes to European
travel. The coming of the railway and the steamer, between 1820 and
1840, had revolutionised perception as well as transport. European
cities, which had earlier been accessible only at the speed of a horse
and at the mercy of the sea-wind, were now to be reached in a single
day. Breakfast in London and dinner in Paris was a reality. Calverley
makes the most of his journey to Munich under such circumstances.

Farewell, farewell! Before our prow
    Leaps in white foam the noisy channel;
A tourist's cap is on my brow,
    My legs are cased in tourist's flannel:

Around me gasp the invalids —
    The quantity to-night is fearful —
I take a brace of so of weeds,
    And feel (as yet) extremely cheerful.

The night wears on: — my thirst I quench
    With one imperial pint of porter;
Then drop upon a casual bench —
    (The bench is short, but I am shorter) —

Place 'neath my head the *havre-sac*
    Which I have stowed my little all in,
And sleep, though moist about the back,
    Serenely in an old tarpaulin.

*

Bed at Ostend at 5 a.m.
    Breakfast at 6, and train 6.30,
Tickets to Königswinter (mem.
    The seats unutterably dirty).

And onward thro' those dreary flats
    We move, and scanty space to sit on,
Flanked by stout girls with steeple hats,
    And waists that paralyse a Briton; —

By many a tidy little town,
    Where tidy little Fraus sit knitting;

(The men's pursuits are, lying down,
　Smoking perennial pipes, and spitting);

And doze, and execrate the heat,
　And wonder how far off Cologne is,
And if we shall get aught to eat,
　Till we get there, save raw polonies:

Until at last the 'gray old pile'
　Is seen, is past, and three hours later
We're ordering steaks, and talking vile
　Mock-German to an Austrian waiter.

*

Königswinter, hateful Königswinter!
　Burying-place of all I loved so well!
Never did the most extensive printer
　Print a tale so dark as thou couldst tell!

In the sapphire West the eve yet lingered,
　Bathed in kindly light those hill-tops cold;
Fringed each cloud, and, stooping rosy-fingered,
　Changed Rhine's waters into molten gold; —

While still nearer did his light waves splinter
　Into silvery shafts the streaming light;
And I said I loved thee, Königswinter,
　For the glory that was thine that night.

And we gazed, till slowly disappearing,
　Like a day-dream, passed the pageant by,
And I saw but those lone hills, uprearing
　Dull dark shapes against a hueless sky.

Then I turned, and on those bright hopes pondered
　Whereof yon gay fancies were the type;
And my hand mechanically wandered
　Towards my left-hand pocket for a pipe.

Ah! why starts each eyeball from its socket,
　As, in Hamlet, start the guilty Queen's?
There, deep-hid in its accustomed pocket,
　Lay my sole pipe, smashed to smithereens!

*

On, on the vessel steals;
Round go the paddle-wheels,
And now the tourist feels
　　As he should;

For king-like rolls the Rhine,
And the scenery's divine,
And the victuals and the wine
    Rather good.

From every crag we pass'll
Rise up some hoar old castle;
The hanging fir-groves tassel
    Every slope;
And the vine her lithe arm stretches
Over peasants singing catches —
And you'll make no end of sketches,
    I should hope.

We've a nun here (called Thèrèse),
Two couriers out of place,
One Yankee with a face
    Like a ferret's:
And three youths in scarlet caps
Drinking chocolate and schnapps —
A diet which perhaps
    Has its merits.

And day again declines:
In shadow sleep the vines,
And the last ray thro' the pines
    Feebly glows,
Then sinks behind yon ridge;
And the usual evening midge
Is settling on the bridge
    Of my nose.

And keen's the air and cold,
And the sheep are in the fold,
And Night walks sable-stoled
    Thro' the trees;
And on the silent river
The floating starbeams quiver; —
And now, the saints deliver
    Us from fleas.

*

Avenues of broad white houses,
  Basking in the noontide glare; —
Streets, which foot of traveller shrinks from,
  As on hot plates shrinks the bear; —

Elsewhere lawns, and vista'd gardens,
    Statues white, and cool arcades,
Where at eve the German warrior
    Winks upon the German maids; —

Such is Munich: — broad and stately,
    Rich of hue, and fair of form;
But towards the end of August,
    Unequivocally *warm*.

There, the long dim galleries threading,
    May the artist's eye behold
Breathing from the 'deathless canvas'
    Records of the years of old:

Pallas there, and Jove, and Juno,
    'Take' once more their 'walks abroad',
Under Titian's fiery woodlands
    And the saffron skies of Claude:

There the Amazons of Rubens
    Lift the failing arm to strike,
And the pale light falls in masses
    On the horsemen of Vandyke;

And in Berghem's pools reflected
    Hang the cattle's graceful shapes,
And Murillo's soft boy-faces
    Laugh amid the Seville grapes;

And all purest, loveliest fancies
    That in poets' souls may dwell
Started into shape and substance
    At the touch of Raphael.

Lo! her wan arms folded meekly,
    And the glory of her hair
Falling as a robe around her,
    Kneels the Magdalen in prayer;

And the white-robed Virgin-mother
    Smiles, as centuries back she smiled,
Half in gladness, half in wonder,
    On the calm face of her Child: —

And that mighty Judgment-vision
  Tells how man essayed to climb
Up the ladder of the ages,
  Past the frontier-walls of Time;

Heard the trumpet-echoes rolling
  Thro' the phantom-peopled sky,
And the still voice bid this mortal
  Put on immortality.

*

Thence we turned, what time the blackbird
  Pipes to vespers from his perch,
And from out the clattering city
  Passed into the silent church;

Marked the shower of sunlight breaking
  Thro' the crimson panes o'erhead,
And on pictured wall and window
  Read the histories of the dead:

Till the kneelers round us, rising,
  Crossed their foreheads and were gone;
And o'er aisle and arch and cornice,
  Layer on layer, the night came on.

J. W. Burgon

WRITTEN ON THE PLAIN OF THEBES

J. W. Burgon (1813–88) was one of many Victorian travellers to
the East whose attention was diverted to Egypt. The route to India,
as well as political control over Egypt in the disintegration of the
Ottoman Empire, were matters of concern to British governments.
Ease of travel also made the cultural riches of Egypt an attraction.
Burgon describes a scene at Luxor that was to become the image of
the Nile for future tourists.

Our boats were moored where Luxor throws
  A seven-fold image in the stream:
In the pale east the morning rose,
  And guided by that slanting beam
We made our way across the plain
  Where Thebes once owned a hundred gates,

With eager eye and slackened rein,
   Like men who know that Memnon waits.

We reached the statue with the sun.
   We listened for the wished-for sound.
In vain, in vain! 'twas heard by none.
   Deep silence brooded all around.
When lo, a lark with wings outspread
   Soared, O how joyfully along,
And poised, it seemed, above my head
   Dissolved herself in sweetest song.

O God (thought I), *Thy* works abide
   While Man's inventions haste away:
Or if these stem awhile the tide,
   Their nobler uses, — where are they?
Thy works not so! These mock at Time.
   The music of the heavenly lute
Will still flow on in strain sublime
   When stones, and even men, are mute.

Sir Edwin Arnold
TO A PAIR OF EGYPTIAN SLIPPERS

Sir Edwin Arnold (1832–1904) reflects another interest in the
ancient world, evoked by the discovery of artefacts. Its results are
seen here in an Egyptian setting but were to be far more evident
after the discoveries by Schliemann in the Grave Circle at Mycenae,
by Sir Arthur Evans at the palace of Knossos in Crete and, of
course, by Howard Carter and Lord Carnarvon at the tomb of
Tutankhamen in Thebes during 1922.

Tiny slippers of gold and green,
   Tied with a mouldering golden cord!
What pretty feet they must have been
   When Caesar Augustus was Egypt's lord!
Somebody graceful and fair you were!
   Not many girls could dance in these!
When did your shoemaker make you, dear,
   Such a nice pair of Egyptian 'threes'?

Where were you measured? In Saïs, or On,
   Memphis, or Thebes, or Pelusium?
Fitting them neatly your brown toes upon,
   Lacing them deftly with finger and thumb,
I seem to see you! — so long ago,
   Twenty-one centuries, less or more!
And here are your sandals: yet none of us know
   What name, or fortune, or face you bore.

Your lips would have laughed, with a rosy scorn,
   If the merchant, or slave-girl, had mockingly said,
'The feet will pass, but the shoes they have worn
   Two thousand years onward Time's road shall tread,
And still be footgear as good as new!'
   To think that calf-skin, gilded and stitched,
Should Rome and the Pharaohs outlive — and you
   Be gone, like a dream, from the world you bewitched!

Not that we mourn you! 'Twere too absurd!
   You have been such a long while away!
Your dry spiced dust would not value one word
   Of the soft regrets that my verse could say.
Sorrow and Pleasure, and Love and Hate,
   If you ever felt them, have vaporized hence
To this odour — so subtle and delicate —
   Of myrrh, and cassia, and frankincense.

Of course they embalmed you! Yet not so sweet
   Were aloes and nard, as the youthful glow
Which Amenti stole when the small dark feet
   Wearied of treading our world below.
Look! it was flood-time in valley of Nile,
   Or a very wet day in the Delta, dear!
When your slippers tripped lightly their latest mile —
   The mud on the soles renders that fact clear.

You knew Cleopatra, no doubt! You saw
   Antony's galleys from Actium come.
But there! if questions could answers draw
   From lips so many a long age dumb,
I would not teaze you with history,
   Nor vex your heart for the men that were;
The one point to learn that would fascinate me
   Is, where and what are you to-day, my dear!

You died, believing in Horus and Pasht,
    Isis, Osiris, and priestly lore;
And found, of course, such theories smashed
    By actual fact on the heavenly shore.
What next did you do? Did you transmigrate?
    Have we seen you since, all modern and fresh?
Your charming soul — so I calculate —
    Mislaid its mummy, and sought new flesh.

Were you she whom I met at dinner last week,
    With eyes and hair of the Ptolemy black,
Who still of this find in the Fayoum would speak,
    And to Pharaohs and scarabs still carry us back?
A scent of lotus about her hung,
    And she had such a far-away wistful air
As of somebody born when the Earth was young;
    And she wore of gilt slippers a lovely pair.

Perchance you were married? These might have been
    Part of your *trousseau* — the wedding shoes;
And you laid them aside with the garments green,
    And painted clay Gods which a bride would use;
And, may be, to-day, by Nile's bright waters
    Damsels of Egypt in gowns of blue —
Great-great-great — very great — grand-daughters
    Owe their shapely insteps to you!

But vainly I beat at the bars of the Past,
    Little green slippers with golden strings!
For all you can tell is that leather will last
    When loves, and delightings, and beautiful things
Have vanished, forgotten — No! not quite that!
    I catch some gleam of the grace you wore
When you finished with Life's daily pit-a-pat,
    And left your shoes at Death's bedroom door.

You were born in the Egypt which did not doubt;
    You were never sad with our new-fashioned sorrows;
You were sure, when your play-days on Earth ran out,
    Of play-times to come, as we of our morrows!
Oh, wise little Maid of the Delta! I lay
    Your shoes in your mummy-chest back again,
And wish that one game we might merrily play
    At 'Hunt the Slippers' — to see it all plain.

Wilfred Scawen Blunt
THE OASIS AT SIDI KHALED

In March 1876, with his wife Anne, his friend Alec Fraser, a servant
and two Egyptian boys as guides, Wilfred Scawen Blunt crossed the
Sinai desert from Cairo to Jerusalem. After being trailed by a
malevolent sheikh and his followers and falling foul of local
Bedouin, half dead from thirst, the party stumbled into the oasis at
Sidi Khaled. Blunt's poem describes their arrival.

How the earth burns! Each pebble underfoot
Is as a living thing with power to wound.
The white sand quivers, and the footfall mute
Of the slow camels strikes but gives no sound,
As though they walked on flame, not solid ground.
'Tis noon, and the beasts' shadows even have fled
Back to their feet, and there is fire around
And fire beneath, and overhead the sun.
Pitiful heaven! What is this we view?
Tall trees, a river, pools, where swallows fly,
Thickets of oleander where doves coo,
Shades, deep as midnight, greenness for tired eyes.
Hark, how the light winds in the palm-tops sigh.
Oh this is rest. Oh this is paradise.

Edward Fitzgerald
THE RUBÁIYÁT OF OMAR KHAYYÁM

Edward Fitzgerald (1809–83) might have remained a very minor
literary figure, friend of Carlyle, Thackeray, and the Tennysons but
little known to the public. In 1859, however, there appeared a
poem that was to become one of the most popular in all English
literature, Fitzgerald's translation of *The Rubáiyát of Omar
Khayyám*. Though he revised it, perhaps in the light of its initial
slow sale, the first edition remains the best known and is reprinted
here in its entirety.

Omar the Tentmaker was a Persian poet of the twelfth century.
Fitzgerald unifies his independent stanzas into a continuous poem
on the philosophy of human existence. Omar's theme might be
summarised as 'Eat, drink, and be merry, for tomorrow we die'.

The poem was apt to be seen as a rival in the Victorian period to Tennyson's *In Memoriam*, in popularity and philosophy. Tennyson, after passing through the dark night of the soul, had come down on the side of belief and immortality. Not so Omar in Fitzgerald's version. 'The Flower that once has blown for ever dies.'

But Victorian readers were able to regard Omar's poem as the product of an alien culture which nonetheless had some attractive points. From the bazaar of good things, they might pick and choose. They would brush aside the theology and enjoy a gentle hedonism, which went little further than a Victorian picnic in its famous loaf of bread, flask of wine, book of verse 'and Thou beside me singing in the Wilderness'. Where was the harm? Once the tiresome theology was disposed of, Omar sounded very much like a Victorian optimist. As Laurence Housman remarked, Fitzgerald's success was in giving the poem 'a reconciling beauty and flavour of his own, which make it more acceptable to all but scholars and pedants'. Its readers derived a little wisdom of the east and a good deal of less esoteric enjoyment.

I

Awake! for Morning in the Bowl of Night
Has flung the Stone that puts the Stars to Flight:
    And Lo! the Hunter of the East has caught
The Sultán's Turret in a Noose of light.

2

Dreaming when Dawn's Left Hand was in the Sky
I heard a Voice within the Tavern cry,
    'Awake, my Little ones, and fill the Cup
Before Life's Liquor in its Cup be dry.'

3

And, as the Cock crew, those who stood before
The Tavern shouted — 'Open then the Door!
    You know how little while we have to stay,
And, once departed, may return no more.'

4

Now the New Year reviving old Desires,
The thoughtful Soul to Solitude retires,
    Where the WHITE HAND OF MOSES on the Bough
Puts out, and Jesus from the Ground suspires.

5

Iram indeed is gone with all its Rose
And Jamshýd's Sev'n-ring'd Cup where no one knows;
   But still the Vine her ancient Ruby yields,
And still a Garden by the Water blows.

6

And David's Lips are lock't; but in divine
High piping Pehleví, with 'Wine! Wine! Wine!
   Red Wine!' — the Nightingale cries to the Rose
That yellow Cheek of hers to incarnadine.

7

Come, fill the Cup, and in the Fire of Spring
The Winter Garment of Repentance fling:
   The Bird of Time has but a little way
To fly — and Lo! the Bird is on the Wing

8

And look a thousand Blossoms with the day
Woke — and a thousand scatter'd into clay:
   And this first Summer Month that brings the Rose
Shall take Jamshýd and Kaikobád away.

9

But come with old Khayyám, and leave the Lot
Of Kaikobád and Kaikhosrú forgot:
   Let Rustum lay about him as he will,
Or Hátim Tai cry Supper — heed them not.

10

With me along some Strip of Herbage strown
That just divides the desert from the sown,
   Where name of Slave and Sultán scarce is known,
And pity Sultán Mahmud on his Throne.

11

Here with a Loaf of Bread beneath the Bough,
A Flask of Wine, a Book of Verse — and Thou
   Beside me singing in the Wilderness —
And Wilderness is Paradise enow.

12

'How sweet is mortal Sovranty!' — think some:
Others — 'How blest the Paradise to come!'
   Ah, take the Cash in hand and waive the Rest;
Oh, the brave Music of a *distant* Drum!

13
Look to the Rose that blows about us — 'Lo,
Laughing,' she says, 'into the World I blow:
　At once the silken Tassel of my Purse
Tear, and its Treasure on the Garden throw.'

14
The Worldly Hope men set their Hearts upon
Turns Ashes — or it prospers; and anon,
　Like Snow upon the Desert's dusty Face
Lighting a little Hour or two — is gone.

15
And those who husbanded the Golden Grain,
And those who flung it to the Winds like Rain,
　Alike to no such aureate Earth are turn'd
As, buried once, Men want dug up again.

16
Think, in this batter'd Caravanserai
Whose Doorways are alternate Night and Day,
　How Sultán after Sultán with his Pomp
Abode his Hour or two, and went his way.

17
They say the Lion and the Lizard keep
The Courts where Jamshýd gloried and drank deep;
　And Bahrám, that great Hunter — the Wild Ass
Stamps o'er his Head, and he lies fast asleep.

18
I sometimes think that never blows so red
The Rose as where some buried Caesar bled;
　That every Hyacinth the Garden wears
Dropt in its Lap from some once lovely Head.

19
And this delightul Herb whose tender Green
Fledges the River's Lip on which we lean —
　Ah, lean upon it lightly! for who knows
From what once lovely Lip it springs unseen!

20
Oh, my Belovéd, fill the Cup that clears
TO-DAY of past Regrets and future Fears —
　To-morrow? — Why, To-morrow I may be
Myself with Yesterday's Sev'n Thousand Years.

21

Lo! some we loved, the loveliest and best
That Time and Fate of all their Vintage prest,
  Have drunk their Cup a Round or two before,
And one by one crept silently to Rest.

22

And we, that now make merry in the Room
They left, and Summer dresses in new Bloom.
  Ourselves must we beneath the Couch of Earth
Descend, ourselves to make a Couch — for whom?

23

Ah, make the most of what we yet may spend.
Before we too into the Dust descend;
  Dust into Dust, and under Dust, to lie,
Sans Wine, sans Song, sans Singer, and — sans End!

24

Alike for those who for TO-DAY prepare,
And those that after a TO-MORROW stare,
  A Muezzin from the Tower of Darkness cries
'Fools! your Reward is neither Here nor There!'

25

Why, all the Saints and Sages who discuss'd
Of the Two Worlds so learnedly, are thrust
  Like foolish Prophets forth; their Words to Scorn
Are scatter'd, and their Mouths are stopt with Dust.

26

Oh, come with old Khayyám, and leave the Wise
To talk; one thing is certain, that Life flies;
  One thing is certain, and the Rest is Lies;
The Flower that once has blown for ever dies.

27

Myself when young did eagerly frequent
Doctor and Saint, and heard great Argument
  About it and about: but evermore
Came out by the same Door as in I went.

28

With them the Seed of Wisdom did I sow,
And with my own hand labour'd it to grow:
  And this was all the Harvest that I reap'd —
'I came like Water, and like Wind I go.'

29

Into this Universe, and *why* not knowing,
Nor *whence*, like Water willy-nilly flowing:
  And out of it, as Wind along the Waste.
I know not *whither*, willy-nilly blowing.

30

What, without asking, hither hurried *whence*?
And, without asking, *whither* hurried hence!
  Another and another Cup to drown
The Memory of this Impertinence!

31

Up from Earth's Centre through the Seventh Gate
I rose, and on the Throne of Saturn sate,
  And many Knots unravel'd by the Road;
But not the Knot of Human Death and Fate.

32

There was a Door to which I found no Key:
There was a Veil past which I could not see:
  Some little Talk awhile of ME and THEE
There seem'd — and then no more or THEE and ME.

33

Then to the rolling Heav'n itself I cried,
Asking, 'What Lamp had Destiny to guide
  Her little Children stumbling in the Dark?'
And — 'A blind Understanding!' Heav'n replied.

34

Then to this earthen Bowl did I adjourn
My Lip the secret Well of Life to learn:
  And Lip to Lip it murmur'd — 'While you live
Drink! — for once dead you never shall return.'

35

I think the Vessel, that with fugitive
Articulation answer'd, once did live,
  And merry-make; and the cold Lip I kiss'd
How many Kisses might it take — and give!

36

For in the Market-place, one Dusk of Day,
I watch'd the Potter thumping his wet Clay:
  And with its all obliterated Tongue
It murmur'd — 'Gently, Brother, gently, pray!'

37

Ah, fill the Cup: — what boots it to repeat
How Time is slipping underneath our Feet:
   Unborn TO-MORROW, and dead YESTERDAY,
Why fret about them if TO-DAY be sweet!

38

One Moment in Annihilation's Waste,
One Moment, of the Well of Life to taste —
   The Stars are setting and the Caravan
Starts for the Dawn of Nothing — Oh, make haste!

39

How long, how long, in infinite Pursuit
Of This and That endeavour and dispute?
   Better be merry with the fruitful Grape
Than sadden after none, or bitter, Fruit.

40

You know, my Friends, how long since in my House
For a new Marriage I did make Carouse:
   Divorced old barren Reason from my Bed,
And took the Daughter of the Vine to Spouse.

41

For 'IS' and 'IS-NOT' though *with* Rule and Line,
And 'UP-AND-DOWN' *without*, I could define,
   I yet in all I only cared to know,
Was never deep in anything but — Wine.

42

And lately, by the Tavern Door agape,
Came stealing through the Dusk an Angel Shape
   Bearing a Vessel on his Shoulder; and
He bid me taste of it; and 'twas — the Grape!

43

The Grape that can with Logic absolute
The Two-and-Seventy jarring Sects confute:
   The subtle Alchemist that in a Trice
Life's leaden Metal into Gold transmute.

44

The mighty Mahmud, the victorious Lord,
That all the misbelieving and black Horde
   Of Fears and Sorrows that infest the Soul
Scatters and slays with his enchanted Sword.

45

But leave the Wise to wrangle, and with me
The quarrel of the Universe let be:
    And, in come corner of the Hubbub coucht,
Make Game of that which makes as much of Thee.

46

For in and out, above, about, below,
'Tis nothing but a Magic Shadow-show,
    Play'd in a Box whose Candle is the Sun,
Round which we Phantom Figures come and go.

47

And if the Wine you drink, the Lip you press,
End in the Nothing all Things end in — Yes —
    Then fancy while Thou art, Thou art but what
Thou shalt be — Nothing — Thou shalt not be less.

48

While the Rose blows along the River Brink,
With old Khayyám the Ruby Vintage drink:
    And when the Angel with his darker Draught
Draws up to Thee — take that, and do not shrink.

49

'Tis all a Chequer-board of Nights and Days
Where Destiny with Men for Pieces plays:
    Hither and thither moves, and mates, and slays.
And one by one back in the Closet lays.

50

The Ball no question makes of Ayes and Noes,
But Right or Left as strikes the Player goes;
    And He that toss'd Thee down into the Field,
He knows about it all — HE knows — HE knows!

51

The Moving Finger writes; and, having writ,
Moves on; nor all thy Piety nor Wit
    Shall lure it back to cancel half a Line,
Nor all thy Tears wash out a Word of it.

52

And that inverted Bowl we call The Sky,
Whereunder crawling coopt we live and die,
    Lift not thy hands to *It* for help — for It
Rolls impotently on as Thou or I.

53

With Earth's first Clay They did the Last Man's knead,
And then of the Last Harvest sow'd the Seed:
    Yea, the first Morning of Creation wrote
What the Last Dawn of Reckoning shall read.

54

I tell Thee this — When, starting from the Goal,
Over the Shoulders of the flaming Foal
    Of Heav'n Parwín and Mushtara they flung,
In my predestin'd Plot of Dust and Soul.

55

The Vine had struck a Fibre; which about
If clings my Being — let the Sufi flout;
    Of my Base Metal may be filed a Key,
That shall unlock the Door he howls without.

56

And this I know; whether the one True Light,
Kindle to Love, or Wrath — consume me quite,
    One glimpse of It within the Tavern caught
Better than in the Temple lost outright.

57

Oh Thou, who didst with Pitfall and with Gin
Beset the Road I was to wander in,
    Thou wilt not with Predestination round
Enmesh me, and impute my Fall to Sin?

58

Oh, Thou, who Man of baser Earth didst make,
And who with Eden didst devise the Snake;
    For all the Sin wherewith the Face of Man
Is blacken'd, Man's Forgiveness give — and take!

59

Listen again. One evening at the close
Of Ramazán, ere the better Moon arose,
    In that old Potter's Shop I stood alone
With the clay Population round in Rows.

60

And, strange to tell, among the Earthen Lot
Some could articulate, while others not:
    And suddenly one more impatient cried —
'Who *is* the Potter, pray, and who the Pot?'

61

Then said another — 'Surely not in vain
My substance from the common Earth was ta'en,
    That He who subtly wrought me into Shape
Should stamp me back to common Earth again.'

62

Another said — 'Why, ne'er a peevish Boy
Would break the Bowl from which he drank in Joy;
    Shall He that *made* the Vessel in pure Love
And Fancy, in an after Rage destroy!'

63

None answer'd this; but after Silence spake
A Vessel of a more ungainly Make:
    'They sneer at me for leaning all awry;
What! did the Hand then of the Potter shake?'

64

Said one — 'Folks of a surly Tapster tell,
And daub his Visage with the Smoke of Hell;
    They talk of some strict Testing of us — Pish!
He's a Good Fellow, and 'twill all be well.'

65

Then said another with a long-drawn Sigh,
'My Clay with long oblivion is gone dry:
    But, fill me with the old familiar Juice,
Methinks I might recover by-and-bye!'

66

So while the Vessels one by one were speaking,
One spied the little Crescent all were seeking:
    And then they jogg'd each other, 'Brother! Brother!
Hark to the Porter's Shoulder-knot a-creaking!'

67

Ah, with the Grape my fading Life provide,
And wash my Body whence the Life has died,
    And in a Windingsheet of Vine-leaf wrapt,
So bury me by some sweet Garden-side.

68

That ev'n my buried Ashes such a Snare
Of Perfume shall fling up into the Air,
    As not a True Believer passing by
But shall be overtaken unaware.

69

Indeed the Idols I have loved so long
Have done my Credit in Men's Eye much wrong:
    Have drown'd my Honour in a shallow Cup,
And sold my Reputation for a Song.

70

Indeed, indeed, Repentance oft before
I swore — but was I sober when I swore?
    And then and then came Spring, and Rose-in-hand
My thread-bare Penitence apieces tore.

71

And much as Wine has play'd the Infidel,
And robb'd me of my Robe of Honour — well,
    I often wonder what the Vintners buy
One half so precious as the Goods they sell.

72

Alas, that Spring should vanish with the Rose!
That Youth's sweet-scented Manuscript should close!
    The Nightingale that in the Branches sang,
Ah, whence, and whither flown again, who knows!

73

Ah Love! could thou and I with Fate conspire
To grasp this sorry Scheme of Things entire,
    Would not we shatter it to bits — and then
Re-mould it nearer to the Heart's Desire!

74

Ah, Moon of my Delight who know'st no wane,
The Moon of Heav'n is rising once again:
    How oft hereafter rising shall she look
Through this same Garden after me — in vain!

75

And when Thyself with shining Foot shall pass
Among the Guests Star-scatter'd on the Grass,
    And in thy joyous Errand reach the Spot
Where I made one — turn down an empty Glass!

THE NINETIES

THE NINETIES

Ernest Dowson

VITAE SUMMA BREVIS

Vitae summa brevis spem nos vetat incohare longam

'Life's brief span forbids us to entertain hope'. This motto at the head of the first of the collected poems of Ernest Dowson (1867–1900) is balanced by the 'days of wine and roses' of which the brief span is to be constituted. If the 1890s are the years of decadence in English poetry, Dowson represents its style by the dim light and fragrant incense in which his Nuns of the Perpetual Adoration live, the dusky grove of profane love, the madder music and stronger wine by which he tries to cloud his memory of Cynara. In such poetry, it seems that the 1890s began where Swinburne had left off in *Poems and Ballads* (1866).

> They are not long, the weeping and the laughter,
>   Love and desire and hate:
> I think they have no portion in us after
>   We pass the gate.
>
> They are not long, the days of wine and roses:
>   Out of a misty dream
> Our path emerges for a while, then closes
>   Within a dream.

NUNS OF THE PERPETUAL ADORATION

In the Catholicism which Dowson describes, imagery and symbolism count for more than doctrine. His vision of such images and symbols recalls something of Keats seventy or eighty years before.

> Calm, sad, secure; behind high convent walls,
>   These watch the sacred lamp, these watch and pray:
> And it is one with them when evening falls,
>   And one with them the cold return of day.
>
> These heed not time; their nights and days they make
>   Into a long, returning rosary,
> Whereon their lives are threaded for Christ's sake;
>   Meekness and vigilance and chastity.

A vowed patrol, in silent companies,
  Life-long they keep before the living Christ.
In the dim church, their prayers and penances
  Are fragrant incense to the Sacrificed.

Outside, the world is wild and passionate;
  Man's weary laughter and his sick despair
Entreat at their impenetrable gate:
  They heed no voices in their dream of prayer.

They saw the glory of the world displayed;
  They saw the bitter of it, and the sweet;
They knew the roses of the world should fade,
  And be trod under by the hurrying feet.

Therefore they rather put away desire,
  And crossed their hands and came to sanctuary
And veiled their heads and put on coarse attire:
  Because their comeliness was vanity.

And there they rest; they have serene insight
  Of the illuminating dawn to be:
Mary's sweet Star dispels for them the night,
  The proper darkness of humanity.

Calm, sad, secure; with faces worn and mild:
  Surely their choice of vigil is the best?
Yea! for our roses fade, the world is wild;
  But there, beside the altar, there, is rest.

AMOR PROFANUS

Dowson's underworld is the shrine of profane love and of spectral
passion. Here, as in much of his verse, contemporaries saw the
reflection of France, Huysmans' novel *A Rebours* (1884) and the
spread of *l'esprit décadent*.

Beyond the pale of memory,
In some mysterious dusky grove;
A place of shadows utterly,
Where never coos the turtle-dove,
A world forgotten of the sun:
I dreamed we met when day was done,
And marvelled at our ancient love.

Met there by chance, long kept apart,
We wandered through the darkling glades;
And that old language of the heart
We sought to speak: alas! poor shades!
Over our pallid lips had run
The waters of oblivion,
Which crown all loves of men or maids.

In vain we stammered: from afar
Our old desire shone cold and dead:
That time was distant as a star,
When eyes were bright and lips were red.
And still we went with downcast eye
And no delight in being nigh,
Poor shadows most uncomforted.

Ah, Lalage! while life is ours,
Hoard not thy beauty rose and white,
But pluck the pretty, fleeting flowers
That deck our little path of light:
For all too soon we twain shall tread
The bitter pastures of the dead:
Estranged, sad spectres of the night.

GROWTH

Dowson acquired an unjustified reputation for preferring very young girls. The truth was that he had fallen in love with one particular young girl, the daughter of a restaurant owner. He courted her for two years but, when she was old enough, she married the waiter instead. The following is one of a number of poems commemorating his feelings for her.

I watched the glory of her childhood change,
Half-sorrowful to find the child I knew,
    (Loved long ago in lily-time),
Become a maid, mysterious and strange,
With fair, pure eyes — dear eyes, but not the eyes I knew
        Of old, in the olden time!

Till on my doubting soul the ancient good
Of her dear childhood in the new disguise
    Dawned, and I hastened to adore

The glory of her waking maidenhood,
And found the old tenderness within her deepening eyes,
    But kinder than before.

NON SUM QUALIS ERAM BONAE SUB REGNO CYNARAE

'I am no more the man I was in the reign of the good Cynara.'
Dowson is best remembered by this poem in which the jaded lover
seeks other pleasures in order to forget Cynara, but cannot put her
from his mind.

Last night, ah, yesternight, betwixt her lips and mine
There fell thy shadow, Cynara! thy breath was shed
Upon my soul between the kisses and the wine;
And I was desolate and sick of an old passion,
    Yea, I was desolate and bowed my head:
I have been faithful to thee, Cynara! in my fashion.

All night upon mine heart I felt her warm heart beat,
Night-long within mine arms in love and sleep she lay;
Surely the kisses of her bought red mouth were sweet;
But I was desolate and sick of an old passion,
    When I awoke and found the dawn was gray:
I have been faithful to thee, Cynara! in my fashion.

I have forgot much, Cynara! gone with the wind,
Flung roses, roses riotously with the throng,
Dancing, to put thy pale, lost lilies out of mind;
But I was desolate and sick of an old passion,
    Yea, all the time, because the dance was long:
I have been faithful to thee, Cynara! in my fashion.

I cried for madder music and for stronger wine,
But when the feast is finished and the lamps expire,
Then falls thy shadow, Cynara! the night is thine;
And I am desolate and sick of an old passion,
    Yea, hungry for the lips of my desire:
I have been faithful to thee, Cynara! in my fashion.

Lionel Johnson
WALTER PATER

As a decadent, Lionel Johnson's characteristics were drink and homosexuality. He performed the doubtful service of introducing Lord Alfred Douglas to Oscar Wilde. Like a number of poets of the 'nineties, he was a Catholic but his true religion was that of Beauty. Here he pays tribute to Walter Pater, an influential figure of the Aesthetic movement in the 1880s, who once said that the prime justification for good actions is that they are beautiful.

Gracious God rest him! he who toiled so well
    Secrets of grace to tell
Graciously; as the awed rejoicing priest
    Officiates at the feast,
Knowing how deep within the liturgies
    Lie hid the mysteries.
Half of a passionately pensive soul
    He showed us, not the whole:
Who loved him best, they best, they only, knew
    The deeps they might not view;
That which was private between God and him;
    To others, justly dim.
Calm Oxford autumns and preluding springs!
    To me your memory brings
Delight upon delight, but chiefest one:
    The thought of Oxford's son,
Who gave me of his welcome and his praise,
    When white were still my days;
Ere death had left life darkling, nor had sent
    Lament upon lament:
Ere sorrow told me how I loved my lost,
    And bade me base love's cost.
Scholarship's constant saint, he kept her light
    In him divinely white:
With cloistral jealousness of ardour strove
    To guard her sacred grove,
Inviolate by unworldly feet, nor paced
    In desecrating haste.
Oh, sweet grave smiling of that wisdom, brought
    From arduous ways of thought;
Oh, golden patience of that travailing soul

So hungered for the goal,
And vowed to keep, through subtly vigilant pain,
From pastime on the plain,
Enamoured of the difficult mountain air
Up beauty's Hill of Prayer!
Stern is the faith of art, right stern, and he
Loved her severity.
Momentous things he prized, gradual and fair
Births of a passionate air:
Some austere setting of an ancient sun,
Its midday glories done,
Over a silent melancholy sea
In sad serenity:
Some delicate dawning of a new desire,
Distilling fragrant fire
On hearts of men prophetically fain
To feel earth young again:
Some strange rich passage of the dreaming earth,
Fulfilled with warmth and worth.
Ended, his service: yet, albeit farewell
Tolls the faint vesper bell,
Patient beneath his Oxford trees and towers
He still is gently ours:
Hierarch of the spirit, pure and strong,
Worthy Uranian song.
Gracious God keep him: and God grant to me
By miracle to see
That unforgettably most gracious friend,
In the never-ending end!

OXFORD

Lionel Johnson's Oxford is more of a Pre-Raphaelite dream than
Matthew Arnold's had been. It is also the city of Art, where Pater
preached Beauty, Wilde and the Aesthetes paraded, and Ernest
Dowson smoked hashish.

Over, the four long years! And now there rings
One voice of freedom and regret: *Farewell!*
Now old remembrance sorrows, and now sings:
But song from sorrow, now, I cannot tell.

City of weathered cloister and worn court;
Grey city of strong towers and clustering spires:
Where art's fresh loveliness would first resort;
Where lingering art kindled her latest fires.

Where on all hands, wonderous with ancient grace,
Grace touched with age, rise works of goodliest men:
Next Wykeham's art obtain their splendid place
The zeal of Inigo, the strength of Wren.

Where at each coign of every antique street,
A memory hath taken root in stone:
There, Raleigh shone; there, toiled Franciscan feet;
There, Johnson flinched not, but endured, alone.

There, Shelley dreamed his white Platonic dreams;
There, classic Landor throve on Roman thought;
There, Addison pursued his quiet themes;
There, smiled Erasmus, and there, Colet taught.

And there, O memory more sweet than all!
Lived he, whose eyes keep yet our passing light;
Whose crystal lips Athenian speech recall;
Who wears Rome's purple with least pride, most right.

That is the Oxford strong to charm us yet:
Eternal in her beauty and her past.
What, though her soul be vexed? She can forget
Cares of an hour: only the great things last.

Only the gracious air, only the charm,
And ancient might of true humanities,
These, nor assault of man, or time, can harm:
Not these, nor Oxford with her memories.

Together have we walked with willing feet
Gardens of plenteous trees, bowering soft lawn;
Hills, whither Arnold wandered; and all sweet
June meadows, from the troubling world withdrawn;

Chapels of cedarn fragrance, and rich gloom
Poured from empurpled panes on either hand;
Cool pavements, carved with legends of the tomb;
Grave haunts, where we might dream and understand.

Over, the four long years! And unknown powers
Call to us, going forth upon our way:

Ah! Turn we, and look back upon the towers
That rose above our lives, and cheered the day.

Proud and serene, against the sky, they gleam:
Proud and secure, upon the earth they stand:
Our city hath the air of a pure dream,
And hers indeed is a Hesperian land.

Think of her so! The wonderful, the fair,
The immemorial, and the ever young:
The city sweet with our forefathers' care:
The city where the Muses all have sung.

Ill times may be; she hath no thought of time:
She reigns beside the waters yet in pride.
Rude voices cry: but in her ears the chime
Of full sad bells brings back her old springtide.

Like to a queen in pride of place, she wears
The splendour of a crown in Radcliffe's dome.
Well fare she, well! As perfect beauty fares,
And those high places that are beauty's home.

BY THE STATUE OF KING CHARLES
AT CHARING CROSS

In Johnson's poetry, there are few more potent symbols than the
statue of a martyred king rising above the traffic of a modern city.
The poem opens rather in the manner of an impressionistic painting
of an urban scene by Camille Pissarro or Atkinson Grimshaw.

Sombre and rich, the skies;
Great glooms, and starry plains.
Gently the night wind sighs;
Else a vast silence reigns.

The splendid silence clings
Around me: and around
The saddest of all kings
Crowned, and again discrowned.

Comely and calm, he rides
Hard by his own Whitehall.

Only the night wind glides:
No crowds, nor rebels, brawl.

Gone, too, his Court: and yet,
The stars his courtiers are:
Stars in their stations set;
And every wandering star.

Alone he rides, alone,
The fair and fatal king:
Dark night is all his own,
That strange and solemn thing.

Which are more full of fate:
The stars; or those sad eyes?
Which are more still and great:
Those brows, or the dark skies?

Although his whole heart yearn
In passionate tragedy,
Never was face so stern
With sweet austerity.

Vanquished in life, his death
By beauty made amends:
The passing of his breath
Won his defeated ends.

Brief life, and hapless? Nay:
Through death, life grew sublime.
Speak after sentence? Yea:
And to the end of time.

Armoured he rides, his head
Bare to the stars of doom;
He triumphs now, the dead,
Beholding London's gloom.

Our wearier spirit faints,
Vexed in the world's employ:
His soul was of the saints;
And art to him was joy.

King, tried in fires of woe!
Men hunger for thy grace:
And through the night I go,
Loving thy mournful face.

Yet, when the city sleeps,
When all the cries are still,
The stars and heavenly deeps
Work out a perfect will.

THE DARK ANGEL

In a mood that contrasts with the earlier stylised poems, Johnson
personifies in his Dark Angel the sexual guilt of 'aching lust'. That
the author's aching lust should now be a topic for verse says much
for the change in poetic frankness since the advent of Dante Gabriel
Rossetti almost half a century before.

Dark Angel, with thine aching lust
To rid the world of penitence:
Malicious Angel, who still dost
My soul such subtile violence!

Because of thee, no thought, no thing,
Abides for me undesecrate:
Dark Angel, ever on the wing,
Who never reachest me too late!

When music sounds, then changest thou
Its silvery to a sultry fire:
Nor will thine envious heart allow
Delight untortured by desire.

Through thee, the gracious Muses turn
To Furies, O mine Enemy!
And all the things of beauty burn
With flames of evil ecstasy.

Because of thee, the land of dreams
Becomes a gathering place of fears:
Until tormented slumber seems
One vehemence of useless tears.

When sunlight glows upon the flowers,
Or ripples down the dancing sea:
Thou, with thy troop of passionate powers,
Beleaguerest, bewilderest, me.

Within the breath of autumn woods,
Within the winter silences:
Thy venomous spirit stirs and broods,
O Master of impieties!

The ardour of red flame is thine,
And thine the steely soul of ice:
Thou poisonest the fair design
Of nature, with unfair device.

Apples of ashes, golden bright;
Waters of bitterness, how sweet!
O banquet of a foul delight,
Prepared by thee, dark Paraclete!

Thou art the whisper in the gloom,
The hinting tone, the haunting laugh:
Thou art the adorner of my tomb,
The minstrel of mine epitaph.

I fight thee, in the Holy Name!
Yet what thou dost is what God saith:
Tempter! should I escape thy flame,
Thou wilt have helped my soul from Death:

The second Death, that never dies,
That cannot die, when time is dead:
Live Death, wherein the lost soul cries,
Eternally uncomforted.

Dark Angel, with thine aching lust!
Of two defeats, of two despairs,
Less dread, a change to drifting dust,
Than thine eternity of cares.

Do what thou wilt, thou shalt not so,
Dark Angel! triumph over me:
Lonely unto the Lone I go;
Divine, to the Divinity.

Michael Field

LA GIOCONDA

Leonardo da Vinci

The Louvre

'Michael Field' was the pseudonym of Katharine Harris Bradley (1846–1914) and Edith Emma Cooper (1862–1913). Their interpretation of the 'Mona Lisa' makes an interesting contrast to the 'vampire' imagery with which Pater invested the picture in his *Renaissance* (1873), though a latent cruelty in the famous face remains a focus of the poet's attention.

Historic, side-long, implicating eyes;
A smile of velvet's lustre on the cheek;
Calm lips the smile leads upward; hand that lies
Glowing and soft, the patience in its rest
Of cruelty that waits and doth not seek
For prey; a dusky forehead and a breast
Where twilight touches ripeness amorously:
Behind her, crystal rocks, a sea and skies
Of evanescent blue on cloud and creek;
Landscape that shines suppressive of its zest
For those vicissitudes by which men die.

A FÊTE CHAMPÊTRE

This poem was written as a commentary on a painting by Watteau in the Dresden Gallery. It is half poetic reconstruction of the scene and half critique of the picture.

A lovely, animated group
That picnic on a marble seat,
Where flaky boughs of beeches droop,
Where gowns in woodland sunlight glance,
Where shines each coy, lit countenance;
While sweetness rules the air, most sweet
      Because the day
Is deep within the year that shall decay.

They group themselves around their queen,
This lady in the yellow dress,
With bluest knots of ribbon seen
Upon her breast and yellow hair;
But the reared face proclaims *Beware!*
To him who twangs his viol less
        To speak his joy
Than her soon-flattered choiceness to annoy.

Beside her knee a damsel sits,
In petticoat across whose stripes
Of delicate decision flits
The wind that shows them blue and white
And primrose round a bodice tight —
As grey as is the peach that ripes:
        Her hair was spun
For Zephyrus among the threads to run.

She on love's varying theme is launched —
Ah, youth! — behind her, roses lie,
The latest, artless roses, blanched
Around a hectic centre. Two
Protesting lovers near her sue
And quarrel, Cupid knows not why:
        Withdrawn and tart,
One gallant stands in reverie apart.

Proud of his silk and velvet, each
Plum-tinted, of his pose that spurns
The company, his eyes impeach
A Venus on an ivied bank,
Who rests her rigorous, chill flank
Against a water-jet and turns
        Her face from those
Who wanton in the coloured autumn's close.

Ironical he views her shape of stone
And the harsh ivy and grey mound;
Then sneers to think she treats her own
Enchanted couples with contempt,
As though her bosom were exempt
From any care, while tints profound
        Touch the full trees
And there are warning notes in every breeze.

The coldness of mere pleasure when
Its hours are over cuts his heart:
That Love should rule the earth and men
For but a season year by year
And then must straightaway disappear,
Even as the summer weeks depart,
                    Has thrilled his brain
With icy anger and censorious pain.

Alas, the arbour-foliage now,
As cornfields when they lately stood
Awaiting harvest, bough on bough
Is saffron. Yonder to the left
A straggling rose-bush is bereft
Of the last roses of the wood:
                    For one or two
Still flicker where the balmy dozens grew.

On the autumnal grass the pairs
Of lovers couch themselves and raise
A facile merriment that dares
Surprise the vagueness of the sun
October to a veil has spun
About the heads and forest-ways —
                    Delicious light
Of gold so pure it half-refines to white.

Yet Venus from this world of love,
Of haze and warmth has turned: as yet
None feels it save the trees above,
The roses in their soft decline
And one ill-humoured libertine.
Soon shall all hearts forget
                    The vows they swore,
And the leaves strew the glade's untrodden floor.

Aubrey Beardsley
THE BALLAD OF A BARBER

A splendidly macabre little piece by Aubrey Beardsley (1872–98), this poem appeared in *The Savoy* in 1896. It has many of the qualities of Beardsley's drawings, the mannered figures and the overblown elegance of decoration. Like some of his drawings, it has also a judicious sense of the improper.

Here is the tale of Carrousel,
The barber of Meridian Street.
He cut, and coiffed, and shaved so well,
That all the world was at his feet.

The King, the Queen, and all the Court,
To no one else would trust their hair,
And reigning belles of every sort
Owed their successes to his care.

With carriage and with cabriolet
Daily Meridian Street was blocked,
Like bees about a bright bouquet
The beaux about his doorway flocked.

Such was his art he could with ease
Curl wit into the dullest face;
Or to a goddess of old Greece
Add a new wonder and a grace.

All powders, paints, and subtle dyes,
And costliest scents that men distil,
And rare pomades, forgot their price
And marvelled at his splendid skill.

The curling irons in his hand
Almost grew quick enough to speak,
The razor was a magic wand
That understood the softest cheek.

Yet with no pride his heart was moved;
He was so modest in his ways!
His daily task was all he loved,
And now and then a little praise.

An equal care he would bestow
On problems simple or complex;

And nobody had seen him show
A preference for either sex.

How came it then one summer day,
Coiffing the daughter of the King,
He lengthened out the least delay
And loitered in his hairdressing?

The Princess was a pretty child,
Thirteen years old, or thereabout.
She was as joyous and as wild
As spring flowers when the sun is out.

Her gold hair fell down to her feet
And hung about her pretty eyes;
She was as lyrical and sweet
As one of Schubert's melodies.

Three times the barber curled a lock,
And thrice he straightened it again;
And twice the irons scorched her frock,
And twice he stumbled in her train.

His fingers lost their cunning quite,
His ivory combs obeyed no more;
Something or other dimmed his sight,
And moved mysteriously the floor.

He leant upon the toilet table,
His fingers fumbled in his breast;
He felt as foolish as a fable,
And feeble as a pointless jest.

He snatched a bottle of Cologne,
And broke the neck between his hands;
He felt as if he was alone,
And mighty as a king's commands.

The Princess gave a little scream,
Carrousel's cut was sharp and deep;
He left her softly as a dream
That leaves a sleeper to his sleep.

He left the room on pointed feet;
Smiling that things had gone so well.
They hanged him in Meridian Street.
You pray in vain for Carrousel.

Arthur Symons
IN BOHEMIA

Arthur Symons (1865–1945) was one of the more detached observers of the decade and its follies. In this poem he celebrates a less restrained bohemia than that of the Pre-Raphaelites, the playground of the 'Nineties.

Drawn blinds and flaring gas within,
And wine, and women, and cigars;
Without, the city's heedless din;
Above, the white unheeding stars.

And we, alike from each remote,
The world that works, the heaven that waits,
Con our brief pleasures o'er by rote,
The favourite pastime of the Fates.

We smoke, to fancy that we dream,
And drink, a moment's joy to prove,
And fain would love, and only seem
To live because we cannot love.

Draw back the blinds, put out the light!
'Tis morning, let the daylight come.
God, how the women's cheeks are white,
And how the sunlight strikes us dumb!

THE GARDENER

Symons' technique is well illustrated by such poems as this which have a craftsmanship and intensity lacking in some of the more extravagant statements of the age.

The gardener in his old brown hands
Turns over the brown earth,
As if he loves and understands
The flowers before their birth,
The fragile childish little strands
He buries in the earth.

Like pious children one by one
He sets them head by head,
And draws the clothes when all is done,
Closely about each head,
And leaves his children to sleep on
In the one quiet bed.

Theodore Wratislaw
THE MUSIC-HALL

Theodore Wratislaw (1871–1933) is an impressionistic artist of the contemporary scene, not unlike Walter Sickert in painting. His description of the music-hall parallels Walter Sickert's sketch of the Bedford.

The curtain on the grouping dancers falls,
The heaven of colour has vanished from our eyes;
Stirred in our seats we wait with vague surmise
What haply comes that pleases or that palls.

Touched on the stand the thrice-struck baton calls,
Once more I watch the unfolding curtain rise,
I hear the exultant violins premise
The well-known tune that thrills me and enthralls.

Then trembling in my joy I see you flash
Before the footlights to the cymbals' clash,
With laughing lips, swift feet, and brilliant glance,

You, fair as heaven and as a rainbow bright,
You, queen of song and empress of the dance,
Flower of mine eyes, my love, my heart's delight!

HOTHOUSE FLOWERS

Wratislaw's poem on the superiority of artifice to nature certainly reflects an important article in the decadents' creed. However, it is so close to being a parody of the 'Green Carnation' culture that perhaps one should not take it too seriously.

I hate the flower of wood or common field.
I cannot love the primrose nor regret
The death of any shrinking violet,
Nor even the cultured garden's banal yield.

The silver lips of lilies virginal,
The full deep bosom of the enchanted rose
Please less than flowers glass-hid from frosts and snows
For whom an alien heat makes festival.

I love those flowers reared by man's careful art,
Of heady scents and colours: strong of heart
Or weak that die beneath the touch or knife,

Some rich as sin and some as virtue pale,
And some as subtly infamous and frail
As she whose love still eats my soul and life.

ORCHIDS

'The air was thick, wet, steamy and larded with the cloying smell of tropical orchids in bloom ... The plants filled the place, a forest of them, with nasty meaty leaves and stalks like the newly washed fingers of dead men.' The repulsion with which the flowers were to affect Philip Marlowe on his visit to Colonel Sternwood's conservatory in Raymond Chandler's novel *The Big Sleep* (1939) had been a cause of fascination to the decadents almost half a century earlier. For Theodore Wratislaw, the exotic blooms in their unnaturally heated air are the companions of subtle thoughts and strange dreams.

Orange and purple, shot with white and mauve,
Such in a greenhouse wet with tropic heat
One sees these delicate flowers whose parents throve
In some Pacific island's hot retreat.

Their ardent colours that betray the rank
Fierce hotbed of corruption whence they rose
Please eyes that long for stranger sweets than prank
Wild meadow-blooms and what the garden shows.

Exotic flowers! How great is my delight
To watch your petals curiously wrought,
To lie among your splendours day and night
Lost in a subtle dream of subtler thought.

Bathed in your clamorous orchestra of hues,
The palette of your perfumes, let me sleep
While your mesmeric presences diffuse
Weird dreams: and then bizarre sweet rhymes shall creep

Forth from my brain and slowly form and make
Sweet poems as a weaving spider spins,
A shrine of loves that laugh and swoon and ache,
A temple of coloured sorrows and perfumed sins!

John Davidson

INSOMNIA

Two principal strands of poetry exist in the 1890s. One is the
preserve of the decadents. The other deals in social and personal
observation, owing more to Arthur Morrison's *Tales of Mean
Streets* than to Huysmans' *A Rebours*. John Davidson (1857–1909)
belongs to the second group. 'Insomnia,' with its images of jewelled
and elaborate torture, is a reflection of his own troubled psychology,
which led him to commit suicide in 1909. A chrysoprase is an
apple-green quartz-like stone.

He wakened quivering on a golden rack
Inlaid with gems: no sign of change, no fear
Or hope of death came near;
Only the empty ether hovered black
About him stretched upon his living bier,
Of old by Merlin's Master deftly wrought:
Two Seraphim of Gabriel's helpful race
In that far nook of space
With iron levers wrenched and held him taut.

The Seraph at his head was Agony;
Delight, more terrible, stood at his feet:
Their sixfold pinions beat
The darkness, or were spread immovably,
Poising the rack, whose jewelled fabric meet

To strain a god, did fitfully unmask
With olive light of chrysoprases dim
The smiling Seraphim
Implacably intent upon their task.

IN ROMNEY MARSH

Few poets at the end of the century equalled John Davidson in his ability to conjure drama from the rural or urban scene. The changing light and scene of Romney Marsh is superbly evoked by his lines.

As I went down to Dymchurch Wall,
    I heard the South sing o'er the land;
I saw the yellow sunlight fall
    On knolls where Norman churches stand.

And ringing shrilly, taut and lithe,
    Within the wind a core of sound,
The wire from Romney town to Hythe
    Alone its airy journey wound.

A veil of purple vapour flowed
    And trailed its fringe along the Straits;
The upper air like sapphire glowed;
    And roses filled Heaven's central gates.

Masts in the offing wagged their tops;
    The swinging waves pealed on the shore;
The saffron beach, all diamond drops
    And beads of surge, prolonged the roar.

As I came up from Dymchurch Wall,
    I saw above the Downs' low crest
The crimson brands of sunset fall,
    Flicker and fade from out the west.

Night sank: like flakes of silver fire
    The stars in one great shower came down;
Shrill blew the wind; and shrill the wire
    Rang out from Hythe to Romney town.

The darkly shining salt sea drops
    Streamed as the waves clashed on the shore;

The beach, with all its organ stops
     Pealing again, prolonged the roar.

IN THE ISLE OF DOGS

Again in contrast to the decadents, Davidson's account of the East
End of London, the river, and the slum tenements, is unashamed
social commentary. The details of the scene are precise and particu-
lar, overlaid by the organ-grinder's stately measure of the Old
Hundredth, 'All people that on earth do dwell, sing to the Lord
with cheerful voice . . .' The poet is carried back in imagination to
a scene of his Scottish childhood and another old man on an island
shore, also playing the Old Hundredth on a barrel-organ in very
different circumstances. John Davidson in the Isle of Dogs is as far
removed from hothouse flowers or Lionel Johnson's Oxford as a
man could be.

While the water-wagon's ringing showers
Sweetened the dust with a woodland smell,
'Past noon, past noon, two sultry hours',
Drowsily fell
From the schoolhouse clock
In the Isle of Dogs by Millwall Dock.

Mirrored in shadowy windows draped
With ragged net or half-drawn blind
Bowsprits, masts, exactly shaped
To woo or fight the wind,
Like monitors of guilt
By strength and beauty sent,
Disgraced the shameful houses built
To furnish rent.

From the pavements and the roofs
In shimmering volumes wound
The wrinkled heat;
Distant hammers, wheels and hoofs,
A turbulent pulse of sound,
Southward obscurely beat,
The only utterance of the afternoon,
Till on a sudden in the silent street
An organ-man drew up and ground
The Old Hundredth tune.

Forthwith the pillar of cloud that hides the past
Burst into flame,
Whose alchemy transmuted house and mast,
Street, dockyard, pier and pile:
By magic sound the Isle of Dogs became
A northern isle —
A green isle like a beryl set
In a wine-coloured sea,
Shadowed by mountains where a river met
The ocean's arm extended royally.

There also in the evening on the shore
An old man ground the Old Hundredth tune,
An old enchanter steeped in human lore,
Sad-eyed, with whitening beard, and visage lank:
Not since and not before,
Under the sunset or the mellowing moon,
Has any hand of man's conveyed
Such meaning in the turning of a crank.

Sometimes he played
As if his box had been
An organ in an abbey richly lit;
For when the dark invaded day's demesne,
And the sun set in crimson and in gold;
When idlers swarmed upon the esplanade,
And a late steamer wheeling towards the quay
Struck founts of silver from the darkling sea,
The solemn tune arose and shook and rolled
Above the throng,
Above the hum and tramp and bravely knit
All hearts in common memories of song.

Sometimes he played at speed;
Then the Old Hundredth like a devil's mass
Instinct with evil thought and evil deed,
Rang out in anguish and remorse. Alas!
That men must know both Heaven and Hell!
Sometimes the melody
Sang with the murmuring surge;
And with the winds would tell
Of peaceful graves and of the passing bell.
Sometimes it pealed across the bay
A high triumphal dirge,

A dirge
For the departing undefeated day.

A noble tune, a high becoming mate
Of the capped mountains and the deep broad firth;
A simple tune and great,
The fittest utterance of the voice of earth.

THIRTY BOB A WEEK

'Thirty Bob a Week' is a useful reminder that, despite the exhibition-
ism of the decadents, Kipling was still a far more popular poet of
the 1890s than they. Kipling is certainly the writer to whom
Davidson seems closest in this poem, though its concern is with the
exploitation of the Queen's subjects at home rather than in her
Empire. A 'hunks' is a miser or hard taskmaster.

I couldn't touch a stop and turn a screw,
   And set the blooming world a-work for me,
Like such as cut their teeth — I hope, like you —
   On the handle of a skeleton gold key;
I cut mine on a leek, which I eat it every week:
   I'm a clerk at thirty bob as you can see.

But I don't allow it's luck and all a toss;
   There's no such thing as being starred and crossed;
It's just the power of some to be a boss,
   And the bally power of others to be bossed:
I face the music, sir; you bet I ain't a cur;
   Strike me lucky if I don't believe I'm lost!

For like a mole I journey in the dark,
   A-travelling along the underground
From my Pillar'd Halls and broad Suburbean Park,
   To come the daily dull official round;
And home again at night with my pipe all alight,
   A-scheming how to count ten bob a pound.

And it's often very cold and very wet,
   And my missis stitches towels for a hunks;
And the Pillar'd Halls is half of it to let —
   Three rooms about the size of travelling trunks.

And we cough, my wife and I, to dislocate a sigh,
 When the noisy little kids are in their bunks.

But you never hear her do a growl or whine,
 For she's made of flint and roses, very odd;
And I've got to cut my meaning rather fine,
 Or I'd blubber, for I'm made of greens and sod:
So p'r'aps we are in Hell for all that I can tell,
 And lost and damn'd and served up hot to God.

I ain't blaspheming, Mr Silver-tongue;
 I'm saying things a bit beyond your art:
Of all the rummy starts you ever sprung,
 Thirty bob a week's the rummiest start!
With your science and your books and your the'ries about
    spooks,
 Did you ever hear of looking in your heart?

I didn't mean your pocket, Mr, no:
 I mean that having children and a wife,
With thirty bob on which to come and go,
 Isn't dancing to the tabor and the fife:
When it doesn't make you drink, by Heaven! it makes you
    think,
 And notice curious items about life.

I step into my heart and there I meet
 A god-almighty devil singing small,
Who would like to shout and whistle in the street,
 And squelch the passers flat against the wall;
If the whole world was a cake he had the power to take,
 He would take it, ask for more, and eat it all.

And I meet a sort of simpleton beside,
 The kind that life is always giving beans;
With thirty bob a week to keep a bride
 He fell in love and married in his teens:
At thirty bob he stuck; but he knows it isn't luck:
 He knows the seas are deeper than tureens.

And the god-almighty devil and the fool
 That meet me in the High Street on the strike,
When I walk about my heart a-gathering wool,
 Are my good and evil angels if you like.
And both of them together in every kind of weather
 Ride me like a double-seated bike.

That's rough a bit and needs its meaning curled.
　　But I have a high old hot un in my mind —
A most engrugious notion of the world,
　　That leaves your lightning 'rithmetic behind:
I give it at a glance when I say 'There ain't no chance,
　　Nor nothing of the lucky-lottery kind.'

And it's this way that I make it out to be:
　　No fathers, mothers, countries, climates — none;
Not Adam was responsible for me,
　　Nor society, nor systems, nary one:
A little sleeping seed, I woke — I did, indeed —
　　A million years before the blooming sun.

I woke because I thought the time had come;
　　Beyond my will there was no other cause;
And everywhere I found myself at home,
　　Because I chose to be the thing I was;
And in whatever shape of mollusc or of ape
　　I always went according to the laws.

I was the love that chose my mother out;
　　I joined two lives and from the union burst;
My weakness and my strength without a doubt
　　Are mine alone for ever from the first:
It's just the very same with a difference in the name
　　As 'Thy will be done'. You say it if you durst!

They say it daily up and down the land
　　As easy as you take a drink, it's true;
But the difficultest go to understand,
　　And the difficultest job a man can do,
Is to come it brave and meek with thirty bob a week,
　　And feel that that's the proper thing for you.

It's a naked child against a hungry wolf;
　　It's playing bowls upon a splitting wreck;
It's walking on a string across a gulf
　　With millstones fore-and-aft about your neck;
But the thing is daily done by many and many a one;
　　And we fall, face forward, fighting, on the deck.

W. E. Henley
from IN HOSPITAL

William Ernest Henley (1849–1903) was a cripple from childhood. One foot was eventually amputated, though the other was saved. He spent some time in Edinburgh Infirmary, as a patient of Lister. The following three sections from his sequence 'In Hospital' describe his experiences before, during, and after a major surgical operation. It was not a subject for the decadents nor, indeed, for any other poets of the day.

Before

Behold me waiting — waiting for the knife.
A little while, and at a leap I storm
The thick, sweet mystery of chloroform,
The drunken dark, the little death-in-life.
The gods are good to me: I have no wife,
No innocent child, to think of as I near
The fateful minute; nothing all-too dear
Unmans me for my bout of passive strife.
Yet am I tremulous and a trifle sick,
And, face to face with chance, I shrink a little:
My hopes are strong, my will is something weak.
Here comes the basket? Thank you. I am ready.
But, gentlemen my porters, life is brittle:
You carry Cæsar and his fortunes — steady!

Operation

You are carried in a basket,
    Like a carcase from the shambles,
    To the theatre, a cockpit
    Where they stretch you on a table.

Then they bid you close your eyelids,
    And they mask you with a napkin,
    And the anæsthetic reaches
    Hot and subtle through your being.

And you gasp and reel and shudder
    In a rushing, swaying rapture,
    While the voices at your elbow
    Fade — receding — fainter — farther.

Lights about you shower and tumble,
   And your blood seems crystallising —
   Edged and vibrant, yet within you
   Racked and hurried back and forward.

Then the lights grow fast and furious,
   And you hear a noise of waters,
   And you wrestle, blind and dizzy,
   In an agony of effort,

Till a sudden lull accepts you,
   And you sound an utter darkness . . .
   And awaken . . . with a struggle . . .
   On a hushed, attentive audience.

After

Like as a flamelet blanketed in smoke,
So through the anæsthetic shows my life;
So flashes and so fades my thought, at strife
With the strong stupor that I heave and choke
And sicken at, it is so foully sweet.
Faces look strange from space — and disappear.
Far voices, sudden loud, offend my ear —
And hush as sudden. Then my senses fleet;
All were a blank, save for this dull, new pain
That grinds my leg and foot; and brokenly
Time and the place glimpse on to me again;
And, unsurprised, out of uncertainty,
I awake — relapsing — somewhat faint and fain,
To an immense, complacent dreamery.

MADAM LIFE'S A PIECE IN BLOOM

Henley at his most robust addresses his reader with the assurance
that Life is a whore, Death is her pimp, and he will get you in the
end. While you choke in his grip, Madam will look on unperturbed.

   Madam Life's a piece in bloom
     Death goes dogging everywhere:
   She's the tenant of the room,
     He's the ruffian on the stair.

You shall see her as a friend,
   You shall bilk him once and twice;
But he'll trap you in the end,
   And he'll stick you for her price.

With his kneebones at your chest,
   And his knuckles in your throat,
You would reason — plead — protest!
   Clutching at her petticoat;

But she's heard it all before,
   Well she knows you've had your fun,
Gingerly she gains the door,
   And your little job is done.

VILLON'S STRAIGHT TIP TO ALL
CROSS COVES

Tout aux tavernes et aux filles

'Everything goes on drink and tarts', as it might be translated now,
'Booze and the blowens cop the lot', in Henley's version. François
Villon was born in 1431. A poet and poor scholar of the University
of Paris, whores, drink and prison played a large part in his life. He
narrowly escaped being hanged for theft. Henley puts Villon into
the underworld slang of the late Victorians. The vigour of the
language speaks for itself.

Suppose your screeve? or go cheap-jack?
   Or fake the broads? or fig a nag?
Or thimble-rig? or knap a yack?
   Or pitch a snide? or smash a rag?
   Suppose you duff? or nose and lag?
Or get the straight, and land your pot?
   How do you melt the multy swag?
Booze and the blowens cop the lot.

Fiddle, or fence, or mace, or mack;
   Or moskeneer, or flash the drag;
Dead-lurk a crib, or do a crack;
   Pad with a slang, or chuck a fag;

Bonnet, or tout, or mump and gag;
Rattle the tats, or mark the spot;
　　You can not bank a single stag;
Booze and the blowens cop the lot.

Suppose you try a different tack,
　　And on the square you flash your flag?
At penny-a-lining make your whack,
　　Or with the mummers mug and gag?
　　For nix, for nix the dibbs you bag!
At any graft, no matter what,
　　Your merry goblins soon stravag:
Booze and the blowens cop the lot.

THE MORAL
It's up the spout and Charley Wag
With wipes and tickers and what not.
　　Until the squeezer nips your scrag,
Booze and the blowens cop the lot.

Vincent O'Sullivan
THE LADY

Vincent O'Sullivan (1868–1940) was a well-known figure in the literary circles of the 1890s. Perhaps it is because he was born in New York, came to England, and was educated at Oxford that his poetry has an anticipatory note of early T. S. Eliot. Like Eliot, he was also much influenced by French poetry of the nineteenth century.

Now, as he listens to the purring noise
Of words she soothes to guests who linger late
When the lights pale, that they may yet rejoice
In the dear sounds which their souls perturbate:
Alas! (he thinks), must this soft satin voice
　　In the death-rattle grate?

And when he feels the glamour of her laugh,
Her red mouth, and her teeth — he tries to shun
Her mocking eyes, and heedless of her chaff,
Thinks how these teeth will rot out one by one,

Under a stone which bears her epitaph,
        Far from the silver sun.

The small white hands she nurses with such care,
While bracelets and old rings their charms confirm,
Ah! lover's kisses have but little share —
But little share and for a little term,
In the atrocious meal she doth prepare:
        Food for the slimy worm.

Great God! he knows that blighting day is near,
A day he often lives in monstrous dreams,
When, in a house where servants move in fear,
And dark men come, while some wretch sobs and
        screams,
'Mid stifling flowers he shall stand by her bier,
        And think how old she seems.

LA DESTRUCTION

The influence of France on England in the 1890s was self-evident.
Few writers, however, bothered to translate French poetry into
English. O'Sullivan is an exception. Here he translates 'La Destruc-
tion' from Baudelaire's *Les Fleurs du Mal*, 'Sans cesse à mes côtés
s'agite le Démon . . .'

The Devil stirs about me without rest,
And round me floats like noxious air and thin;
I breathe this poison-air which scalds my breast,
And fills me with desires of monstrous sin.

Knowing my love of Art, he sometimes takes
The shape of supple girls supremely fair;
And with a wily, canting lie he makes
My heated lips his shameful potions share.

Then far he leads me from the sight of God,
Crushed with fatigue, to where no man has trod —
To the vague, barren plains where silence sounds,

And hurls into my face his foul construction
Of slimy clothes, and gaping, putrid wounds,
And all the bleeding harness of Destruction!

PAPILLONS DU PAVÉ

Another cameo of pavement and café life, this poem once again sees
O'Sullivan at the point of balance between Baudelaire and Eliot.

> A butterfly, a queer red thing,
> Comes drifting idly down the street:
> Ah, do not now the cool leaves swing,
> That you must brave the city's heat?
>
> A butterfly, a poet vain,
> Whose life is weeping in his mind,
> And all the dreaming of his brain
> Is blighted by the dusty wind.
>
> A painted butterfly sits there,
> Who sickens of the café chaff;
> And down the sultry evening air
> She flings her sudden weary laugh.

John Gray
FEMMES DAMNÉES

A further translation of a poem from *Les Fleurs du Mal* is by John
Gray (1866–1934). It is not, however, the poem printed under the
same title which was one of the six that caused the conviction of
Baudelaire's publisher, Auguste Poulet-Malassis, for obscenity in
1857. That decision of the French courts was not reversed until
1949.

> Like moody beasts they lie along the sands;
> Look where the sky against the sea-rim clings:
> Foot stretches out to foot, and groping hands
> Have languors soft and bitter shudderings.
>
> Some, smitten hearts with the long secrecies,
> On velvet moss, deep in their bowers' ease,
> Prattling the love of timid infancies,
> Are tearing the green bark from the young trees.
>
> Others, like sisters, slowly walk and grave;
> By rocks that swarm with ghostly legions,

Where Anthony saw surging on the waves
The purple breasts of his temptations.

Some, by the light of crumbling, resinous gums,
In the still hollows of old pagan dens,
Call thee in aid to their deliriums
O Bacchus! cajoler of ancient pains.

And those whose breasts for scapulars are fain
Nurse under their long robes the cruel thong.
These, in dim woods, where huddling shadows throng,
Mix with the foam of pleasure tears of pain.

Richard Le Galienne
A BALLAD OF LONDON

Richard Le Galienne (1866–1947) is a poet of the 1890s whose
career also overlapped that of T. S. Eliot in the 1920s. His message
in this poem of 1895 that the good times cannot last, if they ever
existed at all, leads him to the image of London as a desert. He does
not yet say waste land. The vision of the two poets and the
particularity of their metropolitan images has at least something in
common.

Ah, London! London! our delight,
Great flower that opens but at night,
Great City of the Midnight Sun,
Whose day begins when day is done.

Lamp after lamp against the sky
Opens a sudden beaming eye,
Leaping alight on either hand,
The iron lilies of the Strand.

Like dragonflies, the hansoms hover,
With jewelled eyes, to catch the lover;
The streets are full of lights and loves,
Soft gowns, and flutter of soiled doves.

The human moths about the light
Dash and cling close in dazed delight,
And burn and laugh, the world and wife,
For this is London, this is life!

Upon thy petals butterflies,
But at thy root, some say, there lies
A world of weeping trodden things,
Poor worms that have not eyes or wings.

From out corruption of their woe
Springs this bright flower that charms us so,
Men die and rot deep out of sight
To keep this jungle-flower bright.

Paris and London, World-Flowers twain
Wherewith the World-Tree blooms again,
Since Time hath gathered Babylon,
And withered Rome still withers on.

Sidon and Tyre were such as ye,
How bright they shone upon the Tree!
But Time hath gathered, both are gone,
And no man sails to Babylon.

Ah, London! London! our delight,
For thee, too, the eternal night,
And Circe Paris hath no charm
To stay Time's unrelenting arm.

Time and his moths shall eat up all.
Your chiming towers proud and tall
He shall most utterly abase,
And set a desert in their place.

Oscar Wilde

THE BALLAD OF READING GAOL

If the test of great poetry is that once a reader picks it up, it is
impossible to put down, then Oscar Wilde's *Ballad of Reading Gaol*
is probably the greatest poem of the nineteenth century. Ironically,
in Wilde's case, it is shorn of artifice, unless of the artifice of
simplicity. The story, like that of the Ancient Mariner or Eugene
Aram, seems almost to tell itself. The facts are plain enough.

On 25 May 1895, Wilde had been sentenced to two years' impris-
onment with hard labour on counts of gross indecency with male
persons. On 21 November he was transferred from Wandsworth to
Reading Gaol, where he remained until he was released from his

sentence in May 1897. At 8 am on 7 July 1896, an execution took place in Reading Gaol. The condemned man was Charles Thomas Wooldridge, a thirty-year-old trooper in the Royal Horse Guards. He had become jealous of his wife, Laura Ellen. On 23 March, he waited for her near her house, not far from Windsor, and slit her throat three times with a razor which he had borrowed for the purpose. It was clear that the crime had been premeditated. Not only was Wooldridge certain to be convicted but the premeditated nature of his crime removed all chance of a reprieve. On 7 July, Billington the hangman pinioned him, pulled the white cap over his head, put the noose round his neck and pulled the lever of the gallows-trap. Wilde could not see or hear anything of the hanging, though he knew it was taking place. On another occasion, however, he heard from his cell the shrieks of a convict being flogged in the basement for malingering. The brutality of prison was inescapable.

Wilde wrote *The Ballad of Reading Gaol* in Dieppe, two months after his release, between 8 and 20 July. It is a powerful indictment of crime and punishment, ostensibly about Wooldridge's case but also suggesting the injustice which Wilde felt he had suffered himself.

The poem was published in February 1898, not under Wilde's name but under his prison number 'C.3.3.'. It was published by Leonard Smithers, better known for issuing high-class pornography. The reviews were excellent, the edition sold out and the poem was reprinted with Wilde's name upon it. Ironically, he who had epitomised the dandy of the decadence was to be known at the end for a poem of harrowing realism.

IN MEMORIAM
C. T. W.
Sometime Trooper of the Royal Horse Guards
obiit HM Prison, Reading, Berkshire
July 7, 1896

I

He did not wear his scarlet coat,
    For blood and wine are red,
And blood and wine were on his hands
    When they found him with the dead,
The poor dead woman whom he loved,
    And murdered in her bed.

He walked among the Trial Men
  In a suit of shabby grey;
A cricket cap was on his head,
  And his step seemed light and gay;
But I never saw a man who looked
  So wistfully at the day.

I never saw a man who looked
  With such a wistful eye
Upon that little tent of blue
  Which prisoners call the sky,
And at every drifting cloud that went
  With sails of silver by.

I walked, with other souls in pain,
  Within another ring,
And was wondering if the man had done
  A great or little thing,
When a voice behind me whispered low,
  'That fellow's got to swing.'

Dear Christ! the very prison walls
  Suddenly seemed to reel,
And the sky above my head became
  Like a casque of scorching steel;
And, though I was a soul in pain,
  My pain I could not feel.

I only knew what hunted thought
  Quickened his step, and why
He looked upon the garish day
  With such a wistful eye;
The man had killed the thing he loved,
  And so he had to die.

*

Yet each man kills the thing he loves,
  By each let this be heard,
Some do it with a bitter look,
  Some with a flattering word.
The coward does it with a kiss,
  The brave man with a sword!

Some kill their love when they are young,
   And some when they are old;
Some strangle with the hands of Lust,
   Some with the hands of Gold:
The kindest use a knife, because
   The dead so soon grow cold.

Some love too little, some too long,
   Some sell, and others buy;
Some do the deed with many tears,
   And some without a sigh:
For each man kills the thing he loves,
   Yet each man does not die.

He does not die a death of shame
   On a day of dark disgrace,
Nor have a noose about his neck,
   Nor a cloth upon his face,
Nor drop feet foremost through the floor
   Into an empty space.

He does not sit with silent men
   Who watch him night and day;
Who watch him when he tries to weep,
   And when he tries to pray;
Who watch him lest himself should rob
   The prison of its prey.

He does not wake at dawn to see
   Dread figures throng his room,
The shivering Chaplain robed in white,
   The Sheriff stern with gloom,
And the Governor all in shiny black,
   With the yellow face of Doom.

He does not rise in piteous haste
   To put on convict-clothes,
While some coarse-mouthed Doctor gloats, and notes
   Each new and nerve-twitched pose,
Fingering a watch whose little ticks
   Are like horrible hammer-blows.

He does not feel that sickening thirst
   That sands one's throat, before
The hangman with his gardener's gloves

Comes through the padded door,
And binds one with three leathern thongs,
    That the throat may thirst no more.

He does not bend his head to hear
    The Burial Office read,
Nor, while the anguish of his soul
    Tells him he is not dead,
Cross his own coffin, as he moves
    Into the hideous shed.

He does not stare upon the air
    Through a little roof of glass:
He does not pray with lips of clay
    For his agony to pass;
Nor feel upon his shuddering cheek
    The kiss of Caiaphas.

2

Six weeks the guardsman walked the yard,
    In the suit of shabby grey:
His cricket cap was on his head,
    And his step seemed light and gay,
But I never saw a man who looked
    So wistfully at the day.

I never saw a man who looked
    With such a wistful eye
Upon that little tent of blue
    Which prisoners call the sky,
And at every wandering cloud that trailed
    Its ravelled fleeces by.

He did not wring his hands, as do
    Those witless men who dare
To try to rear the changeling Hope
    In the cave of black Despair:
He only looked upon the sun,
    And drank the morning air.

He did not wring his hands nor weep,
    Nor did he peek or pine,
But he drank the air as though it held
    Some healthful anodyne;
With open mouth he drank the sun
    As though it had been wine!

And I and all the souls in pain,
  Who tramped the other ring,
Forgot if we ourselves had done
  A great or little thing,
And watched with gaze of dull amaze
  The man who had to swing.

For strange it was to see him pass
  With a step so light and gay,
And strange it was to see him look
  So wistfully at the day,
And strange it was to think that he
  Had such a debt to pay.

*

For oak and elm have pleasant leaves
  That in the spring-time shoot:
But grim to see is the gallows-tree,
  With its adder-bitten root,
And, green or dry, a man must die
  Before it bears its fruit!

The loftiest place is that seat of grace
  For which all worldlings try:
But who would stand in hempen band
  Upon a scaffold high,
And through a murderer's collar take
  His last look at the sky?

It is sweet to dance to violins
  When Love and Life are fair:
To dance to flutes, to dance to lutes
  Is delicate and rare:
But it is not sweet with nimble feet
  To dance upon the air!

So with curious eyes and sick surmise
  We watched him day by day,
And wondered if each one of us
  Would end the self-same way,
For none can tell to what red Hell
  His sightless soul may stray.

At last the dead man walked no more
  Amongst the Trial Men,
And I knew that he was standing up
  In the black dock's dreadful pen,
And that never would I see his face
  For weal or woe again.

Like two doomed ships that pass in storm
  We had crossed each other's way:
But we made no sign, we said no word,
  We had no word to say;
For we did not meet in the holy night,
  But in the shameful day.

A prison wall was round us both,
  Two outcast men we were:
The world had thrust us from its heart
  And God from out His care:
And the iron gin that waits for Sin
  Had caught us in its snare.

3

In Debtors' Yard the stones are hard,
  And the dripping wall is high,
So it was there he took the air
  Beneath the leaden sky,
And by each side a Warder walked,
  For fear the man might die.

Or else he sat with those who watched
  His anguish night and day;
Who watched him when he rose to weep,
  And when he crouched to pray;
Who watched him lest himself should rob
  Their scaffold of its prey.

The Governor was strong upon
  The Regulations Act:
The Doctor said that Death was but
  A scientific fact:
And twice a day the Chaplain called,
  And left a little tract.

And twice a day he smoked his pipe,
  And drank his quart of beer:
His soul was resolute, and held

No hiding-place for fear;
He often said that he was glad
    The hangman's day was near.

But why he said so strange a thing
    No warder dared to ask:
For he to whom a watcher's doom
    Is given as his task,
Must set a lock upon his lips
    And make his face a mask.

Or else he might be moved, and try
    To comfort or console:
And what should Human Pity do
    Pent up in Murderer's Hole?
What word of grace in such a place
    Could help a brother's soul?

With slouch and swing around the ring
    We trod the Fool's Parade!
We did not care: we knew we were
    The Devil's Own Brigade:
And shaven head and feet of lead
    Make a merry masquerade.

We tore the tarry rope to shreds
    With blunt and bleeding nails;
We rubbed the doors, and scrubbed the floors,
    And cleaned the shining rails:
And, rank by rank, we soaped the plank,
    And clattered with the pails.

We sewed the sacks, we broke the stones,
    We turned the dusty drill:
We banged the tins, and bawled the hymns,
    And sweated on the mill:
But in the heart of every man
    Terror was lying still.

So still it lay that every day
    Crawled like a weed-clogged wave:
And we forgot the bitter lot
    That waits for fool and knave,
Till once, as we tramped in from work,
    We passed an open grave.

With yawning mouth the yellow hole
   Gaped for a living thing;
The very mud cried out for blood
   To the thirsty asphalte ring;
And we knew that ere one dawn grew fair
   Some prisoner had to swing.

Right in we went, with soul intent
   On Death and Dread and Doom:
The hangman, with his little bag,
   Went shuffling through the gloom:
And I trembled as I groped my way
   Into my numbered tomb.

*

That night the empty corridors
   Were full of forms of Fear,
And up and down the iron town
   Stole feet we could not hear,
And through the bars that hide the stars
   White faces seemed to peer.

He lay as one who lies and dreams
   In a pleasant meadow-land
The watchers watched him as he slept,
   And could not understand
How one could sleep so sweet a sleep
   With a hangman close at hand.

But there is no sleep when men must weep
   Who never yet have wept:
So we — the fool, the fraud, the knave —
   That endless vigil kept,
And through each brain on hands of pain
   Another's terror crept.

Alas! it is a fearful thing
   To feel another's guilt!
For, right, within, the Sword of Sin
   Pierced to its poisoned hilt,
And as molten lead were the tears we shed
   For the blood we had not spilt.

The warders with their shoes of felt
    Crept by each padlocked door,
And peeped and saw, with eyes of awe,
    Grey figures on the floor,
And wondered why men knelt to pray
    Who never prayed before.

All through the night we knelt and prayed,
    Mad mourners of a corse!
The troubled plumes of midnight shook
    The plumes upon a hearse:
And bitter wine upon a sponge
    Was the savour of Remorse.

*

The grey cock crew, the red cock crew,
    But never came the day:
And crooked shapes of Terror crouched,
    In the corners where we lay:
And each evil sprite that walks by night
    Before us seemed to play.

They glided past, they glided fast,
    Like travellers through a mist:
They mocked the moon in a rigadoon
    Of delicate turn and twist,
And with formal pace and loathsome grace
    The phantoms kept their tryst.

With mop and mow, we saw them go,
    Slim shadows hand in hand:
About, about, in ghostly rout
    They trod a saraband:
And the damned grotesques made arabesques,
    Like the wind upon the sand!

With the pirouettes of marionettes,
    They tripped on pointed tread:
But with flutes of Fear they filled the ear,
    As their grisly masque they led,
And loud they sang, and long they sang,
    For they sang to wake the dead.

'Oho!' they cried, 'The world is wide,
  But fettered limbs go lame!
And once, or twice, to throw the dice
  Is a gentlemanly game,
But he does not win who plays with Sin
  In the secret House of Shame.'

No things of air these antics were,
  That frolicked with such glee;
To men whose lives were held in gyves,
  And whose feet might not go free,
Ah! wounds of Christ! they were living things,
  Most terrible to see.

Around, around, they waltzed and wound;
  Some wheeled in smirking pairs;
With the mincing step of a demirep
  Some sidled up the stairs:
And with subtle sneer, and fawning leer,
  Each helped us at our prayers.

The morning wind began to moan,
  But still the night went on:
Through its giant loom the web of gloom
  Crept till each thread was spun:
And, as we prayed, we grew afraid
  Of the Justice of the Sun.

The moaning wind went wandering round
  The weeping prison-wall:
Till like a wheel for turning steel
  We felt the minutes crawl:
O moaning wind! what had we done
  To have such a seneschal?

At last I saw the shadowed bars,
  Like a lattice wrought in lead,
Move right across the whitewashed wall
  That faced my three-plank bed,
And I knew that somewhere in the world
  God's dreadful dawn was red.

At six o'clock we cleaned our cells,
  At seven all was still,
But the sough and swing of a mighty wing

The prison seemed to fill,
For the Lord of Death with icy breath
    Had entered in to kill.

He did not pass in purple pomp,
    Nor ride a moon-white steed.
Three yards of cord and a sliding board
    Are all the gallows' need:
So with rope of shame the Herald came
    To do the secret deed.

We were as men who through a fen
    Of filthy darkness grope:
We did not dare to breathe a prayer,
    Or to give our anguish scope:
Something was dead in each of us,
    And what was dead was Hope.

For Man's grim Justice goes its way,
    And will not swerve aside:
It slays the weak, it slays the strong,
    It has a deadly stride:
With iron heel it slays the strong,
    The monstrous parricide!

We waited for the stroke of eight:
    Each tongue was thick with thirst:
For the stroke of eight is the stroke of Fate
    That makes a man accursed,
And Fate will use a running noose
    For the best man and the worst.

We had no other thing to do,
    Save to wait for the sign to come:
So, like things of stone in a valley lone,
    Quiet we sat and dumb:
But each man's heart beat thick, and quick,
    Like a madman on a drum!

With sudden shock the prison-clock
    Smote on the shivering air,
And from all the gaol rose up a wail
    Of impotent despair,
Like the sound that frightened marshes hear
    From some leper in his lair.

And as one sees most fearful things
   In the crystal of a dream,
We saw the greasy hempen rope
   Hooked to the blackened beam,
And heard the prayer the hangman's snare
   Strangled into a scream.

And all the woe that moved him so
   That he gave that bitter cry,
And the wild regrets, and the bloody sweats,
   None knew so well as I:
For he who lives more lives than one
   More deaths than one must die.

4

There is no chapel on the day
   On which they hang a man:
The Chaplain's heart is far too sick,
   Or his face is far too wan,
Or there is that written in his eyes
   Which none should look upon.

So they kept us close till nigh on noon,
   And then they rang the bell,
And the warders with their jingling keys
   Opened each listening cell,
And down the iron stair we tramped,
   Each from his separate Hell.

Out into God's sweet air we went,
   But not in wonted way,
For this man's face was white with fear,
   And that man's face was grey,
And I never saw sad men who looked
   So wistfully at the day.

I never saw sad men who looked
   With such a wistful eye
Upon that little tent of blue
   We prisoners called the sky,
And at every happy cloud that passed
   In such strange freedom by.

But there were those amongst us all
   Who walked with downcast head,
And knew that, had each got his due,
   They should have died instead:
He had but killed a thing that lived,
   Whilst they had killed the dead.

For he who sins a second time
   Wakes a dead soul to pain,
And draws it from its spotted shroud,
   And makes it bleed again,
And makes it bleed great gouts of blood,
   And makes it bleed in vain!

*

Like ape or clown, in monstrous garb,
   With crooked arrows starred,
Silently we went round and round
   The slippery asphalte yard;
Silently we went round and round,
   And no man spoke a word.

Silently we went round and round,
   And through each hollow mind
The Memory of dreadful things
   Rushed like a dreadful wind,
And Horror stalked before each man,
   And Terror crept behind.

*

The warders strutted up and down,
   And watched their herd of brutes,
Their uniforms were spick and span,
   And they wore their Sunday suits,
But we knew the work they had been at,
   By the quicklime on their boots.

For where a grave had opened wide,
   There was no grave at all:
Only a stretch of mud and sand
   By the hideous prison-wall,
And a little heap of burning lime,
   That the man should have his pall.

For he has a pall, this wretched man,
    Such as few men can claim:
Deep down below a prison-yard,
    Naked for greater shame,
He lies, with fetters on each foot,
    Wrapt in a sheet of flame!

And all the while the burning lime
    Eats flesh and bone away,
It eats the brittle bone by night,
    And the soft flesh by day,
It eats the flesh and bone by turns,
    But it eats the heart alway.

*

For three long years they will not sow
    Or root or seedling there:
For three long years the unblessed spot
    Will sterile be and bare,
And look upon the wondering sky
    With unreproachful stare.

They think a murderer's heart would taint
    Each simple seed they sow.
It is not true! God's kindly earth
    Is kindlier than men know,
And the red rose would blow more red,
    The white rose whiter blow.

Out of his mouth a red, red rose!
    Out of his heart a white!
For who can say by what strange way,
    Christ brings His will to light,
Since the barren staff the pilgrim bore
    Bloomed in the great Pope's sight?

But neither milk-white rose nor red
    May bloom in prison-air;
The shard, the pebble, and the flint,
    Are what they give us there:
For flowers have been known to heal
    A common man's despair.

So never will wine-red rose or white,
    Petal by petal fall
On that stretch of mud and sand that lies

By the hideous prison-wall,
To tell the men who tramp the yard
That God's Son died for all.

*

Yet though the hideous prison-wall
Still hems him round and round,
And a spirit may not walk by night
That is with fetters bound,
And a spirit may but weep that lies
In such unholy ground,

He is at peace — this wretched man —
At peace, or will be soon:
There is no thing to make him mad,
Nor does Terror walk at noon,
For the lampless Earth in which he lies
Has neither Sun nor Moon.

They hanged him as a beast is hanged:
They did not even toll
A requiem that might have brought
Rest to his startled soul,
But hurriedly they took him out,
And hid him in a hole.

The warders stripped him of his clothes,
And gave him to the flies:
They mocked the swollen purple throat,
And the stark and staring eyes:
And with laughter loud they heaped the shroud
In which the convict lies.

The Chaplain would not kneel to pray
By his dishonoured grave:
Nor mark it with that blessed Cross
That Christ for sinners gave,
Because the man was one of those
Whom Christ came down to save.

Yet all is well; he has but passed
To Life's appointed bourne:
And alien tears will fill for him
Pity's long-broken urn,
For his mourners will be outcast men,
And outcasts always mourn.

5

I know not whether Laws be right,
  Or whether Laws be wrong;
All that we know who lie in gaol
  Is that the wall is strong;
And that each day is like a year,
  A year whose days are long.

But this I know, that every Law
  That men have made for Man,
Since first Man took his brother's life,
  And the sad world began,
But straws the wheat and saves the chaff
  With a most evil fan.

This too I know — and wise it were
  If each could know the same —
That every prison that men build
  Is built with bricks of shame,
And bound with bars lest Christ should see
  How men their brothers maim.

With bars they blur the gracious moon,
  And blind the goodly sun:
And they do well to hide their Hell,
  For in it things are done
That Son of God nor son of Man
  Ever should look upon!

*

The vilest deeds like poison weeds,
  Bloom well in prison-air;
It is only what is good in Man
  That wastes and withers there:
Pale Anguish keeps the heavy gate,
  And the Warder is Despair.

For they starve the little frightened child
  Till it weeps both night and day:
And they scourge the weak, and flog the fool,
  And gibe the old and grey,
And some grow mad, and all grow bad,
  And none a word may say.

Each narrow cell in which we dwell
    Is a foul and dark latrine,
And the fetid breath of living Death
    Chokes up each grated screen,
And all, but Lust, is turned to dust
    In Humanity's machine.

The brackish water that we drink
    Creeps with a loathsome slime,
And the bitter bread they weigh in scales
    Is full of chalk and lime,
And Sleep will not lie down, but walks
    Wild-eyed, and cries to Time.

*

But though lean Hunger and green Thirst
    Like asp with adder fight,
We have little care of prison fare,
    For what chills and kills outright
Is that every stone one lifts by day
    Becomes one's heart by night.

With midnight always in one's heart,
    And twilight in one's cell,
We turn the crank, or tear the rope,
    Each in his separate Hell,
And the silence is more awful far
    Then the sound of a brazen bell.

And never a human voice comes near
    To speak a gentle word:
And the eye that watches through the door
    Is pitiless and hard:
And by all forgot, we rot and rot,
    With soul and body marred.

And thus we rust Life's iron chain
    Degraded and alone:
And some men curse, and some men weep,
    And some men make no moan:
But God's eternal Laws are kind
    And break the heart of stone.

*

And every human heart that breaks,
    In prison-cell or yard,
Is as that broken box that gave
    Its treasure to the Lord,
And filled the unclean leper's house
    With the scent of costliest nard.

Ah! happy they whose hearts can break
    And peace of pardon win!
How else may man make straight his plan
    And cleanse his soul from Sin?
How else but through a broken heart
    May Lord Christ enter in?

*

And he of the swollen purple throat,
    And the stark and staring eyes,
Waits for the holy hands that took
    The Thief to Paradise;
And a broken and a contrite heart
    The Lord will not despise.

The man in red who reads the Law
    Gave him three weeks of life,
Three little weeks in which to heal
    His soul of his soul's strife,
And cleanse from every blot of blood
    The hand that held the knife.

And with tears of blood he cleansed the hand,
    The hand that held the steel:
For only blood can wipe out blood,
    And only tears can heal:
And the crimson stain that was of Cain
    Became Christ's snow-white seal.

6

In Reading gaol by Reading town
    There is a pit of shame,
And in it lies a wretched man
    Eaten by teeth of flame,
In a burning winding-sheet he lies,
    And his grave has got no name.

And there, till Christ call forth the dead,
   In silence let him lie:
No need to waste the foolish tear,
   Or heave the windy sigh:
The man had killed the thing he loved,
   And so he had to die.

And all men kill the thing they love,
   By all let this be heard,
Some do it with a bitter look,
   Some with a flattering word,
The coward does it with a kiss,
   The brave man with a sword!

THE PASSING
OF AN AGE

Rudyard Kipling

RECESSIONAL

June 22 1897

There could be no more appropriate conclusion to the poetry of the age than Kipling's verses written to end the day on which Queen Victoria's Diamond Jubilee was celebrated. The poem itself reflects a sense of awe at the accumulated power of empire, the massed regiments which had paraded through the streets of London, the ironclad battleships of the naval review, the cheering crowds which stopped the procession on the way from Buckingham Palace to St Paul's and broke into choruses of 'God Save the Queen!' Victoria herself was now almost eighty and, as she wrote in her journal, 'very tired' by the end of day. Two days earlier, she wrote, 'How well I remember this day sixty years ago, when I was called from my bed by dear Mama to receive the news of my accession!' The Earl of Rosebery, a former Prime Minister, assured her that 'no capital in the world has ever witnessed such an enthusiasm of devotion to a Sovereign.' Her son-in-law, the Duke of Argyll, reminded her that the military spectacle was proof that 'no Sovereign since the fall of Rome could muster subjects from so many and so distant countries all over the world.' The power was so vast that many, like Kipling, were moved to pray for wisdom in its use and to speculate on the vanity of such pomp.

God of our fathers, known of old,
    Lord of our far-flung battle-line,
Beneath whose awful Hand we hold
    Dominion over palm and pine —
Lord God of Hosts, be with us yet,
Lest we forget — lest we forget!

The tumult and the shouting dies;
    The Captains and the Kings depart:
Still stands Thine ancient sacrifice,
    An humble and a contrite heart.
Lord God of Hosts, be with us yet,
Lest we forget — lest we forget!

Far-called, our navies melt away;
    On dune and headland sinks the fire:
Lo, all our pomp of yesterday

Is one with Nineveh and Tyre!
Judge of the Nations, spare us yet,
Lest we forget — lest we forget!

If, drunk with sight of power, we loose
   Wild tongues that have not Thee in awe,
Such boastings as the Gentiles use,
   Or lesser breeds without the Law —
Lord God of Hosts, be with us yet,
Lest we forget — lest we forget!

For heathen heart that puts her trust
   In reeking tube and iron shard,
All valiant dust that builds on dust,
   And guarding, calls not Thee to guard,
For frantic boast and foolish word —
Thy mercy on Thy People, Lord!

SUGGESTIONS FOR FURTHER READING

Allingham, William, *A Diary, 1824–1889*, H. Allingham and D. Radford (ed.) (Penguin, 1985)

Angeli, Helen Rossetti, *Pre-Raphaelite Twilight: The Story of Charles Augustus Howell* (The Richards Press, 1954)

Baring-Gould, Sabine, *The Vicar of Morwenstow* (Methuen, 1925 and reprints)

Battiscombe, Georgina, *Christina Rossetti* (Constable, 1981)

Beckson, Karl (ed.), *Oscar Wilde: The Critical Heritage* (Routledge and Kegan Paul, 1970)

Beerbohm, Max, *Rossetti and his Circle*, N. John Hall (ed.) (Yale University Press, 1987)

Bell, Quentin, *A New and Noble School: The Pre-Raphaelites* (Macdonald, 1982)

Briggs, Asa (ed.), *William Morris: Selected Writings and Designs* (Pelican, 1962)

Browning, Robert and Elizabeth Barrett, *The Letters of Robert Browning and Elizabeth Barrett Browning, 1845–1846*, Frederic G. Kenyon (ed.) (Harper and Brothers, 1902 and reprints)

Bryson, John, and Janet Camp Troxell (eds.) *Dante Gabriel Rossetti and Jane Morris: Their Correspondence*, (Clarendon Press, 1976)

Doughty, Oswald, *A Victorian Romantic: Dante Gabriel Rossetti* (Oxford University Press, 2nd edition, 1960)

Eliot, T. S., *On Poetry and Poets* (Faber, 1957)

Ellmann, Richard, *Oscar Wilde* (Hamish Hamilton, 1987)

Fleming, G. H., *That N'er Shall Meet Again: Rossetti, Millais, Hunt* (Michael Joseph, 1971)

Ford, Boris (ed.), *Pelican Guide to English Literature: Dickens to Hardy*, rev. edn. (Penguin, 1982)

Fry, Roger, 'Aubrey Beardsley's Drawings,' in *Vision and Design*, rev. edn. (Chatto and Windus, 1928 and reprints)

Gaunt, William, *The Aesthetic Adventure* (Cardinal, 1975)

Gaunt, William, *The Pre-Raphaelite Tragedy* (Cardinal, 1975)

Gaunt, William, *Victorian Olympus* (Cardinal, 1975)

Gosse, Edmund, *Portraits and Sketches* (William Heinemann 1912)

Hopkins, Gerard Manley, *Poems and Prose of Gerard Manley Hopkins*, (ed.) W. H. Gardner, Penguin Books, 1953 and reprints.

Hopkins, Gerard Manley, *Gerard Manley Hopkins: Selected Letters*, Catherine Phillips (ed.) (Clarendon Press, 1990)

Hough, Graham, *The Last Romantics* (Duckworth, 1949)

Huysmans, Joris-Karl, *Against Nature [A Rebours]*, tr. Robert Baldick (Penguin, 1959 and reprints)

Hyder, Clarke K. (ed.), *Swinburne: The Critical Heritage* (Routledge and Kegan Paul, 1970)

Jackson, Holbrook, *The Eighteen Nineties* (Pelican, 1950)

Johnson, Wendell Stacy, *Gerard Manley Hopkins: The Poet as Victorian* (Cornell University Press, 1968)

Leavis, F. R., *New Bearings in English Poetry* (Chatto and Windus, 1932)

MacKenzie, Norman H., *A Reader's Guide to Gerard Manley Hopkins* (Thames and Hudson, 1981)

Mander, Rosalie, *Mrs Browning: The Story of Elizabeth Barrett*, (London, 1980)

Meredith, George, *Letters of George Meredith*, C. L. Cline (ed.) (Clarendon Press, 1970)

Morris, William, *Collected Letters of William Morris, 1848–80*, Norman Kelvin (ed.) (Princeton University Press, 1984)

Morris, William, *Collected Works of William Morris*, May Morris (ed.)(Longmans Green, 1910–15)

Morris, William, *Stories in Prose, Stories in Verse, Shorter Poems, Lectures and Essays*, G. D. H. Cole (ed.) (Nonesuch Press, 1974)

Nicolson, Harold, *Swinburne* (Macmillan, 1926)

Oberg, Charlotte, H., *A Pagan Prophet: William Morris* (University Press of Virginia, 1978)

Praz, Mario, *The Romantic Agony* (Oxford University Press, 1933 and reprints)

Rees, Joan, *The Poetry of Dante Gabriel Rossetti: Modes of Self-Expression* (Cambridge University Press, 1981)

Rossetti, Christina, *Complete Poems of Christina Rossetti*, R. W. Crump (ed.) (Louisiana State University Press, 1986)

Rossetti, Dante Gabriel, *Rossetti's Poems* (J. M. Dent, Everyman Library, 1968 and reprints)

Rossetti, Dante Gabriel, *The Collected Works of Dante Gabriel Rossetti*, William Michael Rossetti (ed.) (Ellis and Scrutton, 1886)

Rossetti, Dante Gabriel, *Letters of Dante Gabriel Rossetti*, Oswald Doughty and John Robert Wahl (eds) (Oxford University Press, 1965)

Rossetti, William Michael, *The Diary of William Michael Rossetti 1870–73*, Odette Bernard (ed.) (Clarendon Press, 1977)

Rossetti, William Michael, *The PRB Journal, William Michael Rossetti's Diary of the PRB 1849–53*, William E. Fredeman (ed.) (Clarendon Press, 1975)

Ruskin, John, *Pre-Raphaelitism and Lectures on Architecture and Painting* (J. M. Dent, Everyman Library, 1906 and reprints)

Sambrook, James (ed.), *Pre-Raphaelitism* (University of Chicago Press, 1974)

Sassoon, Siegfried, *Meredith* (Constable, 1948)

Secker, Martin, and John Betjeman, *The Eighteen-Nineties: A Period Anthology in Prose and Verse* (The Richards Press, 1948)

Silver, Carole, *The Romance of William Morris* (Ohio University Press, 1982)

Swinburne, Algernon Charles, *A Choice of Swinburne's Verse*, Robert Nye (ed.) (Faber, 1973)

Swinburne, Algernon Charles, *The Swinburne Letters*, Cecil Y. Lang (ed.) (Yale University Press, 1959–1962)

Thomas, Donald, *Swinburne: The Poet in his World* (ed.) (Weidenfeld and Nicolson, 1979)

Thornton, R. K. R. (ed.), *Poetry of the Nineties* (Penguin, 1970)

Tompkins, J. M. S., *The Art of Rudyard Kipling* (Methuen, 1959)

Trevelyan, Raleigh, *A Pre-Raphaelite Circle* (Chatto and Windus, 1978)

Turner, Paul, *English Literature 1832–90, Excluding the Novel* (Clarendon Press, 1989)

Wellek, René, *A History of Modern Criticism: 1750–1950*, Vol. 4 'The Later Nineteenth Century' (Cape, 1966)

Wilde, Oscar, *The Picture of Dorian Gray* (Penguin, 1948 and reprints)

Williams, David, *George Meredith: His Life and Lost Love* (Hamish Hamilton, 1977)

Young, G. M., *Victorian England: Portrait of An Age* (Oxford University Press, 1969 and reprints)

INDEX OF FIRST LINES

POETRY
IN EVERYMAN

A SELECTION

Silver Poets of the Sixteenth Century

EDITED BY
DOUGLAS BROOKS-DAVIES
A new edition of this famous
Everyman collection **£6.99**

Complete Poems

JOHN DONNE
The father of metaphysical verse in
this highly-acclaimed edition **£4.99**

Complete English Poems, Of Education, Areopagitica

JOHN MILTON
An excellent introduction to
Milton's poetry and prose **£6.99**

Selected Poems

JOHN DRYDEN
A poet's portrait of Restoration
England **£4.99**

Selected Poems

PERCY BYSSHE SHELLEY
'The essential Shelley' in one
volume **£3.50**

Women Romantic Poets 1780-1830: An Anthology

Hidden talent from the Romantic era,
rediscovered for the first time. **£5.99**

Poems in Scots and English

ROBERT BURNS
The best of Scotland's greatest lyric
poet **£4.99**

Selected Poems

D. H. LAWRENCE
A newly-edited selection spanning
the whole of Lawrence's literary
career **£4.99**

The Poems

W. B. YEATS
Ireland's greatest lyric poet
surveyed in this ground-breaking
edition **£6.50**

£5.99

£4.99

£3.50

PHILOSOPHY AND RELIGIOUS WRITING IN EVERYMAN

A SELECTION

An Essay Concerning Human Understanding
JOHN LOCKE
A central work in the development of modern philosophy **£4.99**

Philosophical Writings
GOTTFRIED WILHELM LEIBNIZ
The only paperback edition available **£3.99**

Critique of Pure Reason
IMMANUEL KANT
The capacity of the human intellect examined **£6.99**

A Discourse on Method, Meditations, and Principles
RENE DESCARTES
Takes the theory of mind over matter into a new dimension **£4.99**

Philosophical Works including the Works on Vision
GEORGE BERKELEY
An eloquent defence of the power of the spirit in the physical world **£4.99**

The Social Contract and Discourses
JEAN-JAQUES ROUSSEAU
Rousseau's most influential works in one volume **£3.99**

Utilitarianism/OnLiberty/Considerations on Representative Government
J. S. MILL
Three radical works which transformed political science **£4.99**

Utopia
THOMAS MORE
A critique of contemporary ills allied with a visionary ideal for society **£2.99**

Ethics
SPINOZA
Spinoza's famous discourse on the power of understanding **£4.99**

The Buddha's Philosophy of Man
Ten dialogues representing the cornerstone of early Buddhist thought **£4.99**

Hindu Scriptures
The most important ancient Hindu writings in one volume **£6.99**

Apologia Pro Vita Sua
JOHN HENRY NEWMAN
A moving and inspiring account of a Christian's spiritual journey **£5.99**

DRAMA
IN EVERYMAN

A SELECTION

Everyman and Medieval Miracle Plays

EDITED BY A. C. CAWLEY
A selection of the most popular
medieval plays **£3.99**

Complete Plays and Poems

CHRISTOPHER MARLOWE
The complete works of this
fascinating Elizabethan in one
volume **£5.99**

Complete Poems and Plays

ROCHESTER
The most sexually explicit – and
strikingly modern – writing of the
seventeenth century **£5.99**

Restoration Plays

Five comedies and two tragedies
representing the best of the
Restoration stage **£7.99**

Female Playwrights of the Restoration: Five Comedies

Rediscovered literary treasures in a
unique selection **£5.99**

Poems and Plays

OLIVER GOLDSMITH
The most complete edition of
Goldsmith available **£4.99**

Plays, Poems and Prose

J. M. SYNGE
The most complete edition of Synge
available **£6.99**

Plays, Prose Writings and Poems

OSCAR WILDE
The full force of Wilde's wit in one
volume **£4.99**

A Doll's House/The Lady from the Sea/The Wild Duck

HENRIK IBSEN
A popular selection of Ibsen's major
plays **£3.99**

£2.99

£2.99

£2.99

AVAILABILITY

All books are available from your local bookshop or direct from
**Littlehampton Book Services Cash Sales, 14 Eldon Way, LinesideEstate,
Littlehampton, West Sussex BN17 7HE.** PRICES ARE SUBJECT TO CHANGE.

To order any of the books, please enclose a cheque (in £ sterling) made payable to
Littlehampton Book Services, or phone your order through with credit card details (Access,
Visa or Mastercard) on 0903 721596 (24 hour answering service) stating card number and
expiry date. Please add £1.25 for package and postage to the total value of your order.

CLASSIC NOVELS
IN EVERYMAN

A SELECTION

The Way of All Flesh
SAMUEL BUTLER
A savagely funny odyssey from joy-
less duty to unbridled liberalism **£4.99**

Born in Exile
GEORGE GISSING
A rationalist's progress towards love
and compromise in class-ridden
Victorian England **£4.99**

David Copperfield
CHARLES DICKENS
One of Dickens' best-loved novels,
brimming with humour **£3.99**

The Last Chronicle of Barset
ANTHONY TROLLOPE
Trollope's magnificent conclusion
to his Barsetshire novels **£4.99**

He Knew He Was Right
ANTHONY TROLLOPE
Sexual jealousy, money and
women's rights within marriage –
a novel ahead of its time **£6.99**

Tess of the D'Urbervilles
THOMAS HARDY
The powerful, poetic classic of
wronged innocence **£3.99**

Wuthering Heights
and Poems
EMILY BRONTE
A powerful work of genius – one of
the great masterpieces of literature
£3.50

Tom Jones
HENRY FIELDING
The wayward adventures of one of
literatures most likable heroes **£5.99**

The Master of Ballantrae
and Weir of Hermiston
R. L. STEVENSON
Together in one volume, two great
novels of high adventure and family
conflict **£4.99**

£3.99

£2.99

£3.99

AMERICAN LITERATURE
IN EVERYMAN

A SELECTION

Selected Poems
HENRY LONGFELLOW
A new selection spanning the whole
of Longfellow's literary career **£7.99**

Typee
HERMAN MELVILLE
Melville's stirring debut, drawing
directly on his own adventures in the
South Sea **£4.99**

Billy Budd
and Other Stories
HERMAN MELVILLE
The compelling parable of
innocence destroyed by a fallen
world **£4.99**

The Scarlet Letter
NATHANIEL HAWTHORNE
The compelling tale of an
independent woman's struggle
against a crushing moral code **£3.99**

The Last of The Mohicans
JAMES FENIMORE COOPER
The classic tale of old America, full
of romantic adventure **£5.99**

The Red Badge of Courage
STEPHEN CRANE
A vivid portrayal of a young
soldier's experience of the
American Civil War **£2.99**

Essays and Poems
RALPH WALDO EMERSON
An indispensable edition celebrating
one of the most influential
American writers **£5.99**

The Federalist
HAMILTON, MADISON, AND JAY
Classics of political science, these
essays helped to found the
American Constitution **£6.99**

Leaves of Grass and
Selected Prose
WALT WHITMAN
The best of Whitman in one volume
£6.99

£5.99

£4.99

£4.99

WOMEN'S WRITING IN EVERYMAN

A SELECTION

Female Playwrights of the Restoration
FIVE COMEDIES
Rediscovered literary treasures in a unique selection **£5.99**

The Secret Self
SHORT STORIES BY WOMEN
'A superb collection' *Guardian* **£4.99**

Short Stories
KATHERINE MANSFIELD
An excellent selection displaying the remarkable range of Mansfield's talent **£3.99**

Women Romantic Poets 1780-1830: An Anthology
Hidden talent from the Romantic era, rediscovered for the first time **£5.99**

Selected Poems
ELIZABETH BARRETT BROWNING
A major contribution to our appreciation of this inspiring and innovative poet **£5.99**

Frankenstein
MARY SHELLEY
A masterpiece of Gothic terror in its original 1818 version **£3.99**

The Life of Charlotte Brontë
MRS GASKELL
A moving and perceptive tribute by one writer to another **£4.99**

Vindication of the Rights of Woman and The Subjection of Women
MARY WOLLSTONECRAFT
AND J. S. MILL
Two pioneering works of early feminist thought **£4.99**

The Pastor's Wife
ELIZABETH VON ARNIM
A funny and accomplished novel by the author of *Elizabeth and Her German Garden* **£5.99**

£4.99

£2.99

£5.99

AVAILABILITY

All books are available from your local bookshop or direct from
Littlehampton Book Services Cash Sales, 14 Eldon Way, LinesideEstate, Littlehampton, West Sussex BN17 7HE. PRICES ARE SUBJECT TO CHANGE.

To order any of the books, please enclose a cheque (in £ sterling) made payable to Littlehampton Book Services, or phone your order through with credit card details (Access, Visa or Mastercard) on 0903 721596 (24 hour answering service) stating card number and expiry date. Please add £1.25 for package and postage to the total value of your order.